PENGUIN BOOKS

IN A STRANGE GARDEN

Lloyd Chapman lives on ten acres on the Kapiti coast with his wife, Ann. They have a boutique nursery growing old roses, while Lloyd strives to breed a thoroughbred horse good enough to win the derby. Lloyd worked for thirteen years in England in North Sea oil exploration before returning to New Zealand and setting up a consultancy offering geophysical services to oil explorers. This is his first book. He hopes the next one will be about roses.

IN A STRANGE GARDEN

The life and times of Truby King

LLOYD CHAPMAN

PENGUIN BOOKS

PENGUIN BOOKS

Penguin Books (NZ) Ltd, cnr Airborne and Rosedale Roads, Albany,
Auckland 1310, New Zealand
Penguin Books Ltd, 80 Strand, London, WC2R 0RL, England
Penguin Putnam Inc, 375 Hudson Street, New York, NY 10014, United States
Penguin Books Australia Ltd, 250 Camberwell Road, Camberwell,
Victoria 3124, Australia
Penguin Books Canada Ltd, 10 Alcorn Avenue, Toronto,
Ontario, Canada M4V 3B2
Penguin Books (South Africa) (Pty) Ltd, 24 Sturdee Avenue, Rosebank, Johannesburg
2196, South Africa
Penguin Books India (P) Ltd, 11, Community Centre, Panchsheel Park, New Delhi
110 017, India
Penguin Books Ltd, Registered Offices: Harmondsworth, Middlesex, England

First published by Penguin Books (NZ) Ltd, 2003

1 3 5 7 9 10 8 6 4 2

Copyright © Lloyd Chapman, 2003
Copyright © photographs as listed

The right of Lloyd Chapman to be identified as the author of this work in terms of
section 96 of the Copyright Act 1994 is hereby asserted.

Editorial Services by Michael Gifkins & Associates
Designed by Mary Egan
Typeset by Egan-Reid Ltd
Printed in Australia by McPherson's Printing Group

All rights reserved. Without limiting the rights under copyright reserved above, no part
of this publication may be reproduced, stored in or introduced into a retrieval system,
or transmitted, in any form or by any means (electronic, mechanical, photocopying,
recording or otherwise), without the prior written permission of both the copyright
owner and the above publisher of this book.

Cover photographs: Truby King and 'Madeline' at Melrose (front)
and the Melrose garden (back).
Alexander Turnbull Library, F3311 and F437 1/4
ISBN 0 14 301879 5
A catalogue record for this book is available
from the National Library of New Zealand.

www.penguin.co.nz

Contents

	Introduction	9
	Chronology	15
ONE	A young man in the colonies	19
TWO	Little Truby	31
THREE	Who am I?	45
FOUR	An asylum by the sea	49
FIVE	Colonising the Catlins	67
SIX	A sound mind in a healthy body	77
SEVEN	Some curious attitudes of his own	83
EIGHT	Conservation at Karitane	103
NINE	The adoption of Mary	113
TEN	A prototype for Plunket	119
ELEVEN	The Plunket movement	127
TWELVE	The elusive Bella	143
THIRTEEN	Taking Plunket abroad	151
FOURTEEN	The later years of Plunket	165
FIFTEEN	A mausoleum in Melrose	173
SIXTEEN	The manic gardener	183
SEVENTEEN	The end	199

Appendix One	The Feeding of Plants and Animals	211
Appendix Two	Constitution and rules of the Plunket Society 1907	217
Appendix Three	Hygeia columns	221
Appendix Four	Karitane products	227
Appendix Five	Truby King's library	235
Appendix Six	The evils of picture shows	241
Appendix Seven	Publications by Truby King	247
Appendix Eight	Truby King's rhododendron correspondence	251

Endnotes	263
Bibliography	271
Index	275
List of Illustrations	283

Thanks to the many people who took the time to help me – you know who you are. My special thanks to my family, and to Barbara Else, Ulrike Hilborn, Margaret Long, Frank Boffa, Paul Crozier, Clare Ashton and James Ritchie.

Introduction

'What do you know about Truby King?' I asked the taxi-driver, hoping to avoid another dissertation on the parlous state of New Zealand cricket or rugby. 'He's the reason I have such a rotten stomach' was the unlikely reply. 'My mother fed me all that scientifically formulated stuff as a baby, and sentenced me to a lifetime of stomach trouble.'

When I was a child my parents encouraged me to collect stamps, perhaps as a calming antidote to more physical activities like rugby and soccer. I still recall grappling with the 1957 carmine image of Sir Truby King celebrating the 50th anniversary of the Plunket Society, aware that this man had played a part in the upbringing of my parents and of subsequent generations, but also feeling unease at his supercilious smirk emanating from the threepenny stamp.

Forty years later, after many years in the oil exploration business, I found myself developing a new career. Collecting roses had become compulsive, and our garden had grown to become one of the biggest collections of old roses in the land. I decided that the only way to justify this was to become an expert, or at least to demonstrate comprehensive knowledge of the subject. Many of the world's old roses had their origins in France, and I travelled there in 1999. Strangely, this led me to a reacquaintance with that authority figure from the New Zealand establishment, Frederic Truby King.

The city of Orléans, strategically placed on the Loire with direct road and rail links to Paris, was an important centre of horticulture, with many *pépiniéristes* (nurserymen) established on the Loiret, south of the city. Armed with Kiwi enthusiasm and high school French, I spent a fascinating month researching the nurseries and the nurserymen who became famous for their roses. The largest and most significant nursery was that of Barbier. He had produced many of the splendid climbing and rambling roses that we still value. From the beginning of the twentieth century, he created such wonders as Albéric Barbier, Albertine, Paul Transon and François Juranville, roses of surpassing beauty, fragrance and style. As was the fashion of the time, the breadth of his nursery encompassed a wide variety of trees, shrubs, vegetables and bedding plants, but the annual catalogue of over 100 pages confirmed his passion for roses.

On my return to New Zealand, I set about solving the puzzle that had challenged me for years. The rambling rose Albéric Barbier was common in Wellington. How had it become so established? On looking at old records supplied by a garden historian, I was surprised to discover that the same Dr Truby King, founder of Plunket, had been an ardent gardener. The surprise increased when I came upon King's vast and detailed plant orders from the Barbier nursery in Orléans, and deepened further when I discovered that although King had imported literally thousands of plants from Barbier, he had not purchased a single rose. Later, I confessed my growing fascination with Truby King to friend Frank Boffa, one of the founding fathers of landscape architecture in New Zealand. He surprised me by describing a similar experience, which had begun with a professional appointment to produce a conservation and management plan for the Truby King garden in Wellington, and ended up as a week-long trawl through the Hocken Library archives, under the spell of this Victorian icon. Frank's notes were all it took to set me on a path of research and revelation. My curiosity, born out of my own obsession, set me off on a journey of discovery.

These explorations have taken me back to my roots in Dunedin, to the Hocken Library's archives, to Seacliff where Truby King was for thirty years director of the country's largest lunatic asylum, and to places that before this I only vaguely knew. I was to discover a powerfully persuasive communicator but also a genuine eccentric, a hunchbacked dwarf, an accomplished scientist. I would also encounter a misogynist, a financial incompetent, a bully and a complex man with attitudes I had little sympathy with.

Throughout my journey I would be haunted by a childhood

INTRODUCTION

memory of sliding on the highly polished linoleum floors of the Roslyn Plunket rooms, risking the wrath of the guardian of Sir Truby's fortress, the imposing figure of the Plunket nurse. The authority vested in her by Truby and his army of upper-class women was enough to instil fear and anti-authoritarian loathing in a small child.

One early step I took was to devour his biography *Truby King – The Man*, published in 1948, ten years after his death. The author, Mary King, his adopted daughter, servant and apostle of Plunket, had devoted years of her life to an account that would set him on a pedestal. He would have been proud of the job that she accomplished. I was annoyed by it and frustrated. I felt even on my first reading that Mary had omitted any negative material, and I later discovered not only her rewriting of history, but that in an archivist's opinion she had expunged critical material before lodging papers with the archives. While there is a great deal of published material about the man and about Plunket, there are very few people still living who have any reliable recall of Truby King. My interpretation of what is still in the archives and the historical record is, I admit, very personal.

While the story of the Plunket Society and how Truby King conscripted the women of Edwardian New Zealand to it has been chronicled, paraphrased and discussed elsewhere, the origins of Plunket are less well known. I was surprised to discover Dr King making an early career decision to become head of the country's largest mental institution while still a young man. It was at Seacliff on the coast of Otago that King seized the opportunity offered by a sprawling baronial estate to develop skills in farming, landscape design and animal husbandry. Showing commendable disregard for regulations and rules, his stewardship of the country's largest asylum gave him the opportunity for considerable personal development as a farmer and scientist.

Behind King was his tiny wife, Bella. Her acceptance of a subservient role was pivotal to Truby's success. When in later life they moved to Wellington, his energies were directed into building a house, developing the Karitane baby food factory and assuming the mantle of Director of Child Welfare. He somehow found time to plan the development of his huge hilltop property, ordering tens of thousands of plants from all over the world. With characteristic fervour he set about developing a garden for his later years. Sadly, Bella would not live to share his dream. By the strength of his personality, the garden on Wellington's exposed hilltop took shape, with Truby often imposing exotic species on an environment to which they were hardly suited. With his personality and commitment, they had no option but to flourish.

On his death, the manic gardener who had narrowly avoided the irony of committal to an asylum was buried in his own garden. It took an act of parliament to sanction this, but it somehow seemed appropriate. This was a man who stole the best years of his adopted daughter's life, the first New Zealander to be given a state funeral, the first private citizen to be enshrined on a postage stamp.

Truby King was a paradox, an enigma. He was the son of a member of the first New Zealand parliament, he rejected a career in banking to train as a doctor, he was dogged by ill-health and a dread of tuberculosis. He married the landlady's daughter and never had children of his own. He was a fierce orator, capable of winning an audience or demolishing an opponent. Truby King's ability to influence people was instrumental in his founding of the Plunket Society, but even his triumphs were clouded in ambiguity. His treatment of women and his extreme and restrictive views on their education and role in life would be ridiculed today. Yet he created a society that empowered women and gave them a world-famous child welfare system.

My interest began with King the gardener, was captured by King the scientist, and was further stimulated by King the farmer, doctor, educator, goldminer and fearsome snob. There is much to admire in what the man achieved, but it is difficult to reconcile his achievements with the complexity of his shortcomings.

Chronology of Truby King's life
1858–1938

Age	Year	
	1858	Truby King born on April Fool's Day in New Plymouth
2	1860	Mother and five children sent to Nelson to escape land wars
6	1864	Brother Francis dies. Truby contracts pneumonia, pleurisy, tuberculosis
15	1873	Truby begins work at the BNZ, New Plymouth, for his father
16	1874	Transfers to Auckland with the bank
18	1876	Moves to Wellington as private secretary to manager of the BNZ
20	1878	Appointed manager, BNZ, Masterton
22	1880	Leaves for London to commence medical studies at Edinburgh University
26	1884	Passes second professional exam with distinction, loses sight in left eye
28	1886	Graduates, winning Ettles Scholarship as top scholar
29	1887	Resident Surgeon, Glasgow Infirmary. Studies for BSc Marries Isabella Cockburn Millar, the landlady's daughter
30	1888	Returns to New Zealand. Commences work at Wellington Hospital
31	1889	Appointed Medical Superintendent, Seacliff asylum
35	1893	Truby's father dies, aged 72
36	1894	Twelve months' leave to study brain pathology in London. Bella accompanies King
38	1896	Extended sick leave, goes back to Edinburgh
39	1897	Back to Seacliff, still unwell, spends winter in Queensland

40	1898	Begins building Karitane house
43	1901	Two 40-foot fishing boats commissioned for Karitane
44	1902	Lecture on Seaside Planting, later published as *Tree Culture in New Zealand*
45	1903	Buys *Argyle* gold dredge in Southland
46	1904	Six months in Japan on paid sick leave
47	1905	Mary King adopted by Truby and Bella
47	1905	*The Feeding of Plants and Animals* published
48	1906	*The Evils of Cram* published
49	1907	First newspaper article on infant welfare published
		First public meeting presaging the formation of Plunket
		King's Karitane house becomes prototype baby hospital
		Society for Health of Women and Children acquire house in Dunedin for hospital
50	1908	Plunket Society officially formed
52	1910	The Fisherman's Cottage and the Sailor's Cottage built at Puketeraki
53	1911	Farm at Tahakopa (Catlins) purchased
		Truby's mother dies, aged 93
54	1912	Truby and Bella on the road preaching the Plunket message for 3 months
55	1913	To London with Bella and Mary, representing New Zealand at medical conference
56	1914	To London to speak at Education and Eugenics Conference
58	1916	Catlins piggery begins using whey from the dairy farm
59	1917	To London, summoned by Lady Plunket. Stays for 15 months
60	1918	Travels to USA, returns to London. With honorary rank, goes to Europe
61	1919	Represents British Empire at Red Cross conference in Cannes
		Returns via Australia, back to work at Seacliff
62	1920	Appointed Director of Child Welfare
63	1921	Leaves Seacliff after 32 years. Moves to Wellington. Bella's health failing.
		Mary, aged 16, starts two-year kindergarten training

CHRONOLOGY

63	1921	Publishes booklet on evils of picture shows
		National tour with Bella, talking to maternity nurses and midwives
64	1922	Purchases 10 acres of land on hilltop at Melrose, overlooking Cook Strait
		Another trip to Australia
65	1923	Building of house begun at Melrose
66	1924	Bella's health fails, she is hospitalised
		Truby and Mary move into Melrose, Bella joins them later
		Begins ordering thousands of plants for the garden
67	1925	Truby King created Knight Bachelor
		Karitane hospital building commences on Melrose land
69	1927	Bella King dies. Truby heartbroken, never really recovers
		Karitane hospital opens
		Truby retires as Inspector-General of Mental Health, Director Child Welfare
		Truby goes to Australia
70	1928	Truby and Mary embark on European trip, returning via USA
71	1929	Truby opens Karitane Products factory in Sydney
72	1930	Conference in London is not a success, Truby's old magnetism is waning
73	1931	Falls ill in Sydney
		Rents out Melrose house, closes Sydney factory
74	1932	Mental state deteriorates. Committed but never hospitalised
76	1934	Confined to bed
78	1936	Permanent nursing support
80	1938	Sir Truby King passes away. Dies bankrupt. Buried with full State honours

CHAPTER ONE

A young man in the colonies

TRUBY KING'S parents were British settlers. His father Thomas arrived in Taranaki in 1841 at the age of twenty, not long after the signing of the Treaty of Waitangi.

Thomas King was not a typical migrant. Most people on the *William Bryan* were in cohesive family groups, mainly from Devon and Cornwall, many with young children. As a single man, Tom was rather isolated. Most passengers travelled below decks in dreadful confinement, while Tom had his own cabin on deck, at a cost of four times the usual passage.

He left behind a secure job, in charge of an office in the London Coal Exchange. His family were middle-class, his father a publican/landlord, his mother an educated woman with some inherited wealth. Unlike most Victorian families, the King's was small. Tom had but one older sister who had married well. A relative of her husband's,

Sir Henry Richardson, took an interest in young Tom, giving him a house when he left school. Life in overcrowded London could be oppressive, but it's likely that the King family lived well. Tom's father Thomas, fifty-one years older than his son, was not well educated. There is no record of any written communication with his son, but his mother Susannah's letters provided him with a much-needed link with home.

Emigrants were characterised as 'enterprising and independent-minded, looking forward to a society far more democratic . . . a chance at last of sun and air, well away from the overcrowded and disease-ridden hovels.'[1] It's hard to know what motivated Tom to leave family, friends and a secure job for remote and unknown New Zealand. He arrived with £200, a reasonable education and in ill-health.

Tom joined the Plymouth Company, an offshoot of the New Zealand Land Company, whose purpose was to acquire land for settlement by migrants from Devon and Cornwall. Notwithstanding his youth, he was elected to the eight member Committee of Colonists at the meeting of intending colonists in Plymouth on 29 October 1840. The chairman reported that their first task was 'to secure for the colony the benefit of a Clergyman of the Church of England'.[2] Principles and high-minded idealism were part of the package. 'The committee will also use every endeavour to establish the nucleus of a Literary Institution and Public Library . . . will also use its best endeavours to establish a Dispensary for the sick, and a Savings Bank.' Harmony between 'Settlers and Native Inhabitants' was also stressed in the wish-list, redolent with Victorian values and attitudes. Tom's joining up with Plymouth people was unusual, given that he was a London lad, and Plymouth was a day's coach ride away from his home. A possible explanation is that his mother's sister Kitty lived in Plymouth. Tom purchased land in Taranaki before leaving England. As with other migrant land 'purchases' of the time, it is questionable whether the land had been surveyed, or if he had title to it.

The five-month journey would have been challenging for the men, women and children, cows, pigs and rats inhabiting the steerage space below decks. The sailing ship of 311 tons had a crew of fifteen men and three boys. The passengers comprised 140, half of them children, all in a vessel of less than forty metres length with no more than two metres standing room below decks. Families were allotted communal berth space of only about a metre wide. Fortunately, the voyage was uneventful. Passengers enjoyed the luxury of dining on deck for half the time, which was infinitely preferable to eating, sleeping and trying to stay sane in cramped squalor below decks. In stormy weather they were confined below, the hatches battened down whether they liked it or not.

Food would have been palatable in the early part of the journey, but as time wore on, the provisions would have succumbed to heat and vermin. To combat the poor water, there was an imaginative selection of drink: 200 litres of lemon juice and 150 kg of sugar to mix with it, 10 bottles port wine, 10 bottles sherry, 1200 litres stout, 120 litres rum, 30 litres brandy. It sounds like a lot of alcohol, but on a 130-day voyage with pretty awful food, one wonders whether it was enough for the seventy bored and apprehensive adult passengers.

On arrival the settlers slept on the Taranaki beach, but the local Maori proved generous and raupo whares were constructed, reportedly for eighteen pounds each. These were crude dwellings, but would have been infinitely preferable to the constraints of shipboard life. One wonders what Victorian Englishmen and women made of this new country, with its high rainfall, 'natives' with whom they would have little empathy, and unfamiliar flora and fauna. Maybe the majesty of Mt Egmont, towering 2500 metres over Taranaki, brought lumps to some throats, or was it just homesickness?

The land that the Plymouth Company had purchased, sight unseen, proved to be difficult. Undulating, lumpy Taranaki terrain, an abundance of streams that were difficult to ford, and lack of suitable transport animals, made any attempt at dominance of this alien land a nightmarish proposition. Tom, the elfin clerk, must have been daunted. He was ill-equipped for this sort of experience. He had no wife or extended family to commiserate with. He probably wanted to go home. His letters paint a picture of an unconfident man.

The first few years would have been hell; it is recorded that a plague of rats swarmed around the settlement in 1843, destroying anything edible. Tom sought solace with Richard Chilman and his family, who had been fellow cabin passengers, and had a whare erected in their garden.

The disputed issue of land ownership was the first problem for these early settlers. Tom had purchased 'one section of suburban land'[3] which was to be balloted for on arrival. In 1842 Governor Hobson issued a proclamation 'prohibiting private European purchase of Maori land'.[4] A commission was set up to establish pre-1840 land sales. The 28,000 hectares of land purchased by the Plymouth Company were eventually downgraded to 1400 hectares by the new Governor FitzRoy in 1844. This threw Tom into confusion. He was not cut out to be a labourer or farmer, and now had little land and insufficient funds, and thus little influence to attract a government position. He was homesick in an alien country, with few ideas and fewer options.

He decided to reinvent himself as a trader, exploiting the one asset he had – a patron back in London. Family friend Sir Henry Richardson was well-disposed to 'young Tom'. Henry allowed him credit of £1000 to purchase goods in London to sell in New Zealand. This was the shaky beginning of Tom the speculator and trader. It wasn't easy, because there was a six-month delay in getting orders to London and receipt of the goods. The credit afforded by his patron was however sufficient to begin. All Tom had to do was obtain the right goods, hope the ship arrived without incident, sell the goods and order more. This might be easy in the days of fax and phone, but was decidedly difficult when a letter took up to six months, in which time fashions could change and demand for goods diminish. To compound matters, he was not functioning well as a single man, and suitable partners were not easy to find. His letters home described a young adult struggling to establish himself in an alien environment.

By 1846 Sir Henry Richardson had lost enthusiasm for financial support of Tom's trading activities. New Zealand was in the doldrums, Tom was on the rocks. He moved to Wellington and took a job with a fellow-trader, but that didn't work out. His health, never robust, was variable. He proposed to Mary Chilman, sister of one of his fellow migrants. She had been enticed to join her brother in 1842, but did not succumb to Tom's charms until 1846. The extended courtship, recorded elaborately in many letters, suggests he was articulate and eventually persuasive. Mary was educated, and knew Tom as a family friend. Her health was also marginal, with rickets and tuberculosis featuring prominently, although this didn't prevent her living to ninety-three. Their courtship was protracted and did not initially win favour with the Chilman family. Perhaps Tom the trader was not good enough?

Eventually he won her over. With accumulated debts, ill-health and a disillusioned patron, he was not succeeding as a trader and may not have been the greatest prospect in the world. Their marriage was forged in friendship and trust against the backdrop of a young unstable country and foundering business ventures. Tom's ill-health and insecurity was not the stuff of a great and prosperous future. He contemplated returning to England or moving to Australia but compromised with Wellington. Things were bleak. He was an ill-equipped loser in a tough land. Mary represented companionship and a fresh start. They married in November 1846 and moved to Wellington shortly thereafter, precipitated by the prospect of a Maori uprising. Wanganui was said to be in a state of war, with 300 soldiers in the stockade and the Taranaki settlers in high anxiety. Tom, with a newly pregnant wife, built a house in Wellington and commenced work with one of his trading associates while continuing his own trading activities. He was out of his depth in the bigger milieu, where traders abounded. He lacked contacts, and above all, influence. This pond appeared to him too large and he was a small fish.

In time Taranaki became less turbulent, so Tom and Mary abandoned Wellington and returned to Taranaki in 1848, selling the Wellington house and using the money to buy a farm adjacent to Mary's brother, Richard Chilman. At this point Sir Henry Richardson died and it is unclear whether Tom settled his loan or used it to finance the next stage of his precarious career.

Tom the tyro farmer, now aged twenty-seven and with a heavily pregnant Mary, began clearing land and learning the elements of pig and dairy farming. It was a precarious if self-sufficient existence.

Children came at regular intervals. Mary was born in 1848, followed by Henry, Sara, then Newton, Truby, Herbert and finally Francis in 1862. In total Mary King would have seven children, spaced at two-yearly intervals.

For Tom, further opportunity came in the unlikely form of politics. He was 'invited' to represent New Plymouth at the first General Assembly, which had been established by the New Zealand Constitution Act of 1852 and provided for the appointment of a legislative council. He jumped at the chance for self-improvement and an opportunity to participate in the making of laws for the government of the colony. He was flattered at the invitation and enough of an intellectual and idealist to realise the importance of the opportunity.

Mary was unimpressed, fearing the consequences of enforced separation. Together with two other Taranaki representatives, Tom set out for Auckland, which was then the seat of government. Unlike many of his aspiring government colleagues, he was not a wealthy man, so the unpaid role would not have been easy. He was diligent, however, working in committees, playing the part of participation rather than a leadership role. To tell the truth, he was out of his depth. He missed his wife sorely but stuck doggedly to the task. His letters are an eloquent record, painting a compelling picture of a deeply private man removed from his wife.

> My own Polly, I am so very tired. We have been six hours tonight and I was 2 in Committee this morning. The debates were most animated and at another time would have gratified me. Still they have rendered endurable a certain number of hours. Wakefield has again been discomfited by 21 to 10. Were he out of the house we would soon get home. Of course we are progressing but at too slow a rate. The overland mail from Taranaki arrived yesterday and this morning I had the pleasure of receiving my darling's letter. Oh my love I do regret my absence . . . I cannot blame myself for acting as I have. I was doubtful

of the wisdom of leaving. I knew it would give pain to both and was yet anxious to serve Taranaki as well as I could. Now darling that I have greater experience I will abandon political life. I believe that I have assisted in doing good though in a very unostentatious way and with my first essay I am content. Hereafter my fond one I will live at home. I will enjoy the society of my wife and children and will strive to do my duty in a way that will not deprive us all of comfort . . . Good night my darling wife. I could write till tomorrow but the candle is waning and I must retire to my solitary couch when I would rather have a night of bliss and embraces from my darling wife . . . Good night my treasure. Another cruel day has gone.[5]

He returned after three months in Auckland. Then followed a period of consolidation. Mary had two more children, Newton in 1856 and Truby in 1858. There were ongoing skirmishes between Maori, but the Kings' standard of living improved because Tom was now remunerated as a politician. He was in Auckland when intertribal war

Mrs Mary King, Truby's mother, c. 1850s and Thomas King, c. 1860s.

came to a head. On 28 August 1860 the following proclamation was posted:

> In communication with His Excellency the Governor and the General Government of New Zealand, and under the absolute necessity that exists for all women and children, without distinction, being as speedily as possible removed from New Plymouth His Honour the acting Superintendent will warn all those drawing rations to be prepared to embark for Nelson about the 1st proximo.
>
> The remaining families, without distinction of rank, will be warned in alphabetical order, and must be prepared to proceed to Nelson on or about the same date. The Government having made arrangements for their reception at that place, and having agreed to maintain them there. Steamers will be provided for the above purpose.
>
> By Command
> R. Carey
> Lieut-Colonel
> Deputy Adjutant-General[6]

Mary King and her five children embarked on the eighty-ton paddle-steamer *Wonga-Wonga* as the sun was setting. The passengers were battened down beneath the hatches, packed sardine-like. The journey to Nelson was a nightmare with seas of monstrous proportions, the passengers arriving the next morning 'more dead than alive'.[7] In truth, the women and children were unwilling refugees anyway, and after a trip of such awfulness, they were unhappy to say the least. Baby Truby, barely a year old, was suffering the effects of infantile diarrhoea, as well as seasickness, and nearly died. The doctor, Isaac Newton Watt, decided against 'bleeding', which was the accepted treatment for many illnesses, and opted for the 'mild' form of treatment, hourly purging with calomel and arsenic. At midnight Mary decided that the suffering of the child was such that the treatment should be discontinued after eight administrations of the purgative, so that he 'might die in peace'.[8] Miraculously he survived. It is said that Frederic Truby's constitution never recovered from this treatment. Like his father, he was destined to be dogged with ill-health for the rest of his life. The long-term harm done by mercury and arsenic purgatives to the wellbeing of our tiny subject is a tantalising question that must remain unanswered.

Life in Nelson was appalling. The townspeople were kindly enough disposed to the Taranaki refugees, but conditions were poor, the families housed in primitive barracks with communal washing and eating facilities. The children were a problem. Mary in her letters noted, 'Our little Fred tires me very much. He gives way to such horrible fits of passion and being weak, of course, hurts himself.'[9] Eldest daughter Mary was also unwell. She eventually died at the age of eighteen of tuberculosis, when Truby, her adoring brother, was eight.

Tom spent little time with the family in Nelson, commuting by precarious sea transport from Taranaki to Auckland, where his fortunes took a turn for the better. He was appointed to one of the nine Provincial Councils, as the member for the Grey and Bell electorate of Taranaki, with an assured income. He spent months at a time away from the family and became a JP, Provincial Treasurer and magistrate, cementing his position in society.

Eventually Tom, Mary and family were reunited in Taranaki after eighteen months of stressful separation. Their homestead was burned to the ground in their absence, so they took up residence in New Plymouth, near the corner of Dawson and Vivian Streets, in a big rambling house with a large garden and orchard. In 1861 Tom was appointed inaugural manager of the New Plymouth branch of the Bank of New Zealand. He remained with the bank for sixteen years. The house was spacious and well furnished. Tom's will reveals that he owned a piano, an extensive library and a collection of books that befitted a man of letters: three English, two French and one German dictionary suggested a multilingual crossword fanatic but it is more likely that he was simply a well-read man.

On his death, aged seventy-two, the *Taranaki Herald* would eulogise:

IN A STRANGE GARDEN

We have lost another of our old Colonists, and one of the leading men of this place, by the death of Mr Thomas King. The colony may, perhaps have had more prominent men in the political arena; but, in less exciting spheres of social and political activity, Mr Thomas King has, during the last half century been amongst the very foremost . . . Since 1880 Mr King has occupied his time with local matters, being Chairman of several local Boards. He has always taken a great interest in the harbour works at Moturoa, and for the last 10 years has been Chairman of the New Plymouth Harbour Board . . . Mr King has been a great reader in his time, and kept himself well posted in all affairs going on at Home and in the Colonies . . . Mr King was universally esteemed and every sign of mourning was visible in town today. The banks and other commercial institutions had their blinds down, and flags at half-mast were to be seen in every direction. Dr Truby King (in charge of the Seacliff Mental Hospital near Dunedin), Mr Newton King (the well-known merchant and auctioneer of New Plymouth) and Mr Henry King (one of the successful farmers in Taranaki) are sons; and the wife of

Truby King's childhood home, New Plymouth.

Mr. F. W. Marchant (Civil Engineer of Timaru) is a daughter of Mr Thomas King.[10]

Not present were children Francis, who died aged eighteen months, and Mary and Herbert who both died of tuberculosis aged eighteen and thirty respectively.

So ended the life of Tom, the elfin, sickly young man who left an assured career in London to experience the hardships of Taranaki, a largely unsuccessful trader turned politician, bank manager and eventually revered public figure. From his letters we know him to be articulate, sensitive, and at times consumed by ill-health, but a caring husband and father. His will indicates that he was fair in his assignment of his estate, the value of which exceeded £13,000, a tidy sum for the time. The oldest son retained the farm; the estate was divided amongst the four surviving children, his wife receiving generous investment income. Tom appointed his three sons, Henry, Newton and Truby, as executors with the proviso that Truby should not be appointed should he be away from the colony of New Zealand at the time of Tom's decease. Truby was at Seacliff at the time, but curiously he 'disclaimed and renounced' the office of executor and trustee that the will conferred. Whether he was uninterested in money or just preferred to leave his father's affairs in the hands of his older brothers in Taranaki is a matter for speculation.

Truby's mother, Mary, lived until she was ninety-three, remaining on good terms with Truby and his wife. Her pioneering contribution, putting up with periods of estrangement and bringing up a family in sometimes dreadful and unsettling circumstances, should not be understated; nor should any early influence on the sickly young Truby, which would have far exceeded that of his father Thomas.

CHAPTER TWO

Little Truby

LITTLE TRUBY got off to an inauspicious start. The nightmare boat trip to Nelson nearly killed him, although the subsequent purging failed to finish him off. His brother Francis died in his second year when Truby was six. Things didn't get much better for Truby. Gastroenteritis preceded attacks of broncho-pneumonia, pleurisy and tuberculosis; but worse still, two years later he lost his sister Mary to tuberculosis in her eighteenth year. She had been Truby's hero, his teacher and mentor, and the little boy was devastated. With his father away for extended periods and his mother distracted by a young family, Truby's relationship with his eldest sibling was unusually close. The tragedy of his sister's untimely death would stay with him all his life.

Truby's formal schooling began when he was eight and a half. It took place in a small barn. His teacher, Mr Beardsworth, lived

IN A STRANGE GARDEN

Frederic Truby King, aged eight years.

upstairs, descending each morning by ladder to instruct his pupils. Later Truby and brother Newton (two years his senior) attended the private school of Mr Crompton who was to become Speaker in the Taranaki Council and then Inspector of Schools for the Taranaki Education Board. Crompton was widely travelled and had taught in France. Truby's appreciation of the French language, in which his father was fluent, blossomed.

> The courses of study ranged well beyond the three 'Rs', to the inclusion of classical and modern languages. The one assistant, Mr Eliot, was responsible for classes in Latin and Mathematics. Although the sciences were not then regularly taught, their value was clearly appreciated by Mr Crompton, an educationalist decidedly ahead of his generation. Often in summer time he would take his pupils on long walks for Nature study. Sometimes to the seaside, sometimes to the bush, or just over the fields. He was never at a loss to classify with appropriate nomenclature the botanical specimens laid before him by indefatigable youth.[1]

Sensitive Truby did not get on particularly well in his first experiences of formal schooling, failing to respond to the physical demands of his peers, who were mostly the children of soldiers. Their games had little appeal for the bookish lad who suffered the consequences of his childhood illnesses and exhibited a marked droop in the right shoulder that would characterise him in later life.

Truby's educational development accelerated with a private tutor, Henry Richmond, a man of some intellect, here described by his biographer:

> He had advanced views on scientific subjects and published more than one pamphlet setting forth theories, which were later recognised, regarding the atom. After establishing a school in New Plymouth, he decided to qualify in Law. Passing his examinations, he was duly admitted at the age of 45 and practised in New Plymouth. He was for a short time Editor of the *Taranaki News*.[2]

Truby formed an instant liking for Richmond, who stimulated an interest in learning. Richmond believed in the value of focusing on one subject until it was fully mastered – a system of single-minded concentration that was to stay with Truby for the rest of his life. Richmond Cottage, where Truby experienced his first delights in learning, was built in 1853 by Richmond and Arthur Atkinson, and is one of New Plymouth's oldest remaining buildings.

At home Tom would read aloud to his family, often in French. With a piano in the house and parents who fostered academic discussion, Truby could only blossom.

At fifteen the quiet diligent young man joined his father's bank, continuing his studies with Richmond through night classes. One of his fellow pupils wrote, 'Nothing would ever divert him from the particular line of thought he was on at the moment.'[3] Perhaps this was the first indication that the thoughtful adolescent had a scientific bent. His clerical progress at the bank was unsurprisingly meteoric, and by the age of sixteen he was ready for something else, or perhaps his father sought to expose him to a bigger, wider world.

In 1874 Truby King transferred to the Bank of New Zealand in

Auckland. Letters home show a voracious reader, a formal and polite lad. His salary was five pounds a month. The hours he worked as a lowly clerk were daunting, often extending late into the night.

In an early letter from Auckland to his father, Truby writes:

> I suppose you have heard that young Brown has been arrested for setting fire to Hobson's building. The case was brought up on the 19th inst., the chief evidence against him being the finding of some Jewish newspapers saturated with kerosine, among other things that had been set fire there, but the case was remanded till Thursday next, bail being given by Isaacs and another Jew.
>
> I have no doubt the Jews will get him off if money will do it, being one of their nation.[4]

Whether this represented an anti-Semitic view inherited from his father, from Tom's clerical days in London, or was Truby's own opinion, it is surprising in its prejudice; Tom's biography gives no indication of anti-Semitism.

Two years later, at the age of eighteen, Truby King was promoted to the position of Private Secretary to Mr George Tolhurst, manager of the Wellington branch of the Bank of New Zealand. Tolhurst, a brilliant if hot-tempered man, had a strong influence on the developing lad. His reported intolerance of fools may well have been developed under the tutelage of Tolhurst.

By 1879, at age twenty, Truby was the assistant manager at the Bank of New Zealand in Masterton, an emerging rural town in the Wairarapa. He worked long hours, often from 8 a.m. to 10 p.m. and boarded with the manager, eventually moving to bachelor quarters with the local headmaster. Mary King records a colleague's comments on the beginnings of Truby as gardener, organiser and orator:

> Truby was a keen gardener, and, with the same love of beautiful surroundings, I soon found myself impressed by Truby into beautifying the school grounds, with the result that despite the long hours at the Bank, we soon had a respectable lot of flowers and vegetables of which we were inordinately proud.

That he retained his love of this delightful occupation, those who have had the opportunity of visiting the grounds of the Seacliff Mental Hospital, which he planted, will realise. One morning I was up early as usual and went into the garden where I found eighteen draught horses disporting themselves, having eaten most of the vegetables and rolled on the flower beds. I called Truby out, and those who know him well can imagine what he said, as, on occasion, he was gifted with a great flow of language.[5]

He was soon manager of the Bank of New Zealand in Masterton where his health problems, never far below the surface, made it necessary to have medical support and he became friendly with Dr Hosking, the local GP. He was not enjoying the banker's role of prosecuting miscreants and dealing with tales of hardship. Managing a bank, even at such a young age, did not suit him. With encouragement from his doctor friend, Truby attempted to seek his father's permission to abandon banking for a medical career. He couldn't bring himself to let his father down, and instead sought his older brother Newton's intercession. Thomas King agreed, with the proviso that Truby waited until he was twenty-one before leaving New Zealand. He offered Truby an allowance of £150 per annum, which was more than his salary at the bank. The option of education at the University of Otago, whose school of medicine opened three years earlier, was apparently not considered.

Truby saw out his time in Wellington, finally making his peace with Mr Tolhurst, who would be instrumental in his first medical appointment when he returned to New Zealand.

In August 1880 Truby King set sail for the mother country. After a short period visiting relatives, he went to Paris. Meeting Robert Smith, a young Scottish doctor, he got to see the city, including a demonstration by the redoubtable Professor Charcot, founder of modern neurology and authority on hysteria and hypnosis. The developing friendship would lead to Truby becoming a lodger with Smith's fiancée's family and, following the untimely death of Smith, King would eventually marry the fiancée himself.

Edinburgh University's medical school was founded in 1726, and became famous as one of the best medical schools in Europe. It was an all-male establishment, having resisted a feminist legal challenge ten years before Truby enrolled. He would be one of a number of New Zealanders studying medicine there when he commenced his studies in 1881.

In his first letter home he wrote:

Edinburgh, March 18, 1881

Dear Pa,
Your letter in which you reply to mine from Paris is so kind, both in words and silence, that I scarcely know how to answer it. You have always been to me the most indulgent and trusting of fathers, but latterly I have almost feared that I should find the limit even of your confiding goodness, and that you would begin to think so weak a nature as mine scarcely worthy of further care.

On this account, as there were examinations to be passed, I have carried your letter about with me, unopened, since Monday, lest it should contain any reproach calculated to upset me; for I am still – as you know I have always been – so over-sensitive, that the slightest hint of any want of confidence or of any dissatisfaction on your part, would have been quite sufficient to render me incapable of doing the work required.

Having finished the examinations for this week, I have just broken the so needlessly dreaded envelope and find it, as I said before, filled only with kindness.

With regard to the allowance of £150 a year, it is of course ample, and if I am able to live for less I shall let you know. Board and lodging is very cheap here – about 25s to 30s per week, and University expenses for Medical classes, etc., amount to only about £35 a year, which is considerably less than it would cost in London.

I shall not know the result of my present examination, which has been on four subjects, until the end of next week, but I am afraid they will pluck me in Mechanics, as I was too excited to be able to do anything, and made a most miserable paper. It is very annoying not to have done better because I had so thoroughly prepared my subject that under ordinary circumstances I could with ease have answered every question put. The other three subjects, which came later, are, I hope all right. The result of the first trial shows clearly that I shall be unable at any time to compete for scholarships, which of course requires a cool head. It is a great test for a nervous man to sit in a large hall with a hundred other students and be forced to think calmly or be plucked.

Your affectionate son
F. T. King[6]

The insecure and introspective son need not have worried. 'Plucked' he was not. In Mechanics he passed. In French and Arithmetic he got 'credit', and in Logic, the most difficult of all, he passed with distinction. His scholarship blossomed, and he passed everything from here on with better than flying colours. He managed to include Botany, Zoology and Greek in his studies, which were not required for a medical degree. Later that year he was awarded the silver medal and a certificate of first class honours. Truby the scholar was on his way. He eventually graduated MB, CM (1st Class) on 1 August 1886, having passed his first, second and third professional examinations with distinction. He decided against writing a thesis, which would have conferred the MD qualification. This he would later regret.

Truby graduated Master of Surgery, winning the coveted Ettles Scholarship as the most distinguished student of Edinburgh University. Curiously, of the 200 graduates that year, the top three were New Zealanders: Drs King, Jeffcott and Lindsay, both of the latter coming from Otago.

Truby's health problems were never far from the surface. Fearing the dreaded quinsy, he had his tonsils removed, which was not then a common operation. Worse was to come, with the vision of his left eye substantially impaired by a side-effect of tuberculosis. Ill-health appeared to prey on his mind.

It was at this point that he announced his engagement, at age twenty-eight, in a poignant letter to his mother.

Edinburgh, Jan 21st, 1886

My Dear Mother
The news of my engagement will no doubt have taken you all very much by surprise, but I trust the announcement was not displeasing. If you knew Bella, there would certainly be no question, for I am quite confident as to your all liking her very much.

How such a good, kind and loving girl comes to care for me I can scarcely understand, and it is almost equally a matter of surprise how a being so indifferent as myself to the charms of ladies' society in general should have become so infatuated with this dearest gentle girl.

Two photos which you will find enclosed may give you some idea as to her appearance, but at best one cannot form much idea of a person from a mere black and white picture, especially when the charms are more mental than physical.

A few words in regard to her family may be of interest to you. It consists of Mrs Millar; her son Robert, a Chartered Accountant; David, Engineer; Bella (future Mrs K) and Thomas, Law Student. [Mr Millar, jeweller and goldsmith was recently deceased.]

The old lady is as fine a specimen of genuine Scotch hospitality and kindness as I have ever met, and from the day I came here, her house has been as open to me as if it had been my very own. Even my friends have been made as welcome as myself, and to several of them, as to myself, Mrs Millar's house will always be their pleasantest recollection of Edinburgh.

As to the rest, Robert is as noble a man as I ever met, trusted by all his relatives, near and distant; and doing, for nothing, enough in the way of investments for them to make him a rich man if he would take any commission. Fortunately he has a very good business indeed.

Naturally, I cannot give you any idea as to when we are to be married, but Bella cannot bear the idea of my leaving Scotland without her, and I must confess that I should be extremely loath to do so myself. The family are averse to our settling in New Zealand, and if it were not for Bella's perfect willingness to accompany me anywhere, I should probably remain on this side of the globe.

However, I have resolved to practise in New Zealand. Remaining in Edinburgh would be out of the question on account of my health, for nothing but great care would enable me to keep at all well here.

Both Mrs Millar and Bella are busy making and getting things for our future, and our engagement is the subject of great temporary interest (as such things always are) to a wide circle of both her friends and mine – the latter mainly students and the London relatives.

With love to all at home,

Your affectionate son,
F. Truby King[7]

The graduation ceremony over, Truby and Bella went on holiday to the country. Bella wrote to her prospective mother-in-law:

This forenoon we went for a long walk round Kinghorn Loch and on the way we gathered a few wild flowers. The roadsides here are perfect flower gardens, they look beautiful. In the afternoon we examined the flowers and found out their names in the Flora. I never can understand how Fred remembers things. Why, he seems to know almost everything, and can always explain things so clearly that one has no difficulty in understanding about them.[8]

Truby would have been exposed to the rich Scottish tradition of gardening while studying in Edinburgh, and would without doubt have visited the city's notable public gardens and parks. The number of famous plant explorers and botanists emanating from Edinburgh at the time is hardly coincidental. His interest in rhododendrons probably dated from this time, developing later to near-obsessive levels. His fondness for the Scots and things Caledonian would also remain with him for the rest of his life.

He decided against returning home, undertaking instead further qualification in the form of a BSc in Public Health, a newly instituted degree. Medicine at that time was hardly an exact science, with many of the principles and techniques still in their infancy. His postgraduate studies included a paper in Lunacy, under Dr Thomas Clouston, later knighted for his contribution to neurology. Clouston's address to the Philosophical Society of Edinburgh on female education contains many of the elements of the contemporary belief in women's inferiority to men, and the ideal of 'healthy, ignorant and happy mothers' that would characterise King's later attitudes and pronouncements.

At the age of twenty-nine Truby was appointed to his first professional position, Resident Surgeon at the Glasgow Royal Infirmary. In recommending him, his superior in Edinburgh wrote:

Royal Infirmary, Edinburgh

April 8th, 1887

I have much pleasure in bearing testimony to the able and efficient manner in which Mr Truby King, M. B., C. M., conducted the administrative duties of the wards allotted to him during his term of office as Resident Physician in the Royal Infirmary.

That Dr King should have obtained the Ettles Scholarship, the blue ribbon of the University, bestowed upon the most distinguished graduate of his year (1886) sufficiently guarantees that his professional attainments are of the highest order. He is most zealous and assiduous in the performance of the duties devolving upon him, kind and attentive to his patients and devoted to his work.

I have no hesitation in expressing my conviction that, in due time, Dr King will take his place in the foremost rank of the profession of his choice; and I need scarcely add that I consider him to be thoroughly fitted for any Hospital appointment for which he may hold himself qualified; and to which he may aspire.[9]

As noted, of the 200 graduates that year the top three students to pass with first-class honours were New Zealanders. It appears that Truby did not feel the need to bond closely with his fellow colonials, as he makes little mention of them in his letters home. He now sported a moustache, as did many young men of the time. It would remain with him for the rest of his days.

In October 1887 Truby graduated BSc, and shortly afterwards married Bella. She was twenty-six, he was twenty-nine. After a short honeymoon, they departed for New Zealand. It was Truby's intention to return home to show off his new wife, but to complete the round trip, returning to Scotland. Leaving the wedding presents behind in Scotland, he signed up as ship's surgeon on the SS *Selembria*, a 3130-ton steam and sail vessel, at a nominal salary of one shilling a month. The ship had a drunken captain and seventy mutinous crew, and the voyage was a chapter of accidents. The cargo was poorly stowed, resulting in a permanent list. It transpired that the propeller was incorrectly fitted. On arrival at Wellington, Truby and Bella jumped ship. The ill-fated vessel eventually caught fire in Montevideo on the return journey.

SS Selembria.

Truby's vacillations regarding where to settle down are interesting. He was to have returned home on completion of his first degree, but chose to complete another, then work as a house surgeon. He was undoubtedly under pressure from the Millar family not to take Bella away to New Zealand. His love of Scotland and things Scottish will become apparent as we progress, but he was acutely aware that the Scottish climate was not good for his often frail constitution and his tubercular disposition.

Truby's passport is deposited in the Hocken archives. Aside from the large number of stamps that attested to his prodigious travels, is

Three top Edinburgh medical graduates, 1886. Truby King is on the left.

LITTLE TRUBY

Truby and Bella King, c. 1887.

the notation of his height as five feet eight inches. In 1900 this would have been regarded as average, whereas references to his size ('slight', 'tiny', 'short' were phrases often associated with the man) are confirmed by photographs. It seems that Truby King suffered from 'small man's syndrome' and was economical with the truth; or rather, optimistic when declaring his height on his passport application.

So it was that the trim, one-eyed doctor with a drooped shoulder and his new wife began the next chapter of their adventure.

CHAPTER THREE

Who am I?

TRUBY KING had planned to visit New Zealand, fulfil his responsibilities to show off his new bride, and explain to his parents why he wasn't staying, before returning to the 'mother' country on the ill-fated SS *Selembria*. Mary King tells how, twenty years later, Bella opened her purse at a social function, and out fell the return part of the Edinburgh-London railway ticket, corroborating this intention.[1] In any event, the Kings remained in New Zealand, thus necessitating the wedding presents, languishing in Edinburgh, being packed in zinc-lined cases and sent to the distant colony.

> Wellington
> February 11th, 1888
>
> Gentlemen,
> I beg to offer myself as a Candidate for the position of Resident

Medical Officer to the Wellington Hospital, and submit the following facts in support of my application.

I was born in New Plymouth, and am now in my 30th year, and am married.

My medical curriculum at Edinburgh University began early in 1881. I passed the First Professional Examination in October, 1882, with First Class Honours. In April, 1884, I passed the Second Professional Examination, also with First Class Honours, and in October of the same year the First Examination for the degree of Bachelor of Science (Public Health). I graduated as Bachelor of Medicine and Master in Surgery (M. B. and C. M.) at the University with First Class Honours in August, 1886, and obtained the 'Ettles Scholarship', which is awarded to the most distinguished graduate of the year.

During the above period I obtained eight Medals, including the First Medals in Pathology, Practical Anatomy, and Practice of Medicine.

In 1888 I was for the session a Demonstrator of Practical Physiology in the University, under Professor Rutherford, and in 1885, a Demonstrator of Anatomy under Dr Macdonald Brown, in the College of Surgeons.

After graduation I acted for a short time as *locum tenens* for Dr Matthew of Corstophine. In October, 1896, I was appointed a Resident Physician to the Edinburgh Royal Infirmary, in charge of Professor Greenfield's Wards; and, at the expiration of my term of office, in April, 1887, was appointed a Resident Surgeon to the Glasgow Royal Infirmary, under Dr Neilson Knorr, which appointment I also held for six months.

Since then I have passed my Final Examination for the degree of B. Sc. (Public Health), and arrived here yesterday a Surgeon to the s. s. 'Selembria'.

Should you honour me with your appointment, I shall devote myself entirely to the work of the Hospital.

WHO AM I?

I am, Gentlemen,
Your obedient Servant,
(Signed) F. Truby King
M.B., C.M., B.Sc.

To the Trustees
of the Wellington Hospital.[2]

What is particularly interesting is that this letter is dated the day after Truby and Bella arrived back in New Zealand, which suggests some behind-the-scenes manoeuvring on the part of family or friends. Mary King suggests that Mr Tolhurst, his previous employer at the bank in Wellington, was responsible.

Given the position that King's father had achieved in New Plymouth society, it's unlikely that there was financial pressure for Truby to seek a job immediately on arrival. He could have chosen from a number of medical positions in any New Zealand city. His choice of Wellington Hospital seems unusually hasty. For a bright, newly married young man embarking on a profession in a now-unfamiliar country, his actions are difficult to rationalise. One presumes Mrs King did not contribute to the decision, and may not have even been consulted.

In 1888 Wellington was the dominion's fourth city, with a population of around 30,000. Auckland, with over 50,000 people, Christchurch and Dunedin were all larger. Wellington Hospital, in Riddiford St, Newtown, was not large, catering for old people and accident cases. The quality of care was not high and there were a number of other hospitals operating in Wellington at the time. Standards were reportedly frightful. The hospital was starved of money and apparently nobody wanted the job that Truby applied for.

Medical Superintendent sounds an exalted position, but the history of the hospital says otherwise: 'The rapid succession of medical officers was therefore due to a system something similar to that of applying to house surgeons of the present day. They came for experience for a short period and passed out into practice or other public appointments.'[3] The hospital had thirteen Superintendents before Truby King; in the thirty-eight years from 1850, their average stay being less than three years.

Truby's acolyte, Dr Gray, gives us a glimpse of Truby's ability to investigate and rectify problems:

> Youthful as he then was to hold such a responsible post, King was already showing signs of the earnestness, the courage and the combativeness which characterised his whole after career. At that time typhoid fever was very prevalent in this comparatively new hospital and King reported to his board that he considered that the fault lay with the sewerage system. The members of the board rejected the suggestion with scorn, pointing out that the new sewerage had just been installed and could not be at fault, but King stuck to his guns. On his own initiative and at his own expense he carried out an investigation and discovered that the drains had not been connected up, but discharged into a foul cesspit in the foundations.[4]

Curiously, he would make the same investigation when he went to his next position, suggesting an early preoccupation with sanitation.

In Wellington, we find the first evidence of Truby King the educational crusader. Prior to his time, there was little formal training for nurses. Parliament would not pass the Nurses Registration Act, the first in the world, for another thirteen years. King led a movement to organise a training school for nurses. He instituted a four-month training course, the students graduating with a certificate.

Evidence of his idiosyncratic personality was beginning to emerge. It was a source of some amusement for the patients to see 30-year-old Truby in 'night wrap and carpet slippers'[5] doing his evening rounds of the wards.

Truby stayed a scant fifteen months before applying for the position of Medical Superintendent at Seacliff. This would be a position he would hold for over thirty years, making it, in the words of Barbara Brookes, 'his personal fiefdom'.

CHAPTER FOUR

An asylum by the sea

LUNACY AND troubles of the mind have never been easy topics. The early days in the colony of New Zealand saw gaols as the repository for society's misfits. Lunatics took their place alongside military deserters, convicts, delinquents, debtors, drunkards, vagrants and prostitutes.

Early gaolers apparently tolerated lunatics. There is no reported instance of the mentally disturbed being punished while in gaol. Those who became violent were restrained by irons, fetters and occasionally straightjackets. However, the imposition of the insane on the prison system was seen as unsatisfactory, leading to demands for separate housing and proper treatment for those of troubled mind. Prior to the 1870s, asylum-keepers noted that nothing could be done for many patients, except to watch them 'at the full of the moon'.[1] Humoral treatment (relating to the four bodily fluids) was still in vogue, as were techniques like head-shaving and bowel control. It is possible that Truby King's famous obsession with bowel regularity in children, frequently encountered in Plunket literature, derives from this.

Fear of lunatics, prompted by celebrated cases both in New Zealand and abroad of their murdering attendants, was reflected in public concern, culminating in the 1876 Act of Parliament to have asylums run by central government. This predated the centralisation of Education (1877) and Prisons (1880).

The first Inspector of Lunatic Asylums, Frederick Skae, was a Scot, establishing a tradition that would find ready acceptance in Truby King, who would exhibit a near-obsessive Caledonian bias. Skae's initial problem was that of overcrowding. He was required to accommodate nearly 800 patients, yet had institutional room for only 270. His long-term solution was the development of rural asylums, of which Seacliff was to be the largest and grandest. This afforded the removal of the disturbed from the purview of society, with their incarceration in the country away from prying eyes. The further appeal was undoubtedly the measure of self-sufficiency, achieved through institutional farming, which offered both employment of the (unpaid) inmates and provision of food from the asylum farm, all of which helped keep costs under control.

Situated some forty kilometres north of Dunedin, on the isolated Otago coast, Seacliff was an ideal spot to house the unwanted victims and dregs of Victorian colonial society. The twisty coastal road was arduously primitive, but the main trunk railway gave easy access to Dunedin and the north. The Seacliff Lunatic Asylum was designed by Lawson, who was the architect for Dunedin's brooding Knox church. It was to be New Zealand's largest building, an imposing Scots baronial edifice of three storeys, 225 metres long by sixty-seven metres wide, with an 'observation tower' nearly fifty metres tall. The Victorians may not have wanted their lunatics living in close proximity to them, but they certainly housed them grandly. The design was based on the Norwich County Asylum in England. Using local clay, over $4^{1}/_{2}$ million bricks were manufactured on the asylum site. Work commenced in 1878, but by the next year reports began to emerge of 'site slippage'. James Hector, director of the Geological Survey, was called in to report. He noted that the site sloped ten degrees towards the sea, with the North Wing situated on a different geological formation to the rest of the building. He cast doubts as to the wisdom of the location and recommended drainage work. The architect refused to reconsider the site, and amidst a public outcry, building continued. As the main building neared completion, grave anxiety was expressed at the continual movement in the foundations, plaster was constantly falling and alarming noises were heard in the timbers of the roof. And this without any lunatics in residence!

Seacliff was the country's largest mental institution, with fifty staff and 500 of the country's 1600 inmates, of which 37 per cent were women. In 1886, Duncan MacGregor, Inspector of Mental Hospitals, would describe Seacliff as 'inexpressibly dreary and dispiriting'.[2] He would become one of Truby King's greatest allies and supporters in the years to come. Dr MacGregor, a forthright Scot, then recently retired as Professor of Mental and Moral Philosophy and Political Economy at Otago University, held views coincident with King's. MacGregor was a Social Darwinian, believing that New Zealand was rapidly becoming contaminated with low-quality immigrants and their offspring. He was an advocate of hard work for mental patients and would be a consistent mentor to Truby King.

Following a major slip in 1887, when all female patients were evacuated from the North Wing, a Royal Commission concurred with Hector, citing poor drainage and unequal settlement. They were scathing in their condemnation of both architect and builder. The resignation of the Medical Director next year was hardly surprising.

Against this background, it is interesting to ponder Truby King's application for the position. His academic qualifications far exceeded the requirements, although his knowledge of care of the insane was 'only a fortnight's post-graduate training in psychiatry at Edinburgh University'[3] as a cynical commentator tartly observed. Truby would have been well aware of the terms of reference of the job, and should have been able to comprehend what it offered him in terms of

IN A STRANGE GARDEN

Seacliff, the grand baronial asylum.

personal and professional development. Medically, it could only have been a backwater. Orthodox medical men of the time (there were no women) regarded the choice of psychiatry as 'evidence of eccentricity more appropriate to a patient'.[4] His work at Wellington Hospital could hardly have been called unorthodox, and there is evidence, in the form of a glowing testimonial from his hospital staff, that his tenure there was satisfactory. So why did King turn away from the conventional practice of medicine in Wellington, to become director of the country's largest asylum in the remote South Island countryside?

The salary was larger, the title grander, the responsibilities broader. We shall see that money meant little to King, who died a pauper and invariably gave away more than he earned. With the appointment came a number of other grand titles: Lecturer in Mental Diseases, Examiner in Public Health and Examiner in Medical Jurisprudence at the University of Otago (then New Zealand's only medical school) in Dunedin. While these may have been flattering to his ego, the main thrust of his chosen occupation was to be the care of people loosely classified as 'mentally ill'. Did he have a vocation for this?

His colleague, successor and long-time admirer, Dr Gray saw it thus:

> Truby King was, I think, the only person I have known intimately who could, without any reservation, be called a genius, and exemplifying the unexpectedness of genius, although he held the position of Medical Superintendent of a mental hospital for thirty-two years, his real interests lay, not in mental hospitals or patients, but in the nurture and care of infants, in which field of medicine he became an international authority. I have no doubt that Truby King could have excelled in almost any career, as an actor he would have reached the top flight, as a criminal lawyer in the wider scope of the English bar he would have without doubt have attained eminence.[5]

What prompted King's career change, we'll never know. All we can do is to examine his *modus operandi* and judge him from his results.

The hospital that Truby King inherited was structurally unsound and the inmates mentally unsound. Truby's task was to impart harmony and to foster soundness. Historian Frank Tod reported thus:

> In a matter of months, the entire landscape surrounding the hospital was changed. The virgin bush rapidly cleared to make way for lawns, flower gardens and playing fields. For inmates whose liberty was more restricted, recreational grounds were specially prepared to enable them to enjoy the outdoor scenery and benefit from the fresh air. These grounds, or recreational yards as they were later called, were surrounded by brick or wooden walls, but care was taken in their construction not to obstruct the view.[6]

Over a period of years Truby King would articulate and develop his holistic beliefs in a healthy environment, in exercise and fresh air; themes that he would revisit, restate and refine. The environment in which he worked was flexible and unfettered. The guidelines for running the institution were few, beyond the need to satisfy the

Inspector of Asylums. King had a virtually free hand in his treatment of the insane, and in the management of a large agricultural enterprise.

Initially he set about correcting some of the outstanding deficiencies. Firstly, the water supply was replaced, with an elaborate piped system from a distant spring. Sanitation, drainage and ventilation came under scrutiny, were rectified and upgraded. King could do little but complain at the overcrowding, but with the resolution of the North Wing's problems, the physical environment became more tolerable.

The farm came in for considerable scrutiny, to produce the right dietary ingredients to fulfil his idea of what a patient should eat. The previous 'three meat meals a day' regime was drastically reviewed to a more balanced healthy diet. Patients, unless physically incapable, were turned into farm workers, neatly achieving King's goals of improved fitness and exposure to fresh air, as well as occupying minds with healthy outdoor pursuits.

Dr MacGregor's 1889 annual report to parliament is instructive. He noted 'greatly improved appearance and health of the inmates, all but forty-eight males out in the open air, 217 males working on the farm, much higher than any other New Zealand institution'.[7] A year later his report was more effusive: 'Seacliff is no longer a prison where crowds of men and women are confined in close courtyards doing nothing but brooding over their morbid feelings.' He observed that: 'The administration is vigorous and careful. The farm is steadily being cleared and is increasing yearly in its productiveness . . . the best spirit prevails among the staff . . . I have offered King an assistant but he prefers for the present to keep the whole of the medical treatment in his own hands.' Here, perhaps, is the first clue that Truby was unwilling to have anyone meddling in 'his' social experiments.

Of the 142 patients committed to Seacliff in a typical year (1905), the reason for their interment were given as:[8]

Reason	total	women	men
Congenital & heredity	27	9	18
Unknown	22	4	18
Epilepsy	21	3	18
Alcoholism	16	3	13
Senility	15	5	10
Domestic troubles	7	7	0
Masturbation	5	0	5
Childbearing	4	4	0
Climacteric	4	4	0
Injury	3	1	2
Adolescence	2	2	0
Diabetes	2	2	0
Overwork	2	2	0
Puberty	2	2	0
Syphilis	2	2	0
Apoplexy	1	1	0
Chorea	1	0	1
Dissolute	1	1	0
Fright	1	0	1
Ill health	1	1	0
Influenza	1	0	1
Surgical operations	1	0	1
Worry	1	0	1

A 'lunatic' as defined in law was someone 'judged unable to manage their own affairs.'[9] King had no control over who was committed. Aside from the genuinely mentally ill, he had to cope with the aged, alcoholics and those committed by unscrupulous families.

He instituted a number of employment changes. The privileges regarding priority assignment of food were withdrawn, with staff eating the same meals as patients. 'Inferior Chinese tea' was replaced by 'good Ceylon tea' for staff and patients alike. Staff were subject to instant dismissal for any acts of violence against patients. Democratically, the billiard table that was previously reserved for staff was made available to patients by day, with staff access only when patients were in bed.

Inevitably, King's reforms met with some dissent, culminating in complaints from a disaffected staff member, via *The Globe,* and newspaperman W. F. Kitchin, whose complaints prompted a parliamentary inquiry. Truby King's replies to the ten charges, although lengthy, are worth reading. His character resonates through the eloquent, carefully worded retort, which is reproduced in full in Frank Tod's history of the Seacliff district.[10] With a measure of gravity, tempered with wit, Truby King analysed and demolished the charges brought against him. Naturally the Department stood firmly behind their Doctor King, the charges all being dismissed.

Barbara Brookes noted:

> Truby was, above all an individualist, 'not a clubman' and as superintendent of an isolated asylum aiming for self-sufficiency, he was able to develop his theories to the full, untrammelled by the constraints of collegiality. He refused an early offer of an assistant, preferring to keep the whole of the medical treatment in his own hands. Seacliff became his personal fiefdom in which he attempted to create a world based on the principle of 'hygiene for the body, hygiene for the mind'. This implied external improvements to the living conditions of the patients, and close attention to their moral welfare. The former could be achieved by improvements in plumbing, ventilation and diet, while the latter relied on exercise, suitable recreation, rest and the greatest amount of liberty consistent with safety.[11]

Not content with solving the building's shortcomings, King set out to extend the scope of the asylum. Realising the untapped potential of the sea, he established a fishing station at Karitane, some six kilometres north of Seacliff. The resident attendant and three patients caught over 3½ tons of fish, of which half was smoked and used at Seacliff, the balance going to other public institutions. King used his own money to provide a cottage for his fishermen. Ten years later, the fishing boat had increased in size, and doubled as a pleasure boat to amuse patients. The annual catch had grown to over 100 tons. This would approximate three kilograms of fish per patient per week, so one assumes King managed to turn the other institutions in Otago into compulsive fish-eaters, all of this before the advent of refrigeration. The inspector's report for 1903 details a month's production of four tons being distributed to: Christchurch Asylum (1675 lb), Burnham Asylum (120 lb), Caversham Industrial School (150 lb), Dunedin Hospital (100 lb), Ashburn Hall (100 lb), Orokonui Home (60 lb), Benevolent Institution, Dunedin (200 lb), Salvation Army Refuge (10 lb), Old Men's Home, Ashburton (100 lb), Samaritan Home, Christchurch (100 lb), after providing two days dinner per week for Seacliff patients and staff. He insisted that fish was dispatched fresh, which meant the day it was caught. A recent (2001) article in the *Otago Daily Times* suggests that Truby King was responsible for the development of Karitane's fishing industry, which at its peak saw sixty fishing boats working from the town.[12]

Now aware of the scope of his job, King saw no difficulty in including property development within his portfolio. Recognising the need for staff accommodation in the Seacliff village adjacent to the asylum, he bought land and erected houses. Where a lesser person would have first sought approval from his superiors, he adopted the direct approach. Land was purchased, eight cottages erected, staff installed, and repayments deducted from their wages. Sometimes the simplicity of King's methods defies contradiction. As an afterthought, he bought adjacent land as a park for the attendants' children. Today, faced with Crown Health Enterprises, District Hospital Boards, Resource Consents and local council mandarins, King might well be driven insane.

His thoughts for his staff extended far beyond his responsibilities as an employer. His medical position gave him access to all employees, and he would think nothing of invading a worker's house at any time of day or night. Kath Lonie recounted to me how he was well-known for appearing in the small hours of the morning, to demand a stamp for the letter he had just written.[13] Truby King's staff belonged to him.

After five years at Seacliff, King had the asylum running efficiently. Bursts of feverish activity were, however, punctuated by long periods of poor health. The family curse of tuberculosis continued to hang over him, to his continual anxiety. Deaths from tuberculosis in the

Truby and Bella in the Seacliff garden, 1890s.

family were a grim reminder. Francis had died at eighteen months, Mary his beloved sister at eighteen years, younger brother Herbert had recently succumbed at the age of thirty, and Truby himself had lost most of the sight in his left eye with tubercular complications some years earlier. He had long spells confined to bed – six months in 1892, running the hospital by proxy, doubtless driving Bella and his acolytes madder than usual.

Between bouts of illness, Truby still managed to achieve a lot, both at the hospital and elsewhere. In 1893 he and Bella went on a tour of the Catlins, in remote South Otago, where later he would buy property and indulge himself as a farmer, sawmiller and goldminer. The following year he and Bella returned to England for Truby to study brain pathology, and to qualify as a member of the Psychological Society. On his return to Seacliff he was once more confined to bed for the winter. Late in 1896 Truby and Bella took extended leave, returning to Edinburgh, coming back via Queensland. Despite his frailty, Truby managed to travel extensively. His mentor, MacGregor, Inspector of Asylums, looked after him handsomely. In May 1904, he wrote:

> I have the honour to inform you that the Cabinet has granted you six months sick leave on full pay. Arrangements will be made to relieve you of duty as soon as possible, and I shall be glad if you will remain in charge until these can be effected. I deeply regret the cause which has rendered cessation of work on your part necessary, and trust that at the end of the period you will return to your duties with fully restored health.

With an often unwell King in sole charge of the asylum, it's a credit to the staff that it functioned at all. That the Inspector sought cabinet approval for six months' paid sick leave suggests remarkable sympathy on behalf of his superiors.

In August Truby and Bella set sail for Japan. Despite the convalescent intent, it was hardly a relaxing trip. Stopping in Sydney, Brisbane and Darwin, then on to Manila and Hong Kong, they finally arrived in Japan. The autumn heat was trying but Bella and Truby saw all the tourist sights. They subjected themselves to a strenuous regime, travelling from one end of the country to the other, staying not always in tourist hotels but frequently in Japanese accommodation. In four months they saw and experienced more than the average healthy tourist might have attempted. Truby managed to interview professors of agriculture, visit hospitals, see nurseries and obtain seeds of new plants. Being a keen photographer, he managed to infiltrate Japanese photographic studios to develop his plates, this being before the days of modern cameras and processing. Nothing apparently was too difficult for him.

As a relaxing health cure it was a disaster, but as a window on another culture it was enlightening. Bella and Truby King were impressed with the degree of 'natural' feeding practised by the Japanese, with every baby being breast-fed, generally far more than six months, often to two years. They were also impressed with the fitness of the Japanese, taking note of the diet that apparently contributed to their wellbeing. King, the inquisitive intellectual, managed to absorb enough of the Japanese culture for the experience to remain with him forever. He accumulated a large number of Japanese prints, artefacts and mementoes, and even managed to acquire an ornate Japanese musical instrument. It is unclear how this seriously unwell man even contemplated a trip of such magnitude. Tuberculosis would have substantially diminished his energy. A more sane, less frenetic person might have contemplated a health resort, or a quiet convalescent holiday with a pile of books.

Shortly after returning from Japan, Truby, who was then aged forty-seven, and Bella, forty-five, adopted Mary. This was an event that would set him on a new path of infant nutrition, and would eventually lead to the formation of the Plunket Society. It had its genesis at Seacliff, but is covered in later chapters.

Notwithstanding his enforced leisure due to recurrences of poor health, King wrote prodigiously. Not long after his return from the Japan trip, he published *The Feeding of Plants and Animals*, which by itself would have ensured lasting fame. The next year came one of his more extreme works, *The Evils of Cram*. This was a particularly odd and trenchant attack on 'over-pressure' in schoolchildren's study, which he believed responsible for adolescent insanity. In a later chapter, this theme is explored at length.

Back at Seacliff, King's classification of mental patients advanced, allowing better tailoring of treatment and rehabilitation. One of his goals was to get patients ready to be discharged out to a job. He recognised early in his career that 'unless a patient was discharged within six months he was there for life'.[14] Those ready for discharge would go out with a letter describing what they were suited to, and what they should avoid. It was favourably commented upon by his inspectors that King always knew every patient, and could recite their symptoms, treatment and prospects without reference to notes.

King's attitude to alcoholism was unequivocal. He had read widely and considered alcoholism a vice, not a disease. While his father kept alcohol in the home, Truby is believed to have been virtually teetotal. He advocated the compulsory detention of alcoholics, believing that recovery inside twelve months was unlikely. He did not believe that alcoholism was inherited. His distaste for alcohol, and for alcoholics, was marked. 'It is a commonplace of medical experience that men often give up drink after years and years of habitual excess, and when all hope of reformation has been abandoned, but that this hardly ever takes place in the case of women' noted Truby in a letter to Mrs Cracroft Wilson of the Plunket Society in Christchurch.[15] His views of women's differing abilities extended to their susceptibility to alcohol.

With the passing of the Voluntary Boarders at Mental Hospitals Act, King instituted the Orokonui Home for Inebriates at Waitati, some ten kilometres south of Seacliff, staffed with special attendants, hand-picked from Seacliff for their staunchness and insensitivity to the perceived habits of alcoholics. This sounded like an early form of alcoholic Tough Love. King had patients referred to him from all over New Zealand, and is recorded as never having refused entry to anyone.

Was he a good and conscientious doctor to the insane? Undoubtedly, yes. The annual reports to parliament from the various inspectors who supervised his thirty-two years at Seacliff were always effusive in their assessment of Truby King's work. He treated his staff more than fairly, going out of his way to ensure their housing and ongoing education were looked after. He went to considerable lengths to improve the conditions that his patients lived under, with accommodation that was bright and cheerful, and grounds that were inspiring in their beauty. He provided fresh, nourishing food, with due consideration to the best nutrition and most appropriate ingredients.

There are many instances of King's creativity. He replaced the drab institutional décor with more cheerful colour schemes. He ensured that the gardens produced adequate supplies of fresh flowers for the wards. He developed staff training schemes where attendants could advance their qualifications and therefore salaries. He introduced the nursing of male patients by women, which had a measurable soothing effect. He was liberal in giving patients restricted liberty. He developed the library and persuaded newspapers to donate their daily organs. He built, at his own expense, cottages where patients nearing release could live more normal lives. He encouraged patients to dress not in drab institutional garb, but in clothes more akin to those worn by 'normal' people. In essence, his was a very 'Kiwi' approach. He rejected the mumbo-jumbo of early psychiatry, opting instead for down-to-earth, common-sense treatment of his inmates as people to be helped with holistic natural treatment.

Mention should be made of King's most famous patient at Seacliff, one Lionel Terry, poet, author and artist. Terry was Eton and Oxford educated, emigrating to New Zealand in 1901 after roaming the world. He was an imposing man of six feet four inches, towering over the diminutive Truby. Terry was King's most celebrated patient, and a genuine eccentric. He embarked on a walking tour of the country, covering 900 miles in forty days, giving lectures in every town he came upon, camping at night in the sleeping bag that always accompanied him. His first New Zealand publication[16] warned against the 'yellow peril': the advent of the Chinaman and alien immigration to the colony. In Wellington, in an act of premeditation, he shot and killed an innocent Chinese before dramatically turning himself in to the police. The case aroused much public interest, and Terry was found guilty and sentenced to death. Public interest was intense, and a petition of 50,000 signatures sought his release. The sentence was later commuted to life imprisonment, and Terry eventually found his way to Seacliff, having dramatically set fire to his prison cell and serially escaped from the Sunnyside asylum. An habitual escaper, he led the authorities a merry chase, refusing King's offer of the freedom of Seacliff in return for his word not to escape. Truby King eventually resorted to giving Terry his own exercise yard, in which he was always accompanied by two guards. At his most difficult, Terry had to be force-fed by a tube, which necessitated six men. After a spell in gaol following yet another escape, Terry relented and accepted King's offer, giving his word that he would not escape. Thereafter he lived a rather exalted life, with his own suite, his own guards, and meals specially prepared to his instructions. Truby King took a personal interest in Terry, often inviting him to his house for a meal and game of cards. A later Medical Superintendent offered the opinion that Truby King did not realise the unique difficulties that Terry posed.[17]

AN ASYLUM BY THE SEA

Two of Terry's poems are worth review:

Emotional Insanity

Oh let us sing the praises of the Medical Profession!
Those sleek, silk-hatted gentlemen of smiling self-possession!
It doesn't matter who you are, nor what you do or say,
They'll diagnose your symptoms in a most amazing way.
For instance, if a blackguard cheats your daughter or your wife
And you seize a handy shooting-iron and end his little life.
Rash man! Your actions won't accord with Mercy or Humanity!
You prove yourself a victim of Emotional Insanity!
Or, if a swarm of Jews or Chows, invade your native land
And spread a few diseases of an extra special brand.
And if they teach your boys and girls the latest thing in vice,
And gen'rally prevent your getting peace at any price.
And if, at last, you rise against a state of things chaotic,
And give foul play to feelings which, are mainly patriotic.
Alas! Such conduct won't conform with Modern Christianity!
Most clearly, you're afflicted with Emotional Insanity!
Then let us bow our heads in awe, and crawl in abject meekness
Before these wondrous Medicos who probe our mental weakness!
They'll analyse the minds of men, of highest reputations
And prove that all are victims of some awful aberration!
In fact, although it seems to smack of blasphemy and libel,
Anent a little tragedy that's mentioned in the Bible.
They'll glance above their spectacles and state with bland urbanity,
That Holy Moses suffered from Emotional Insanity![18]

Truby King himself suffered Terry's poetic jibes. This poem addresses his Plunket period:

> Hark the Herald Angels sing
> Glory to our Truby King.
> He has humanised the cow;
> She will feed our babies now.
> Joyful all ye people rise,

> Fattest brat takes Plunket prize.
> Hear his lectures, read his tracts,
> Study all his latest facts;
> Then unite with us and sing
> Glory to our Truby King.[19]

King, not noted for his sense of humour, commented that 'I was more interested in bone and muscle than fat'.[20] Whether Truby had the ability to laugh at himself is captured in a story found in the memoirs of Eleanor McLagan, one of the first women doctors, who Truby employed briefly at Seacliff.

> Later, Sir Truby left Seacliff and was promoted Inspector of Asylums. On one occasion he visited Seacliff on an inspection. Sir Truby was accommodated in two semi-detached rooms near the entrance to the asylum. A conscientious nightwatchman noticed the door unlocked, looked in, saw someone sleeping and locked the door. In the morning Sir Truby found himself locked in. He called and called, he banged and banged. An attendant came by, heard the row and unlocked the door. A furious King cried 'Let me out! Let me out! I'm Sir Truby King'. The attendant who didn't know Sir Truby by sight, thought he'd got a particularly raging lunatic here. 'Yes, yes,' he answered soothingly, 'We've got two more Sir Trubys upstairs,' and locked him in again. Later the Superintendent came to see why Sir Truby hadn't turned up for breakfast, and rescued him. Sir Truby could not see any humour in the situation.[21]

Did Truby King succeed at Seacliff? Undoubtedly, his patients were better fed, fitter and very likely happier. In the context of mental health, the answer is less clear, and as far as the curative record is concerned, the results are more equivocal. Statistics from the annual reports to parliament, over the most significant period of King's tenure (1889–1907) show that nationally the average recovery rate of patients in all asylums other than Seacliff was 9.4 per cent. The Seacliff recovery rate of 6.7 per cent is substantially lower. Significantly, Seacliff never exceeded 7 per cent discharge:recovery, while other asylums frequently exceeded 10 per cent. Previous commentators have claimed King's success rate was much higher but this is not supported by the facts. As King was in charge of more than a quarter of New Zealand's insane, this statistic must be seen as significant, notwithstanding the high number of residents who for a variety of reasons were unlikely ever to be released. Given the continual overcrowding pressure on asylum space, it's unlikely that King would have been permitted to allow his patients to stay longer than in other institutions. A more robust analysis of statistics from the twenty-year period from 1902 to the year he left Seacliff, shows that Truby King's Seacliff was the least successful of all major mental institutions, as measured by the discharge:recovery statistics reported annually to parliament through the Appendix to the Journals of the House of Representatives. Over that period, the four major institutions reported:

Auckland	1781	11% recovered or discharged
Wellington	1547	9%
Christchurch	1077	8%
Seacliff	1033	6%

The inescapable conclusion, therefore, is that under Truby King Seacliff had the poorest record of major New Zealand asylums of curing or discharging its inmates. Curiously, in all the annual reports to parliament, this statistic was never amplified or remarked upon, despite annual tabulation of a variety of indicators of performance. It should, however, be noted that Truby King always enjoyed the effusive confidence of every Inspector of Mental Asylums.

Seacliff finally ceased to be an asylum in 1970. The unstable baronial mansion was demolished in 1959. Its patients were transferred to the new facility nearby at Cherry Farm while treatment of patients in the other Seacliff facilities continued. Much of the land and newer buildings have gone back into private ownership. The Otago Regional Council now maintains some of the land as Truby King Park. It has a serene and haunting atmosphere.

Dr Eleanor McLagan recalls her time working at Seacliff:

Seacliff's beautiful farm not only supplied much of the asylum's food, but also provided occupation for patients who were able and happy to work under supervision but unable to look after themselves in the outside world.

Sir Truby's brilliant mind and catholic interests rapidly made him a master of many aspects of farming – particularly in the breeding of prime stock, in which he succeeded so well, and the asylum took so many prizes, that the farmers objected to the competition as unfair. After that, asylum stock went to shows 'for exhibition only' and for sale as studs. If one wanted a pamphlet on how to rear calves, for instance, the Agriculture Department gave one written by Dr King. How to get a good percentage of eggs – ditto. When the potato blight first hit New Zealand, his was the pamphlet on how to combat it. All this interest and the knowledge gained on rearing young animals was afterwards switched to babies. But exactly why he switched to babies is not altogether clear.[22]

In truth, Truby's greatest success came as a farmer, as we shall see in Chapter Six.

CHAPTER FIVE

Colonising the Catlins

OF ALL Truby King's strange exploits, the Catlins venture might well be the strangest.

In the early days of Seacliff the Kings took a holiday in the Catlins area of South Otago. Today, the Catlins remains one of the least-known treasures of New Zealand, a wilderness nature reserve of magnificent native bush, wild coastlines, abundant birdlife and some imaginative tourist tracks and facilities. Even in the twenty-first century, many of the roads remain unsealed. In its uninhabited state one hundred years ago it must have been very wild, inhospitable and extremely challenging.

In 1893, when the Kings visited, the Catlins were feeling the benefits of the new railway that was pushing south from Balclutha. New Zealand needed timber and the Catlins was a rich source of rimu and other native timber, ready for exploitation. The railway made it possible. The 295-metre rail tunnel at McDonalds had just been completed with the labour of gangs of unemployed from Dunedin, working in conditions that were little better than those of the goldrush. Despite the terrain, the Catlins were being tamed. The climate was described as 'winter for nine months, rain for the other three'.[1] Sandflies and mosquitoes terrorised intruders in the summer months; clinging mud was the winter attraction.

Against this unlikely backdrop, Truby and Bella King apparently fell in love with the Catlins. In typical pioneering fashion, and despite their poor health, they ventured up the Catlins River for a three-day camping trip in a flat-bottomed boat. The area had only recently been settled, with pioneers still battling to clear bush to establish their farms. Notwithstanding the rain and some dismal camping experiences, Bella wrote, 'The Doctor is looking and feeling very well indeed, and says he has never enjoyed a holiday so much.'[2]

With native bush on the low hills and broad valleys, and more than occasional rain, the Catlins would have daunted all but the most

Travel in the Catlins wasn't easy, c. 1912.

Truby King's timber mill at Tahakopa.

optimistic. The railway had only just reached Owaka but in 1911 Truby King purchased the nine-hectare Lauriston farm at Tahakopa, thirty kilometres from anywhere, along barely formed rutted tracks that challenged horse-drawn transport. Rivers had to be forded and comfort would have been minimal. The logic of his purchase is hard to explain. King, at fifty-two, was enjoying the first success of Plunket, but he had a lot more to do. Before him was the task of touring the nation and selling the Plunket message, after which he would embark on substantial overseas travel. He already had the Seacliff farm to indulge his agricultural fantasies, together with a horde of 'volunteer' workers — why would he want a farm in such an inaccessible and inhospitable place? He could easily have bought land near Seacliff if he had wanted. The only explanation was that this land was cheap, but then Truby was hardly a cheapskate, certainly not a pragmatic investor. Was this a challenge that he really needed? The trip from the Catlins to Dunedin was daunting. Even when the railway reached Tahakopa, the trip from Seacliff was a considerable undertaking for a healthy man, let alone a hyperactive director of New Zealand's biggest asylum.

With his usual zeal, King undertook challenges that few would have considered. When the railway eventually reached Tahakopa in

1915, he decided that he would extend it across the river to Lauriston. Not content with a makeshift bridge, he used imported Australian hardwood and constructed a magnificent edifice – a bridge that remains today, a curious anachronism now stripped of its railway line. Reputedly, the Lauriston extension was one of the few private railway lines in the country constructed to Railways' satisfaction and served to link King's Lauriston timber mill to the outside world. The mill was extensive and modern, the first to use steam-powered locomotives and an overhead [skyline], logging haulage system. Unusually, the railway lines were steel, not the wooden ones of less ambitious mills.

King's timber-milling venture had his older brother Newton and New Plymouth doctor Syd Allen as partners. Syd Allen had briefly worked for Truby King at Seacliff and would eventually marry King's niece. While Allen played a passive role, Newton took an active and practical interest, perhaps keeping brother Truby's excesses somewhat curbed. The mill failed to pay expected dividends. Nevertheless, it produced over a million super feet of timber each year, which made it one of the larger mills operating in the area. Less than competent management took its toll, competition from imported timber didn't help and the depression provided the final death knell. The mill ceased operation in 1929, two years after Newton King and Bella King had died.

Initially, milled timber was used to construct houses as King set about stamping his manic personality on Tahakopa. More land was acquired until King owned six farms: Lauriston, Valley Farm, Jersey Vale, Scotts, Homestead and Township farms, totalling over 600 hectares. This land is amongst the most fertile in the country and it is a sad commentary to see such prime farmland now used for exotic trees for chip-milling.

Twenty-four houses were built to provide rent-free accommodation for the mill workers, to a considerably higher standard than elsewhere. For married workers they comprised four or five rooms, with ranges and baths; single workers had huts.

Oblivious to the expense, King drained the river flat land and brought it into cultivation. Farming was initially cropping, then changed to mixed farming and finally dairy farming for the butter and cheese factory. The most technically advanced dairy farm was constructed, with the first herring-bone milking shed, electric lighting, hot water, machine-milking, concrete underfoot and innovative animal handling.

Power was required for the dairy venture, so King constructed a water-wheel using an adjacent stream as prime motive power for the electric generator. Then he built a steam auxiliary generator, just in case the hydro power failed. It is perhaps fortunate that nuclear power had not yet been invented.

The milking herd exceeded 100 cows. In best King tradition, they were the finest milking stock: Jersey and Friesian. In accordance with the best hygiene, cows walked through a disinfecting water-bath before entering the milking shed. Never were there such coddled cows.

Over 1.5 tons of milk went daily to the cheese factory, of which King was the largest shareholder. From the cheese factory came whey as a by-product, so he built a piggery. Whey was piped to the piggery, which produced over thirty pigs a month that fetched top prices at market.

Even the swedes lined up for Truby King.

King is remembered at Tahakopa for 'the best of the best'. He reputedly had the ability to get the best out of his employees and his 'people problems' were minimised. They must have been a compliant lot, for he saw no problem in invading their houses to ensure that his high standards were not being breached, just as he did at Seacliff. Were they unconsciously being socially uplifted by King? Competitions were organised for 'the best-kept house and garden'.[3] Points were awarded by the triumvirate (King, farm manager Murphy and another employee, O'Byrne) who would randomly visit, scoring such attributes as cleanliness, housekeeping, hygiene, home improvements and garden. Prizes (typically ten pounds) were awarded, with larger families being awarded bigger prizes.

On his regular trips to Tahakopa, Truby King visited everyone from farm workers to mill workers to bushmen, dispensing advice, medical treatment and undoubtedly a heavy dose of patronage. As the community grew, the schoolhouse became too small. He immediately donated land and supervised the design and construction of the new school himself, donating timber from the Lauriston mill. He rejected the Education Board's plans, on the grounds of not enough fresh air and light. He undoubtedly knew best.

King would stay overnight at the mill manager's house. An outside door allowed access to the porch, where he would hatch more plans for a better world. Locals remember the 'thump, thump, thump' of King pacing at night as he grappled with another scheme.[4]

Not even King's Seacliff patients were free from servitude at the Catlins. How he managed to construe this as occupational therapy we'll never know, but locals remember with amusement the stories of mental patients shovelling lime onto his paddocks. The unofficial record was 100 tons of lime spread fifteen centimetres deep on a small paddock.[5]

At its peak Tahakopa thrived as a mill town at the end of the Catlins railway line. Population peaked at over 400 people but the end was not far away. King realised that his extravagant investments were not going to pay off and saw the timber running out. The depression was not far off, and he was moving to Wellington. He sold his farms in 1921. For the grand sale, a special train was commissioned to bring buyers from Dunedin to Tahakopa, with over 600 people attending. The stock sold well above expectation: 124 head of cattle averaged 21 pounds 18 shillings, high prices for the time; 500 lambs averaged 23 shillings, fat sheep 34 shillings. The farms were sold, but collection of the money proved less simple. King's terms of payment were kind, if unwise. Interest payments fell into arrears and yet another King venture failed to deliver financially. By 1929 five of his farms had come back into his ownership with the default of the tenants. King wrote to Andrew Sutherland, his trusted farm manager, 'There is with me something more than the mere matter of money. I want to be able to feel for the rest of my life (which may not be a very long time) that I have left my old property in a creditable state . . .'[6]

Mary King records, 'Perhaps the man who made the most out of the farm venture was a patient from the Mental Hospital at Seacliff who was paid 14 shillings a day as a farm labourer, and had £1,400 in the bank when the farm was sold.'[7]

Today, Truby King's ghost has all but departed the Catlins. The mill closed in 1929 and the mill houses were moved to other places. The mill manager's house remains as a comfortable farmhouse on Lauriston farm, which like most Catlins farms struggles to make sense of the 'new' realities of farming in the twenty-first century. Many Catlins farms are now foreign-owned, growing exotic gums. Only the railway bridge stands proud but bemused, bereft of railway line and shrouded by willows. A solitary rhododendron struggles valiantly in the overgrown front garden of a deserted worker's cottage while the Tahakopa school faces dwindling rolls and threats of closure.

The company was incorporated in September 1911 and dissolved in 1925.

And if it wasn't enough to be a doctor, farmer and timber miller, Truby King wanted to be a goldminer. Mary King wrote of 'an unsuccessful gold-dredging venture, beginning in 1903 and ending with the burning of the dredge about 1908 (thought to be the revengeful act of a dismissed employee), the Argyle Gold Dredging

Memorandum of Association
Railhead Dairy Factory Company[8]

name	occupation	shares
Frederic Truby King*	physician, Seacliff	175
Charles Crowe	cheesemaker, Tahakopa	25
William Wilson*	farmer, Papatowai	40
Herbert Philp	farm hand, Tahakopa	20
Hugh Galbreath	farmer, Tahakopa	20
David Brown Fea*	farmer, Tahakopa	25
Arthur Stoddart*	farmer, Tahakopa	25
David Neill*	farmer, Tahakopa	25
Colin Martin*	farmer, Papatowai	25
Archibald Skey*	farmer, Wharuarimu	10
John Dunlop	farmer, Wharuarimu	20
Archibald Galbreath	farmer, Tahakopa	25
John Harris	farmer, Tahakopa	25
David Bond	farmer, Tahakopa	25

* director

Company, operating near the head of the Waikaka Valley was wound up'.[9] Her disapproval of the venture is palpable, probably in proportion to Truby's gung-ho enthusiasm.

Why did he do it? We'll never know, although there is a handwritten reference in Mary's files to 'mad gold speculators Sir L and Lady B, who took dad and mum for a fortnight's tour of the goldfields in a wagonette'.[10] Maybe Truby just couldn't avoid the lure of a venture stimulated by a titled acquaintance? He wouldn't have been the first to be seduced by a speculative gold proposition, especially if suggested by 'someone smart'. He was involved in at least three gold-dredging ventures on or near the Waikaka River, not far from the Catlins. These were: Sheddon's Freehold 1901–1904, on the Sheddon property, in partnership with the landowners (King commissioned the dredge and largely financed the venture); Rex 1901, again in partnership with the Sheddon family (this venture ended acrimoniously, in the courts); and Argyle 1902–1907. The Argyle Gold Dredging Company was incorporated in December 1902, with nominal capital of £6000. Partners were Truby and Bella King, Dr Alexander and Miss Beswick (matron of Seacliff Mental Hospital). Monthly meetings took place at Seacliff, with Truby in the chair.

The Argyle dredge was purchased by Truby for £3900 and relocated from near Beaumont on the Clutha River. In cavalier King fashion, no expense was spared. He set up the headquarters office on site, with electric light and floor coverings to counter the winter cold. The dredge was regarded as one of the best constructed and equipped in the district. In the seven years of its existence, the Argyle dredge paid dividends of over £7000, which makes it one of the more successful ventures of the era; of the twenty-seven companies registered in 1902, fewer than half paid any form of dividend. Allister Evans quotes from the Chairman's August 1906 monthly report: 'In consideration of the large returns for the past few weeks, the dredge master [Caithness] and secretary [Mutch] receive a bonus of £1. The 10 dredge hands each receive a bonus of 10/-.'[11] The Argyle dredge by then had recovered 3385 oz of gold, for a return of £13,517. The weekly cost of running the dredge was £50. The dredge eventually met an untimely end in flames.

Truby carried on a most amiable correspondence with his dredge master David Caithness, giving him a glowing reference at the end of the dredging project. Caithness may also have been involved with Truby on the Maori Gully dredge, which is mentioned in the archives, along with some evidence of sluicing, yet another money-consuming and potentially gold-recovering method. Despite the fiery demise of the Argyle dredge, King and Caithness parted on good terms.

Truby the environmentalist was, however, sensitive to the destruction of farmland by dredging. Dredges were grotesque machines that munched their way through farmland, spewing the sorted 'tailings' (gravel and soil) out the back. Little attempt was made to restore the dredging scars, and much of Central Otago still bears the lumpy, undulating waves of infertile and desolate, stony, dredge tailings adjacent to good, undredged farmland. King instigated a planting project to establish larch trees in the tailings, in a move that was well before its time.

CHAPTER SIX

A sound mind in a healthy body

SEACLIFF AFFORDED Truby King some unique opportunities. The asylum was remote from the mainstream of society, although he maintained links with the real world by way of his lecturing at Otago university.

He had a large captive workforce which benefited from being kept busy. He was the commander and they were his troops in the development of a scientific theory of farming. Seacliff also offered him another interesting cameo role, that of landscape architect, on the grand scale of Capability Brown.

The forbidding appearance of the asylum and grounds had been noted prior to King's arrival. 'The whole external aspect of the place is dreary and depressing because it is dense bushland, just in the process of being cleared, and the laying out of the grounds about the building is, at present, in a state of chaos,' wrote MacGregor, the inspector.[1] Truby King's philosophy from the outset was one of sympathy and compassion for the troubled mind; he believed a harmonious and peaceful environment was implicit in the recovery of the mentally ill.

This was before the time of psychotherapy and psychiatric drugs, and his first act was to decorate the main Seacliff building. Many of the staff were hired for their trade skills and designated 'tradesmen/attendants'. The wards, in their previous sombre 'green and strong blue', were all repainted, with each corridor and room being a colour different from its neighbour. Plants, ferns, flowers and paintings were added, many being donated by Dr and Mrs King.

Truby's father Tom was, amongst other things, a farmer and it is likely that Truby would have been acquainted with many aspects of 'the land'. He already had some gardening experience, but it was as a large-scale farmer that he saw the greatest challenge. Seacliff was designated a Farm Asylum. Its land extended to 400 hectares and was designed to be self-sufficient and to occupy patients' minds and bodies. Truby already had well-developed views on fresh air and the therapeutic value of work. This was the canvas on which to paint his grand landscape. One can imagine the Seacliff farm manager's wry delight when his employers began to take an interest in the grounds.

Pleasant grounds and landscape were considered an adjunct to recovery, as they provided ample opportunity to stimulate a renewed interest in life. King replaced the existing 'gardener/attendant' with the more grandly titled 'landscape gardener', to the accompaniment of grumblings in the press. Whether or not the gardener was a Scot is not recorded, but it's a reasonable assumption. Male patients were put to work with picks, shovels, handcarts and barrows. The high corrugated-iron perimeter fences and 'airing courts' that restricted views of the ocean and the landscape were replaced with more appealing picket fences, and even a ha-ha (a concealed ditch, beloved of Victorian landscapers). King's abhorrence of straight lines saw meandering paths and soft curved edges bounding the parks and gardens. Trees, shrubs and flowers were extensively planted.

A SOUND MIND IN A HEALTHY BODY

While the able-bodied men were away working on the farm, the women were not. Being 'more excitable than men' in his view,[2] the best they could hope for was employment in the laundry or kitchen or other more menial support work. Whether this arose from an innate belief in women's place in the grand scheme of things, or a pragmatic desire to avoid the sexes fraternising, King recognised the need to provide harmonious surroundings for his women patients too. Croquet greens, tennis courts and meandering leafy walks were constructed for them.

It would be easy to characterise King as a wholesale reformer, but the institution was still in its early phase of development, and the philosophies he espoused were already well appreciated. What is more remarkable is the whole-hearted way that King tackled the work. His belief that the health of the mind depended on the health of the body and that the mentally ill were entitled to the best possible conditions characterised his approach to the environment of Seacliff. His work to enhance the physical surroundings for his patients was of the highest quality since he saw it as an integral part of the process of recovery. If he had gone no further than the sympathetic humane treatment of the insane, he could have rested on his laurels. But he had to push on . . .

While being careful to stress that work was voluntary, King provided outside employment for the patients: clearing bush, chopping wood, mowing lawns, digging and planting, as well as work in the orchards, vegetable gardens, piggery, sheep and dairy farms. Work was restricted to five or six hours a day, with two spells for 'smoking'. Over 80 per cent of the male patients were thus employed. Supervision was by the tradesmen/attendants, who were expected to participate and join in with the patients in order to bring about a 'spirit of hearty comradeship and friendliness'.[3] Staff were expected to carry out the work of the institution, with the patients rendering assistance. King was particularly strict about considerate treatment of patients, and would dismiss any staff member guilty of violence against a patient. This appeared to work well, as the rate of staff dismissal dropped significantly once his regime became accepted.

His relationship with his staff was firm. He expected absolute obedience from his subordinates. The anti-King *Globe* newspaper noted that 'Doctor King is of a very irritable disposition, easily roused to anger, and remarkably autocratic in his bearing towards officials under him'.[4] It would be fair to assume that he had a rather short fuse, and did not suffer fools gladly. Doubtless the *Globe* saw the eccentric doctor as a ready source of controversy. The chief attributes sought by King of his nursing staff were consistency, honesty, hard work, sobriety, kindness and obedience. It is worthy of note that there was always demand for positions at Seacliff, at least on the staff.

Seacliff was an ideal laboratory for a scientific farmer to experiment, practise and refine his techniques. With a ready supply of inmates, he never had to worry about labour or his projects being questioned. The famous 'blue ribbon' example illustrates his approach:

> I remember going into a very extensive byre about milking time, and being intensely amused and interested to watch a cow wearing a blue label round its neck being turned into a blue-labelled stall and fed from a blue-painted bucket; others with red labels being turned into red-labelled stalls and fed from red buckets, an ingenious device of Dr King's to prevent any mistake on the part of mental patients who acted as farm labourers, and who might otherwise have confused the food intended for each. I was told that neither the cow nor the men ever made a mistake, and in this way each cow got the proper amount of food specially adapted to her grade or class.[5]

It was the care of young calves that was to produce one of the principles that would underpin Plunket. When King arrived at Seacliff, the farm had a 20 per cent death rate in calves, due to 'scouring', which was analogous to diarrhoea in babies. Calves were denied their mother's milk for economic reasons – it was deemed more profitable to feed calves cheaper artificial substitutes and sell the higher-value cow's milk. The bucket-fed regime had the consequence that calves did not thrive to the same extent as did those suckled by their mothers. The challenge to Truby King was to devise a scientific formulation that would result in healthy bucket-fed calves.

He looked at work done in British and American universities and, studying the nutritive components of milk, particularly protein and fats, he devised an equivalent artificial feeding regime that resulted in calves achieving the same weight gain as those raised naturally. Scouring and the associated deaths vanished. King had shown that a scientifically formulated artificial feeding regime could produce equivalent results to those of natural feeding.

The significance of this breakthrough may not have been immediately obvious, but was to provide King with the platform from which to launch the next phase of his career.

During his time at Seacliff King built up an impressive dossier of results from his holistic approach to farming. His application of sound, common-sense, scientific principles resulted in blight-free potatoes, aphid-free crops and increased crop yields. Seacliff supplied eggs to hospitals throughout Otago and potatoes to as far away as Avondale in Auckland. Animals from the Seacliff farm won so many prizes at local A&P shows that competing farmers complained, and the asylum stopped entering competitions. His *Feeding of Plants and Animals* was enthusiastically received when published in 1905 (see Appendix One). This was to become the fundamental theme for the rest of his life – the simple belief that plants and animals, with the right care and right nutrition, were better equipped to cope with the demands of life. Nearly 100 years later the theory underpins much of the world's organic farming practices.

Truby extended this philosophy to an assertion that insanity was a consequence of inadequate diet and rearing, and that a good, balanced, wholesome diet could cure it. His dietary reforms had the support of his Mental Health superiors, and by 1906 his 'healthy food' regime was the norm in all New Zealand asylums.

From the questionable assumption that insanity was a disease of imperfect nutrition, it was a simple step for King to conclude that insanity would not occur with a well and properly nourished brain. Extending the argument further, he reasoned that good nutrition must begin at birth. In his annual report to parliament in 1906 he went further: 'If women were rendered more fit for maternity, if

IN A STRANGE GARDEN

Mary King and Matron Charlotte Beswick in the Seacliff garden, c. 1910, dwarfed by giant Cardiocrinum, a rare member of the lily family from China. The photograph was taken by Truby King.

instrumental deliveries were obviated as far as possible, if infants were nourished by their mothers, and boys and girls were given rational education, the main supplies of our asylums, hospitals, benevolent institutions, gaols and slums would be cut off at the sources.'[6] As time progressed, he became more convinced of the infallibility of his pronouncements.

King had observed the harm that poor feeding brought to plants and animals. He knew that the weakest were the ones to suffer, and from observation of his mental patients he believed that their incapacity had its beginnings in poor nutrition at an early age. It has been suggested that the realisation that most forms of insanity could not be cured by environmental engineering was responsible for King's shift toward infant welfare.[7] Whether or not Truby King was a pragmatist, he was about to set off in a new direction. It was the beginning of the child-care crusade.

Chapter Seven

Some curious attitudes of his own

There is an incongruity in Truby King's attitude to women and his prescriptive approach to baby care that warrants comment at this stage. While his treatment of women doctors passed as gentlemanly, and he could on occasion be more than courteous, some of his advocacy borders on the lunatic, when viewed from the standpoint of the twenty-first century.

Victorian attitudes were notably conservative. King, as the scion of an early migrant family, inherited many of the beliefs of his English parents, conditioned by their trying pioneer times in Taranaki. His upbringing, with its private schooling and a multilingual father, was hardly working-class. King's teacher, Richmond, who concentrated on exploring individual subjects exhaustively, provided him with a unique private education. His wife's Edinburgh upbringing was similarly privileged. As a boarder in her family for the formative part of his university education, Truby would not have felt out of place. He was often described as an 'awful snob',[1] and by his persuasive influence on those who wielded the instruments of power, we must assume that he moved easily among the more important members of Victorian and Edwardian New Zealand 'society'. His seven years in Scotland gave him a strong empathy with 'Home' and 'Empire', and his conservative medical education would have done its best to mould him into a decent chap. While Truby was often at loggerheads with the medical profession, there are no recorded instances of his public distaste or contempt for his chosen occupation.

At Seacliff this decent fellow showed commendable concern for the less-advantaged inmates. His record on the treatment of the insane is laudable. His concern for the underdog and his knowledge of his patients was exemplary. Truby's farming practice at Seacliff showed him to be a good scientist, to have holistic views and a conservative empathy with nature. His belief that 'in plants, just as in the case of animals, the inroads of disease are best prevented by keeping the organism well nourished'[2] was further refined to become one of the tenets of the Plunket movement, extolling the merits of breast-feeding:

> Nutrition given by the mother is always best, and the wisest breeders will always continue to let Nature have her way where they wish to keep their purebred stock at the highest pitch of health for the perpetuation and improvement of the best strains. When the farmer resorts to hand rearing he does so simply because there is a profit in removing butterfat valued at a shilling a pound and replacing it with vegetable starches and fats which cost him about a penny. But this is not the attitude or feeling of the mother who rears her child by means of a bottle. For the most part she is densely ignorant of the duties of maternity, and does not realise the injustice she is doing to herself and her offspring.[3]

This masterful seven-page document shows King at his best and worst. At best, he was a good scientist, skilfully communicating his investigative techniques, explaining clearly his results. At worst, he succumbed to bombast, berating the education system and straying from the subject in hand.

He knew that Parisian mothers in the Great War, without access to cow's milk, were forced to breast-feed, producing babies significantly healthier than their bottle-fed counterparts. He satisfied himself of the merits of natural feeding and wanted to tell the women of New Zealand the folly of incorrect artificial feeding.

His description of women as 'densely ignorant' of the duties of maternity helps explain his simplification of feeding schedules. King wanted a simple regime for baby feeding that could be taught by Plunket nurses and adhered to by nursing mothers. Often disorganised himself, he stipulated 'feeding by the clock' and regular weighing, not because he was a stickler for routine but because the routine could be simply communicated and understood. Many of the 'old school' Plunket nurses became high priestesses of his teachings, themselves feared as 'old battleaxes' and it may be they who should bear some, if not most, of the blame for what was perceived as a prescriptive regime. Certainly the more permissive, relaxed Plunket nurses of the latter part of the twentieth century would have been out of place in Truby King's day.

His views on the place of women are often coupled with those of an influential Dunedin medical colleague and obstetrician, Dr Batchelor, who said in a public lecture: 'It is essential that the State recognise the necessity for a racial divergence in the education of boys and girls about the age of puberty: after passing the standard usually attained at this age, let the girls' studies be chiefly directed to domestic management, domestic economy, physiology and hygiene . . .'[4] Batchelor prepared the way for King, who spoke next, delivering his famous 'preposterous farce' speech: 'It is impossible for me to convey how strongly I feel that the common education of men and women upon similar lines was one of the most preposterous farces ever perpetuated . . .'[5]

This infuriated the women's movement, particularly two of the more vocal woman doctors, Emily Siedberg and Agnes Bennett. They would have ongoing battles with King and Batchelor over the years. Agnes Bennett later scored a significant victory over King at the 1913 BMA conference in Auckland, when she observed that he had slipped a motion onto the last day's agenda to the effect that education of women was a disadvantage to the nation. King had gone home early, expecting his motion to be passed unopposed. Bennett, in a rousing speech which was greeted by applause, argued forcefully against this. The motion was defeated. She would later describe King and Batchelor as 'The greatest obstacle to women's progress and emancipation that New Zealand has known'.[6]

Then there are his views on raising adolescents.

In 1906, preceding the foundation of the Plunket movement and as his star was meteorically rising, he produced a publication entitled *The Evils of Cram*. The previous year he had published *The Feeding of Plants and Animals,* his synthesis of the successful farming experiments at Seacliff. Truby King was beginning to realise his potential, but more importantly he was beginning to realise that people listened to him.

The Evils of Cram sought reforms of the education system. The debate on education was intensifying at this time, drawing on similar critical sentiments in the United States and Britain, fuelled by the concerns throughout the white Commonwealth about Anglo-Saxon fecundity. Truby King was by no means the originator of this debate, but was able to exploit it as a vehicle for his own views. In the preamble to a dense ninety-three-page document he defined Cram as follows:

> A *Cram* system of Education is one which neglects the body for the sake of the mind, and neglects the mind as a whole for the sake of displaying what can be put into and be taken unchanged out of one corner of it.
>
> *Cram* centres its attention on superficial fugitive memory and narrow formal scholastic reasoning and attainments, with a view to the passing of examinations. It fails to produce even a good memory, since the development of that faculty depends in the long run on interesting

or useful associations. Cram ultimately impairs memory and receptiveness, and it stifles independent thought and initiative, along with the natural desire for knowledge.

Cram exalts the 'learner' above the 'thinker' and the 'doer', and gives its prizes to the crammer rather than to the honest worker. Its main end is the passing of examinations, and has no broad human outlook.

Cram is wrapped up in the schoolroom, and forgets the world of men and women outside its walls. It lives and dies in the present, and does not concern itself with the practical needs of the community or the country.

Cram and examinations have ruled China for thousands of years, and have dominated Education throughout the civilised world with disastrous results during our time.

Cram is recognised as a leading factor in the production of degeneracy, making many women unfit for maternity and both sexes more or less incompetent. We are using up the strength and energy of the rising generation at the very time when we ought to be developing our future men and women, with a view to the creating of a healthy, capable race and a great country.[7]

King was well supported in his arguments on educational pressure. His widely respected Dunedin contemporary, ophthalmologist Dr Lindo Ferguson, had previously shown a link between nervous strain and eyesight problems. King knew he could count on many well-qualified educators for support. While he was not alone in railing against the education system of the day, which placed undue value on passing examinations, it is the content of this remarkable document that gives clues to what made Truby King tick. The six paragraphs above began perfectly sensibly, defining the object of his attention. By the time he has reached the final paragraphs, he had been deflected into one of his failings, that of stating of opinion as fact. Whether or not Cram was a significant factor in China was hardly the point; it gave King the opportunity to allude to the Chinese menace, a theme ever-present in the Victorian mind.

The leap to another Victorian bogey, degeneracy, was not too hard for him to make, allowing him to flirt with his old friend Eugenics. 'A healthy capable race and a great country' were recurrent themes never far from his lips and always calculated to win him applause.

The structure of *The Evils of Cram* is interesting. The introduction mentions response to King's comments on 'over-pressure in education' and says, 'To facilitate reference, a synopsis of contents has been drawn up, which will enable each reader to readily pick out any section of the subject in which he may happen to be personally interested. A few reprints from leading newspapers outside Otago are included, because they show that there is a consensus of opinion throughout the colony in favour of reform in our scheme of Education. The views of a few leading authorities outside the colony are printed at the end of the pamphlet.'

The first section reports Truby King's lecture to the Froebel Club on 10 May 1906, entitled *Lecture on the Science of Education with Criticism of our Methods*. (Friedrich Froebel, a teacher trained in Botany and Biology, was born in Germany in 1782 and was the founder of the Kindergarten movement. Froebel believed that 'we must cultivate women, who are the educators of the human race, else the new generation cannot accomplish its task'.)[8] King used the address to deliver a review of the education system and an attack on youthful 'over-study'. The report of his lecture covers five pages, beginning with the history of education and ending with two cases of children admitted to the Seacliff asylum. By reprinting the newspaper report, King could further massage his reputation: 'Mr Mark Cohen presided over a large and intensely-interested audience, and in introducing the speaker said that he was one of the best educators of public opinion in Dunedin. He took time to think his subject out thoroughly, and arrived at conclusions as the result of deep and earnest study. Moreover he had the courage of his opinions, and was not afraid to express them.'

King began his address by tracing the history of education and the responsibilities of the teaching profession, acknowledging the contributions of Rousseau, Pestalozzi, Froebel and Herbert Spencer.

In five pages of historical preamble, King had brought the audience to where he could launch into his chosen topic. In passing, he made mention of some of his favourite themes: sunshine, fresh air, healthy exercise and recreation, noting that without these, girls could not develop into 'women capable of suckling their own children'. These are themes he would weave into the fabric of Plunket.

Developing the theme of overwork in children, King quoted the cases of two children who had been referred to Seacliff, a boy and a girl. He quoted from his report of 1897 on the girl.

> In the apparent causes of insanity among patients admitted, that of 'over-study' is of special interest. It is extremely important that parents and guardians should clearly recognise that prolonged and excessive mental strain and neglect of exercise, recreation, and rest, especially among girls, during the period of rapid growth and development, cannot be continued without an ultimate dwarfing of both mind and body, and grave peril to the integrity of the organism. In the stress of competition for honours and prizes the brain is so often worked at the verge of the breaking strain, to the neglect of everything else, that one is inclined to wonder that entire mental collapse does not result more frequently. If the secondary effects of over-pressure among girls is impairing the potentialities of reproduction and healthy maternity were more widely known, it would possibly prove a greater incentive to moderation than the more striking but comparatively rare causation of insanity.

He summarises the girl's history:

> No hereditary diseases in the family. Parents temperate, and not nervous; no tendencies to insanity; clever; great powers of concentration; was Dux of a High School; used to work till three o'clock in the morning, and get up again at six a.m.; good memory; very strong will; good power of self-control; affectionate; very energetic and industrious with regard to everything, study, housework, etc. Had good health, but was very sedentary in her habits. Did not go in for games or any recreation.

Of the boy, King reported:

> Some five years before he came to the asylum I was sent for by the boy's mother, who said that he had become paralysed. I went to see him, and found him in bed, very feverish. His mother said he had fainted on the way to school. To my surprise, on examining him I found him to be suffering from acute rheumatic fever. I said: 'This did not come on suddenly.' She said: 'Oh, yes: he fainted going to school.' After she had gone I questioned the boy, and he admitted that he had been suffering for some time. 'Oh, yes,' he said; 'but I was going for a scholarship, and I tried to walk to school.' Rheumatic fever causes the most damnable agony, and it is hardly bearable by an adult; and this boy tried to walk to school with that damnable pain, and to conceal it, because his one ambition was a scholarship.

Continuing, the doctor pointed out that these were extreme cases:

> The injury done to the thousands of others was apparent in impaired mental and bodily capacity, and in the case of women in weakly offspring or no offspring at all. Spencer said: 'Success in life depends more on energy than information'; and no system which sacrificed energy for information was good. In this life the physical underlay the mental, and the mental must not be temporarily developed at the expense of the physical. He would make some practical suggestions for a start. The syllabus should be greatly cut down; no child should be taught a lot of subjects at once. There should be teachers abreast of modern and fundamental requirements. There were certain things which every teacher ought to do in physical examination of the children under his charge. For example, every child ought to be weighed at school at least every three months; if possible, every month. The children could weigh each other. In that way they would get to be proud of their physical condition, and ashamed of any falling away of it.

Whether two cases of juvenile insanity are adequate proof of wholesale mental breakdown of the youth of the country due to overpressure at school is arguable. King, however, with his forceful oratory managed to persuade his audience without difficulty.

SOME CURIOUS ATTITUDES OF HIS OWN

Under the heading 'Some Press Criticisms' followed three pages of eulogistic reviews from Dunedin's *Evening Star*, long a crusader against Cram, the *Christchurch Press* and *Lyttleton Times*. Newspapers saw him as being eminently newsworthy and would enjoy this symbiotic relationship for many years to come.

> In the history of New Zealand newspapers there have been two men who were heartily disliked by reporters and sub-editors, even though they may have admired them. They were Truby King and Viscount Bledisloe, Governor-General during the depression years. Both had the habit of arriving in newspaper offices demanding to see proofs. And both were wont to interpolate phrases and views that they had forgotten to express from the platform. In Dunedin the *Otago Daily Times* staff used to scuttle for cover when they saw King coming.[9]

The next section, titled 'Some Expert Opinions', covers ten pages, and comprises favourable published reactions to King's reported address. The quoted experts included many professors, teachers and academics. All the opinions were supportive of King. Many took the opportunity to reiterate all they believed to be wrong with the education system. Truby King had tapped a deep vein of public disquiet, one in which he knew his opinion would be well received and appreciated.

There is only one dissenting voice, that of Mr Alexander Wilson, Rector of Otago Boys' High, who felt obliged to refute King's implicit attack on his school, which the boy in King's address had attended. Wilson, described as 'sensitive and discerning', was an experienced principal, having previously spent twelve years in charge of the Girls' High School. He took King to task for the dramatic method of his presentation and distortion of the facts for the sake of rhetoric. This was too much for Truby King. In his characteristic prose, he set Wilson up as the villain, the oaf, the apostle of everything he despised in the system of education, using his considerable vocabulary to dismiss the dissenting principal. It is not recorded when Mr Wilson's career terminated, but few could but fail to wilt under the attack of Truby King in full voice. In twenty-eight pages King dissected, analysed, refuted and condemned the hapless Rector. Sadly, King didn't publish Wilson's letter, instead making reference to sections that he particularly disagreed with. Warming to the task, he exposed four 'fallacies' that Wilson has committed. With the luxury of a self-published treatise, King could not resist the temptation to expound all of his theories, exposing as he went some of his more outrageous attitudes.

Leaving aside the padding, here are some of the gems contained in his explanation of the 'fallacies'.

> *Weighing and Measuring*
> Such vital questions should not be left to mere conjecture, especially in a school where the headmaster virtually countenances and upholds over-pressure for examination purposes. The rector could easily arrive at a sufficiently accurate estimate of the degree of impairment of growth induced by stress in his own school by having his pupils weighed and measured at the beginning and end of each session, in accordance with the recommendations made in England by Sir James Crichton-Browne a quarter of a century ago, and since so strongly insisted on by Dr Francis Warner and the medical profession in general. By this simple means, a teacher gets warning ahead of almost every case where the health of the pupil is beginning to succumb to over-pressure.

'Weighing and measuring' would become a recurring, almost obsessive theme with King, finding its way into Plunket methodology, but failing to find the same acceptance from educators.

King took particular note of Crichton-Browne:

> The necessity for games and exercises was pointed out strongly enough by Sir James Crichton-Browne a quarter of a century ago in his now classical popular work 'Education and the Nervous System', and has been insisted on by every educational authority worthy of the name since that date . . . The value of physical education does not now require to be vindicated. It is generally recognised that 'to be a good animal' is one of the first requisites to success in life . . . As health is

essential to education, and exercise is essential to health, exercise has come to be regarded as essential to education.

Unfortunately, the Scottish Sir James Crichton-Browne (1840–1937), famous self-publicist, Victorian psychiatrist, and once an assistant to Charles Darwin, is nowadays not viewed so favourably. His work was substantially discredited by J. G. Fitch, Principal Inspector of Schools, who, in a critical memorandum attached to Crichton-Browne's report that King refers to, noted: 'Every one of his judgements is hasty and inaccurate, arrived at by a loose and partial method of inquiry.' Fitch further observed that he had 'the habit of stating an opinion as if it represented a fact'. Perhaps King saw him as a kindred spirit? I. M. Ingram noted of the research methodology:

> Crichton-Browne would stand before these large classes with his notebook, and ask pupils to raise their hands if they suffered from headaches. He would note the result in his book, then similarly ask if the headaches were at the front, top or at the back of the head, and whether they occurred early or late in the day. He then claimed in his report that 46.1% of the pupils in elementary schools in London suffered from habitual headache, and linked this to 'overpressure'. No individual examinations of children were made, and the inspector points out that that most of the children seemed bewildered by the questions.

King continued his exhortation on the importance of fitness:

> Speaking many years ago to the students of Yale University, Julian Hawthorne earnestly exhorted them to keep themselves always in the fittest physical condition, as the only effective means by which they could maintain supremacy over themselves and those innate tendencies which have to be fought with and mastered. As a doctor, one cannot overstate the medical importance of this aspect of the case, though it cannot be discussed in a public newspaper. I may mention, however that I have a letter from Dr Levinge, late superintendent of the asylum at Christchurch (the physician who has had the most

extensive experience of insanity in this colony) in which he gives his opinion that over-pressure in connection with our school life tends to set up a vicious circle by lessening the power of nervous control, and so paving the way to general instability of the nervous system, sexual irregularities and insanity itself.

He often seems to be concerned with 'those innate tendencies which have to be fought with and mastered'. Beneath his refined language, he could well be suggesting that too much study leads to masturbation.

He continued the theme to consider puberty:

The harmful influence of faulty hygienic arrangements, particularly in regard to open air, sunlight, exercise and recreation, tells more gravely on the organism at the momentous period of puberty than at any other time of life. The reason is obvious. Growth is taking place more rapidly than at any period after infancy – everything is in a state of transition. There is necessarily considerable disequilibration, and the awakening into intense activity of wide areas of the brain tissue previously dormant does not take place without some tendency to loss of control. Any undue mental stress brought to bear at this critical turning point will express itself in further loss of the power of control, and may lead to disaster in the case of either sex. Wrong habits are liable to be contracted and though insanity itself is essentially a disease of adult life, and scarcely arises after birth before the age of twenty is reached, yet we frequently have the seeds of future disabilities in men and women sown during school life. Where insanity supervenes before twenty it is almost invariably associated with sexual accompaniments, which show clearly to the physician where the lines of defence should be set up. All the greatest schoolmasters of our times, from Arnold of Rugby to Almond of Loretto, have been keenly alive to these considerations, and no one can afford to ignore them who has at heart the welfare of any class of boys or girls. Safety lies in high spirits, good vigorous normal health, and plenty of physical activity. Hysteria or any other manifestation of lack of control is the natural accompaniment of a jaded system and feeble vitality.

SOME CURIOUS ATTITUDES OF HIS OWN

When there is defective nutrition the highest and most delicate brain cells associated with the noblest functions are the first to suffer.

There are admitted to the Seacliff Mental Hospital (exclusive of congenitals), say, 110 patients per annum. Of these, so far as we can ascertain, there is an average of four per annum originally of average or more than average intelligence who have become insane before the age of twenty-one. Of these four I am satisfied that one patient becomes insane through the direct effects of faulty conditions of education [four-fifths of such cases are girls]. About an equal number of cases is associated with marked sexual irregularities. As will be understood, from what I have already indicated, it is impossible to state what proportion of these [nearly all males] would be saved under a rational education system. I may say, however, that the almost invariable history one gets regarding such lads is that they have been sedentary, not given to playing games and inclined to be bookish. [Truby King was described as a bookish lad who hated taking part in games.] Lads made to take part in school games rarely go seriously wrong in this way. Regarding the other half, some factor, such as injury to the head, sunstroke, seduction or marked heredity, has been ascertained in the majority of cases, but there are few instances where no cause is forthcoming . . . However, as I have always maintained, it is not as a cause of actual insanity that school over-pressure concerns us most, but as a potent factor in giving rise to widespread degeneracy and a more or less universal dwarfing of the ultimate physical, mental and moral stature of the whole community.

He went on to quote extensively from two other sources; J. M. Guyau (Education and Heredity) and Herbert Spencer.

'The life of a woman, generally sedentary and under more or less unhealthy conditions, gives no time for recuperation to a constitution exhausted by an irrational education, whereas in the case of man recuperation may take place; on the other hand, the mother's health is of much more importance to the child than the health of the father.

> The man's expenditure in paternity is insignificant compared to the woman's; the latter needs a considerable reserve of physical and moral energy during gestation, maternity, and afterwards during the early education of the child. The mothers of Bacon and Goethe, though both very remarkable women, could not have written either the 'Novum Organum' or 'Faust'; but if they had ever so little weakened their generative powers by excessive intellectual expenditure, they would not have had a Bacon or a Goethe as a son. If during life the parents expend too much of the energy they have drawn from their environment, so much the less will be left for their children . . . Herbert Spencer says, 'If we consider that the regimen of girls of the upper classes is much better than that of girls belonging to the poorer classes, while in most other respects their physical treatment is not worse, the deficiency of reproductive power among them may be reasonably attributed to the overtaxing of their brains – an overtaxing which produces a serious reaction on their physique. This diminution of reproductive power is not only shown by the greater frequency of absolute sterility, nor is it only shown in the earlier cessation of child-bearing, but it is also shown in the very frequent inability of such women to suckle their infants.'

King was particularly fond of quoting Spencer, a Victorian who thankfully is no longer accorded much credence. Spencer was a contemporary of Charles Darwin, an engineer by training who once worked as a sub-editor on *The Economist*. He died celibate, taking to his grave beliefs that the weak, poor and unintelligent should be discouraged from breeding. He had a strong belief in science, but it is said that he didn't really understand Darwin and misunderstood some of the fundamentals of science. His biographer, Kieran Egan, said of him: 'What we have is a set of ideas that by the end of the nineteenth century were shown to be wrong, or were outmoded, eccentric, confused and flawed.'[10] While Spencer's reputation came crashing down, the educational ideas derived from his flawed theoretical structures soldiered on tenaciously.

King appears obsessively drawn to gender differences:

Now, let me draw Mr Wilson's attention to a matter which he has persistently ignored. My lecture at the Froebel Club was addressed to an audience composed almost entirely of women [the newspaper reports of the meeting failed to note this, too]: the bearing of my remarks was pointed especially to the education of girls; and the extract which I read from my public report in 1897 dwelt almost exclusively on school over-pressure as affecting the potentialities of motherhood. Let me repeat the extract in question:

'In the apparent cause of insanity amongst patients admitted that of "over-study" is of special interest. It is certainly important that parents and guardians should clearly recognise that prolonged and excessive mental strain, and neglect of exercise, recreation, and rest, especially amongst girls, during the period of rapid growth and development, cannot be continued without an ultimate dwarfing of both mind and body, and grave peril to the integrity of the organism. In the stress of competition for honours and prizes the brain is so often worked at the verge of the breaking strain, to the neglect of everything else that one is inclined to wonder that entire mental collapse does not result more frequently. If the secondary effects of over-pressure among girls is impairing the potentialities of reproduction and healthy maternity were more widely known, it would probably prove a greater incentive to moderation than the more striking but comparatively rare causation of insanity.'

Mr Wilson does not seem to realise, when he admits that school over-pressure is doing harm to girls, that he is conceding precisely what I specially tried to impress upon my audience at the Froebel Club, and I think I may fairly say *succeeded* in impressing on them. Even here, however, there are essential differences between Mr Wilson's views and my own. It never seems to occur to the rector that anything short of an actual breakdown is to be regarded as evidence of harm done. He does not seem to have ever given a thought to such injuries as are referred to by the authorities I have quoted, and he is quite willing to let things drift indefinitely, in spite of his half-hearted admission that we are doing a great wrong to girls in allowing them to strain themselves in too exacting competitive examinations.

King devoted another four pages to detailed examination of the shortcomings of Wilson's case, to the point of dissecting his reports when principal of the Girls' High some thirteen years previously. Given that King's lecture to the Froebel club was widely and enthusiastically reported, one is inclined to wonder whether an errant high school principal warranted such extravagant treatment.

In conclusion, King listed his ten-point Proposed Fundamental Reforms. They were (in abbreviated form):

1. Adequate open-air playgrounds for every school.
2. Proper provision for heating, ventilating and lighting schools, and a supply of suitable furnishings.
3. The devotion of a reasonable time daily to open-air occupations and recreations, as compulsory part of every school curriculum.
4. Restriction of the quantity of mental work (especially memorising of unimportant matters and excessive quantitative demands made in connection with arithmetic, mathematics, grammar, languages, etc.).
5. Reduction in the number of subjects studied during any one term. The recognition of quality rather than quantity of work.
6. A proper adjustment of studies to meet the respective necessities and aptitudes of boys and girls, the future man or woman always being kept in view.
7. The safeguarding of pupils from mental or physical breakdowns by encouraging open-air games, by simple, practical instruction in elementary hygiene and the laws of life, and by careful adjustment of school burthens by competent teachers trained to detect almost intuitively the first signs of failure in body, mind or spirits. All pupils should be measured and weighed at regular intervals, and a proper register should be kept.
8. The removal of temptation to cram now held out in the form of scholarships.
9. A properly organised and systematised scheme directed towards

fitting pupils attending schools in certain localities for avocations specially related to the main occupations or industries of the districts — e.g., farming, gardening, fruit-growing, fishing, mining, and crafts or trades.

10. A broad, thorough training of all teachers in the fundamental requirements for educating youth to the best advantage in accordance with modern knowledge.

He concluded modestly, 'I am confident that the resultant decrease in disease, degeneracy, and ineptitude would be important, practical and economic considerations for the colony.'

The fifth and penultimate section of *The Evils of Cram* comprises text of further Truby King addresses. They included:

> *The Teacher as a Creative Agent* (thirteen pages).
> *Play Games as Education* (five pages of an address to the Free Kindergarten Association).
> *The Fit and the Unfit — Improving the Race* (two pages devoted to his crusade to raise the general standard of health). 'It is possible to centre our attention too much upon disease and forget that the positive, the natural, and the more important thing is health. We are all ready to endow hospitals, and the sentiment is excellent, but we could do more if we bent our efforts towards preventing the necessity for hospitals.'

The final twenty pages of this marathon document are devoted to reprints of information supportive of Truby King's cause, including:

> Dr Almond, principal of Loretto school, Edinburgh: *True Education Versus Cram*. (Almond's support for Herbert Spencer and the perils of examinations.)
> *Cram and Neglect of the Body* by Herbert Spencer. 'On women, the effects of this forcing system are, if possible, even more injurious than on men. Being in great measure debarred from these vigorous and enjoyable exercises of body by which boys mitigate the evils of excessive study, girls feel these evils in their full intensity. Hence the much smaller proportion of them who grow up well-made and healthy

. . . And this physical degeneracy hinders their welfare far more than their many accomplishments aid it. Mammas anxious to make their daughters attractive could scarcely choose a course more fatal than this, which sacrifices the body to the mind. Either they disregard the tastes of the opposite sex, or else their conception of these tastes is erroneous. Men care little for erudition in women, but very much for physical beauty, good nature and sound sense.'

A Woman's Views on Boys, Girls, Marriage and Herbert Spencer by Mrs Earle, in *Pot-pourri from a Surrey Garden*, 27th edition. 'Mr Herbert Spencer's book has fortunately reached a very cheap edition (published at 6d). It is a book created by the hand of genius, and not the result of personal experience. I humbly bow to it in grateful thanks for all the good I derived from its perusal.'

Overstrain in Schools by Robert Lee, Chairman Wellington Education Board.

The Training of the Human Plant by Luther Burbank. (A treatise on sunshine, good air and nourishing food.)

The Education of Women by W. L. Felter, Brooklyn, New York. 'Marriage and maternity the natural goal . . . education must not spoil for maternity.'

Truby King had proved by now that he was a good scientist, the author of a well-researched treatise on plants and animals. He had demonstrated that he could formulate artificial feeding regimes that would produce animals every bit as good as ones reared on their mother's milk. Much of this was work of a high calibre, and formed the basis for what would become Plunket. His trenchant advocacy against over-pressure in schools was neither original nor was it particularly robust, mixing his opinion with dubious work of later-discredited 'experts', presented forcefully as axiomatic. King's lengthy attacks on a high school principal who sought to stand up to his criticisms is not only petulant and bullying; it is also unwarranted if one accepts the generally favourable response accorded by public and profession to King's anti-cram pronouncements.

The greatest concern emerging from *The Evils of Cram* are King's views on women. The proposition of women being 'densely ignorant' and thus unsuitable for further education was hardly popular or widely supported. While it might be argued that he was merely espousing Victorian attitudes widely held at the time, the truth is that he appears to have been at the very forefront of their promotion. How he would move on to found a system of care for babies administered by woman volunteers is not immediately obvious.

CHAPTER EIGHT

Conservation at Karitane

KARITANE is one of the older coastal settlements in the South Island, being associated with whaling in the 1830s. The area is known as Te Awakoeo (stream of the small paua) and there is evidence of a fortified Maori pa. Dominant features are the Waikouaiti River, Blueskin Bay and the peninsula. Seacliff is up the long, twisty, hill road, five kilometres to the south of Karitane.

A year after he commenced his tenure at Seacliff, Truby and Bella bought land on the Karitane peninsula, and three years later built a holiday house. Firstly, he had to solve the problems of nature and the regular incursion of the sea, which threatened to isolate the peninsula. Mary King tells of her father's Canute-like exploits:

> By act of God the peninsula was several times doomed to become an island; but by the tireless energy of Dr. King and his helpers it

remained a peninsula. A storm would arise in the night, and suddenly the waves would sweep through the marram grasses, swirl down the sandy road and out into the river. It seemed as if all his work would be demolished in an hour. With lantern in hand, Dr. King would arouse every villager out of his bed, and with wheel barrows, carts, shovels and every available vehicle, set to work to beat the waves at their game.[1]

That King would seek to mobilise the people of Karitane is interesting enough: that they would turn out in the middle of the night speaks volumes for his determination and powers of motivation.

In 1902 King gave a lecture on Seaside Planting to describe his Karitane conservation efforts. The government duly published it in *Tree Culture in New Zealand*.[2] King's description of his work is illuminating, and worth reading in full:

> The area dealt with at Karitane consisted of two entirely distinct parts: (1) a sand isthmus about 4 chains wide and 8 chains long, connecting the Karitane peninsula with the mainland, and (2) the peninsula itself.
>
> In the early days of the colony some half-dozen whalers had their huts erected on the isthmus, and the sand was securely held against wind and sea by a natural growth of flax and native grasses. Later the huts were abandoned, and cattle soon destroyed the vegetation both of the isthmus and the neighbouring sandhills along the coast of the mainland.
>
> Up to this time the peninsula, which rises steeply to a terrace about thirty or forty feet above sea-level, had been quite free from drifting sand, and was closely covered with a luxuriant growth of grass and clover. Now the sand commenced to drift along the beach and across the isthmus, some finding its way into the estuary and contributing to the shoaling and ruining of the port; and another portion travelling up the slopes of the peninsula, killing all the vegetation in its path except a gorse bush here and there. Sometimes the ground was so deeply covered with sand that a dray could be driven over the remains of the

Numéro 19 / Issue 19

Lemony Snicket's: A Series of Unfortunate Events

Previews
ON COMMAND
Canada

NATIONAL TREASURE
Nicholas Cage

Movies & games in your room. Press Menu on your TV remote.

Des films et des jeux dans votre chambre. Appuyez sur le bouton Menu de votre télécommande.

If you accidentally exit your movie, press MENU immediately to return to your movie.

En cas d'interruption accidentelle du visionnement de votre film, appuyez immédiatement sur la touche MENU pour revenir au film.

Action • Action
National Treasure

A treasure hunter is in hot pursuit of a mythical treasure that has been passed down for centuries.

Nicholas Cage
Rated PG   2 hrs. 12 min.

Action • Action
Ocean's Twelve
(AVAILABLE IN ENGLISH AND FRENCH/DISPONIBLE EN FRANÇAIS OU EN ANGLAIS)

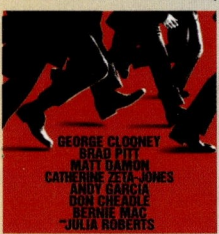

Danny Ocean recruits one more team member so he can pull off three major European heists in this sequel to Ocean's 11.

Brad Pitt
Rated PG-13   2 hrs. 6 min.

Experience High Speed TV Internet in the comfort of your guest room.
Internet is not available in all hotels.

Faites l'expérience de la télévision par Internet à haute vitesse dans le confort de votre chambre d'hôtel.
L'accès Internet n'est pas offert dans tous les hôtels.

Ordering Information/ Renseignements sur la location

Order A Movie Today – It's Easy!
Commandez sans tarder! C'est facile!

1. To order an On Command movie, press the "MENU" button on the remote for instructions and a complete listing of movies and prices.
2. Billing is IMMEDIATE and automatic. There is a separate charge for each movie ordered.

1. Pour commander un film On Command, appuyez sur le touche « MENU » de la télécommande et consultez la liste des titres et des frais de location.
2. La facturation est IMMÉDIATE et automatique. Chaque film commandé est facturé séparément.

> Not all movies, video games or TV internet are available in all hotels. If you exit your movie or turn the TV off, you will lose your movie.
>
> Certains films et jeux vidéo ainsi que l'accès Internet ne sont pas offerts dans tous les hôtels. Si vous arrêtez votre film ou éteignez la télévision, vous perdrez votre film.
>
> **Parents:** Some movies contain material intended soley for adults (18 and older). To prevent the showing of any movie in your room, call the front desk.
>
> **Avis aux parents:** Certains films contiennent des scènes destinées exclusivement aux adultes (18 ans et plus). Pour éviter qu'un film soit commandé, avisez la réception.

Please send your comments to:/Veuillez faire parvenir vos commentaires à:
telloncommand@ocv.com

Games Unlimited
Now Available in Many Hotels.
Play games using TV remote control or Internet keyboards. Select Games on your menu for titles.
Games not available in all hotels.

Jeux à volonté
De nombreux hôtels offrent maintenant Jeux à volonté.
Jouez à l'aide de la télécommande ou du clavier Internet. Choisissez un jeu dans le menu.
Les jeux ne sont pas offerts dans tous les hôtels.

fences, and at others, the bare earth, devoid of any sign of plant life, was exposed. The isthmus became so much lowered that from time to time it was submerged during high tides, and the river threatened to resume its ancient course straight through the neck, which would have completed the ruin of the port.

At this stage, in 1899, the matter was taken in hand by the Karitane District Improvement Society. The isthmus was fenced, and manuka scrub was lashed to the bases of the posts which skirted high-water mark, in order to accumulate a sand barrier. The scrub was maintained at about a foot or more above sand level, and as the sand rose other layers were added from time to time.

A second similar line of scrub defence, parallel to and a quarter of a chain back from the first line, was erected later. In the meantime, marram grass had been planted; and a clay embankment and roadway, protected by the scrub and a fringe of marram, was carried across the isthmus from the mainland to the peninsula.

At the present time an uninterrupted sand dune stands as an effective barrier to all further sea encroachments. This dune, eight chains long by over a quarter of a chain wide, and averaging from six to seven feet high at the crest, is densely covered with marram grass, the leaves of which carry the wind shelter two feet higher. This sand ridge is increasing in height at the rate of fully two feet a year, and it has raised the level of the ocean beach in an inclined plane stretching several chains down to low-water mark.

Three things have been accomplished – (1) some thousands of tons of drift sand, in transit to shoal the estuary and prevent plant growth on the land, have been arrested, bound together and laid down in the desired position as a sea wall sheltering a permanent roadway. (2) A wind barrier has been formed 8 feet high. This now shelters plantations of Olearias, Box-thorns, Pines, Cypress, Willows and Cabbage-trees, which are making good growth to the north of the roadway. Clover has sprung up wherever the sand is not occupied by marram grass or shrubs – all this taking place where only a few years ago sea wreckage was strewn at every specially high tide. (3) The portion of the peninsula which has been rendered for the time being valueless by drifting sand has clothed itself with the most luxuriant covering of grass and clover wherever we have not planted shrubs and trees.

The peninsula, some 43 acres in extent, rises abruptly from the sea to a height in places of 130 feet; and the problem before us was how to clothe it with shelter most expeditiously and economically. The Domain Board had practically no funds, and certainly nothing to expend in experimenting.

The property immediately adjoining the isthmus belonged to myself, and I decided to give a fair trial to the methods which had been found effective on the islands and sea coast of Scotland. Fortunately ample data were available in a series of essays on the subject, published in the Transactions of the Highland and Agricultural Society.

With these before us, screens of palings, manuka scrub, etc., were erected round the margin of the terrace, and, under cover of these shelters, belts of Conifers, Gums and the harder deciduous trees, with some native evergreens such as Ngaio and Cabbage-tree were planted. These now form dense established thickets, in which the Blue-gums reach 20 feet in height, Pinis Insignis 16 feet, Silver Birch and Rowans 8 feet, etc.

The success of these plantations could not have been greater, but the initial cost of providing a shelter rendered them expensive. There can be no doubt that shelter is the first consideration for seaside planting, and that no form of shelter quite equals a 'dead fence' of palings or scrub if it be desired to raise a belt of trees to a given height in a minimum of time.

We find it of inestimable advantage to work the whole of the soil thoroughly beforehand, and where this is feasible we never resort to pit-planting. Trenching by hand is, of course, out of the question on the score of expense, and is unnecessary (in this district at least) because special ploughing and cultivating prove equally effective.

CONSERVATION AT KARITANE

We plough shallow in the summer, clean well with cultivator and harrows, plough deeply with a digger-plough in the autumn, crop with potatoes the following spring where suitable, and realise a profit. Where too exposed for potatoes, we sow down crimson clover or annual red clover.

Once shelter has been established, a wide range of trees and shrubs will flourish at the seaside as well as, or even better than, inland. The baneful influence of the sea breezes laden with salt ceases when we moderate the rate of the air currents to a certain degree, and diminishes as the trees grow taller on account of acclimitisation and the increased toughness and strength of the leaves and twigs of mature plants. If ground space, time and expense were of no importance, the ideal seaside shelter would commence with marram or lyme grass on the low-lying sands, and rise gently up the slopes through graded Veronicas, Flax, Senecios, Olearias and Pittosporums to plantations of loftier Conifers, Gums and deciduous trees.

In experimenting with screen formations at Karitane we lost much time and were put to considerable expense, in places, by the more or less complete failure of the majority of the plants relied on at Home. Sea-buckthorn, Tamarisk, Snowberry and Dogwood are universally recommended as pioneers by all Home authorities; yet, with the exception of Tamarisk, none of these plants have made as much headway in fully exposed situations here in three years as some other shrubs have done in a single season. Even the Tamarisk has proved capricious, and has done well only under comparatively favourable conditions. None of our evergreen Oaks have made and sustained more than a few inches of growth per annum, and the same applies to the English Maple. In this district these trees are useless as pioneers. Gorse, broom and briar, in spite of their thriving cannot be recommended, on account of their coming under the Noxious Weeds Act.

New Zealand Flax has proved one of the hardiest and best shelter plants of moderate height. For rapidly-effective temporary shelter,

Lupins are unequalled, but they are comparatively short-lived, though the Lupin will keep on re-sowing itself. The Lupin does not rob the ground to so great a distance as the Mallow, will flourish in almost pure sand and has the further advantage of storing up additional organic matter in the soil. It must be borne in mind that when the windward side of the screen is composed of Mallow or Lupin planted close up to permanent shrubs, the latter are left bare on the death of the former for a number of feet above ground level, and are then apt to suffer severely from the effects of wind whistling through them. In spite of these objections, no shelter has proved more useful than Lupin and Mallow when used judiciously. A fringe of either or both, placed a sufficient distance away from other shrubs, is invaluable.

If limited to one kind of plant for the rapid and economical formation of a dense permanent shelter screen up to 12 feet, I should choose Veronica Elliptica. Cuttings can be propagated by the thousand with a minimum of trouble, and the young plants need no protection or shelter of any kind when placed in their permanent positions. Stray plants of this Veronica form an indigenous growth here almost to the water's edge, on the cliffs fully exposed to the south-west wind laden with sea-spray. Other hardy Veronicas such as Arborea and Colensoi-major also do well here.

The hardier Senecios and Olearias have proved not only indifferent to wind, but are found to be more healthy and vigorous when exposed. Like the Veronicas, well-rooted cuttings may be planted out directly into exposed situations without being sheltered.

Among exotic shrubs, the Escallonia Macanthra has proved one of the hardiest and best, but propagation is much more troublesome than in the case of the foregoing plants, and is less easy to establish.

The best of the Pittosporums (P. Ralphi) and the best of the Coprosmas (C. Lucida) make rapid growth, and are thoroughly hardy and reliable.

Nothing we have tried with the exception of Olearia Traversii, outstrips the Cabbage-tree in rapidity of growth, and the extreme case of propagation by seed renders it one of the best trees for extensive planting at the seaside.

Goat-willow and Box-thorn have both proved very hardy, quick-growing and satisfactory. The Broadleaf, on account of its hardiness and permanence, is one of the most desirable seaside shrubs. We consider it a good pioneer to plant on the windward side of any shrubs of doubtful permanency. The Broadleaf can be relied upon for ultimate shelter and continuous steady growth.

The Ngaio, which is so valuable in the north, has proved almost a failure, owing to the severe cutting-back of young plants by frost, and the ravages of aphides in summer, though there are some good adult specimens in the district. When it is added that adult trees here are much infested by borers, many of them dying from this cause, it will be realised that the Ngaio is of doubtful value in this locality.

The Pohutakawa is killed outright in cold winters, and the Taupata and Karaka are too much cut by frost to make any satisfactory progress as pioneers.

Of lofty evergreen trees, the Pinus Muricata and hardier Gums promise to serve our purpose best. Some of the hardier wattles are expected to form good shelter quickly. Cupressus Macrocarpa and Pinus Insignis grow fairly satisfactorily, but are more cut by the sea breezes than Pinus Muricata.

This tends to indicate that King had growing confidence in his ability to understand nature, to interact with it, to influence it, if not to dominate it. The report cannot be dismissed as plagiarism, showing instead a clear understanding of natural processes and how to work within them. He was never afraid to seek the public stage and tell people about his work.

King's property, later named Kingscliff, was built as a holiday house, while the Kings continued to live at the asylum. He would

IN A STRANGE GARDEN

Kingscliff, the house at Karitane.

later use it as a therapeutic outreach for his 'recoverables', as well as encouraging his more trustworthy cases to walk from Seacliff to Karitane and picnic there under attendant supervision.

The house, which still exists today, is visible across the estuary from Karitane. An imposing two-storey building with white weatherboards, it nestles against a grove of trees. Its original construction reinforces a commendable aspect of Truby's character:

> Set in beautiful grounds of trees and flowerbeds, the house was not only pleasing to the eye, but extremely interesting. It had been built round a tree, which grew up through the livingroom, spreading its shady branches over the roof. Dr King was eccentric: he would rather live with the tree than commit the sin of cutting down so fine a specimen. That he would have to live with its inevitable inhabitants, spiders and grubs, didn't worry him; he was the first conservationist. The new owners had no qualms about removing the tree to make a more conventional but still charming livingroom.[3]

CONSERVATION AT KARITANE

The garden covered at least an acre, and incorporated a rhododendron dell, one of his gardening trademarks, together with a grove of hazelnuts, a daffodil garden for Bella, various flowering shrubs, roses and a large stand of gum trees. In her oral history recollections,[4] Mary tells of Truby frequently renting the house out, and the Kings camping under the gum trees in a tent, with access to the bathroom in the house. It is unclear whether they camped by choice or because Truby forgot he'd already tenanted the house.

CHAPTER NINE

The adoption of Mary

FROM A multitude of sources arose four conflicting stories of Mary's adoption.

Mary herself explains in her book: 'It was a great sorrow to them both that Mrs King was incapable of child-bearing, and so, on 17 February 1905 they adopted a baby girl, whom they called Mary – the child of esteemed friends.' The Kings had just returned from a six-month convalescent visit to Japan.

Then in her oral history recorded by Jim Sullivan in 1992, Mary White (née King) at the age of eight-eight recalled her youth. Her mother, she said, was a maternity nurse, her father a painter at Seacliff. Father had died and mother couldn't cope with new-born Mary, who was the second of two children. 'Fred [Truby] and Bella were off to Japan, collected [me] when they returned.' According to Mary, she was born on 25 January 1904. Truby and Bella returned from Japan in February 1905. Is it possible that Mary had been boarded out for the best part of a year?

Mary's account of how Truby and Bella forbade contact with her mother or sister Ngarita is heart-rending. She was instructed to return gifts of a New Testament and wrist-watch, and was forbidden to communicate with her blood relatives. While at Archerfield boarding school in Dunedin, she would sometimes see her birth mother at Knox church, where she came hoping to catch a glimpse of Mary with the other schoolgirls.

The second source is from the great-aunt of a personal friend of the author's, who at the age of 101 was still regarded as having keen and reliable recall.[1] She trained as a Karitane nurse, both at Karitane and at Christchurch, and met Truby King half a dozen times, remembering him as 'a wee man, very kind and gentle, the kind of person who would come into a room very quietly, and be noticed'. She remembers stories of Mary being a twin, her father being a warder and unable to afford the expense of two children. People, she said, were very much against Truby adopting only one twin and Mary was apparently the more delicate of the pair. I have been unable to corroborate this information through birth records.

Mr Moss, who was on the staff at Seacliff, had a very different perspective on Mary's adoption. He has it that one O'Connell, an attendant at Seacliff, had been found drunk on duty. In order for O'Connell to retain his position, King 'persuaded' him to allow one of his many children to be adopted by the Kings, who had no children of their own. This theory also cannot be verified from legal records of births.

Lastly, Dr Eleanor McLagan, one of New Zealand's first women doctors, whom Truby employed at Seacliff, tells another story:

> A favourite male attendant had married a favourite female attendant. He got acute diabetes, and insulin being unknown at the time, died in a very short while. The widow with her baby was taken back on the staff. One of my duties was to watch the baby carefully and see that all was well with it. Eventually the Kings, who had no children of their

THE ADOPTION OF MARY

own, adopted that baby. Dr King trained the widowed mother in the routine he had evolved for artificial baby feeding, and put her in Dunedin to give free advice to distracted mothers on a salary paid out of his own pocket. Some years later he told me he could not have done this if he had been in practice himself, but as a civil servant, and out in the country, he could do it without infringing medical ethics.[2]

Which, if any, of the stories do we believe and what information can we deduce even from the more improbable sources? While there are elements of truth in McLagan's story, my research suggests that she had confused the widowed mother with another King acolyte, although the diabetic death is likely.

Truby was at the time, along with his mentor, MacGregor, a propounder of the Eugenic theories which were very much in vogue. Whether a true eugenicist would consider adoption is arguable. Whether King would steal the child of a drunken attendant, given his distaste for drunks, is even less believable.

Adoption at the beginning of last century was shrouded in the stigma of illegitimacy.

In April 2002 Mary White died in Adelaide, aged ninety-eight. Some months later I was fortunate to make contact with both of her sons. Michael had been made aware of my interest by a third party, while Stephen had become friendly with a nursing acquaintance of my wife, who was then located with her doctor husband in a small Australian opal-mining town where he lived. Until this time, my research had been almost entirely deductive. The role of the biographer can become complicated when forced to confront the subject's relatives, and while I am grateful for their candour and willingness to pass on information, I must confess discomfort when confronted with opinions with which I cannot agree. I am aware of Robert Graves' scornful assessment of biography in his poem 'To Bring the Dead Back to Life' where he suggests that biography is a branch of character-acting in which the subject is diminished by the biographer's limited acting skills. The information provided by the White brothers gave this impoverished actor further evidence to dissect and more puzzles to solve.

While some of the pieces of the jigsaw remain stubbornly misplaced, I feel that the adoption of little Mary sheds significant light on Truby King. With the blessing of his superiors, he was in 1904 about to go off to Japan on sick leave. His fifteen years work at Seacliff had established him not only as a talented if dogmatic asylum director, but also as a scientist and farmer. His *Feeding of Plants and Animals* would be published in the following year, and there is no doubt the thinking that would lead to the foundations of Plunket was well advanced.

Bella and Truby King were childless. Bella was aged forty-three, and apparently unsuited to the rigours of childbearing due to infantile rickets. Without children, King's credibility in infant welfare may have been compromised. Sources close to the family suggested that King sought to adopt a child to validate his position. As a physician his choice of adoption subject would not have been limited, and given his Caledonian predisposition, it's hardly surprising that he chose the child of a Scottish-born mother.

Esther Loreena Gordon was born to Leilah and William Gordon in Dunedin on 25 January 1904. She was the younger of two girls, her sister being christened Ngarita Inez (hardly Scottish names). They met while working at Seacliff where Leilah was a nurse/attendant and William, Irish by birth, was a painter. Before their second child was born, William developed diabetes and soon after the birth he departed to Dunedin to live and eventually die with his mother. Leilah, who later became celebrated as a nurse, midwife and welfare worker, was put under considerable pressure by Truby King to yield up her youngest for adoption. As the *Dictionary of New Zealand Biography* notes:

> She was left in financial difficulties and was vulnerable to pressure when the superintendent at Seacliff, Frederic Truby King and his wife Isabella, both in their mid 40s, offered to adopt baby Esther around July 1904. King was impatient and insistent, and Leilah Gordon had few other choices. Consenting to the adoption was a decision she was

Mary King in her early twenties.

bitterly to regret – it became the 'lasting event' of her life. Before the adoption papers were signed, the Kings went to Japan for six months leaving the baby in care and Gordon working as a nurse at Seacliff.[3]

Leilah Gordon unsurprisingly left Seacliff, returning to Dunedin where she enrolled as a midwife. It is unlikely that she did so with King's support, as he took the strange and unusual step of a court order forbidding any communication with the child now known as Mary King.

Recent American research has highlighted the trauma of infant-maternal separation, christening it the 'Primal Wound'. Statistics have shown a very high incidence of social problems in adopted children, leading to the conclusion that the severing of the bond established *in utero* can give rise to depression, anxiety and behavioural problems in those adopted. It is not my proposition that Mary suffered any of these difficulties, only to stress that her start in life was far from normal. Adoption, yes; but being boarded out while the Kings were in Japan for six months, then injunctions against communication with her birth mother, does not impress with normality. Mary's children talk of her in the most devoted and loving terms, but a nervous breakdown before she eventually married suggests some residual difficulties.

As Truby King's life unfolds, we will see Mary playing a number of pivotal roles in support of the great man. She appeared to enjoy a privileged childhood: boarding school, doting parents, training as a kindergarten teacher; then with Bella's death, she was thrust into a number of supporting roles as social secretary, companion, taker of dictation, interpreter of commands and edicts.

Mary's birth mother, still regretting the surrender of her daughter, tried to persuade her to rejoin the family when she turned twenty-one, but by then Mary was too involved with her adoptive father and declined.

CHAPTER TEN

A prototype for Plunket

Mary at thirteen months old was described by Bella as 'a very delicate baby . . . almost a skeleton'. As the breast-feeding option was unavailable, Mary was fed from a bottle with a mixture of cow's milk and cane sugar. Bella was not happy with her progress and, frustrated with her husband's apparent lack of interest, chided: 'Fred, you're more interested in your animals than your own child.' Bella suggested that he should devise a more suitable food, as he had done for his animals. She knew that Truby the scientist would accept the challenge.

He devoured everything he could about the feeding of infants to supplement his previous medical knowledge. He would have been impressed with the pioneering work of Budin in France, von Reubner in Germany and Strauss and Rotch in America, who were all working on aspects of infant feeding and medical care. Better still, Truby had just been joined at Seacliff by Dr Falconer, fresh from studying Public Health at University College, London. Falconer told him of the work at the Battersea Milk Depot, where Dr McCleary had a cure for infant diarrhoea. For Truby King, fresh from his triumphs of creating artificial dairy feed substitutes for calves, this struck a chord. In characteristic fashion he delved into Falconer's reports from Battersea, then into the literature from France and the United States. The topic that most arrested King was the American approach of 'humanising' cow's milk, which required the modification of fat, protein and sugar levels to more closely mimic human milk. Given the new information and the need to devise a practical feeding regime for little Mary, he set to.

Later in 1905 Truby took the opportunity to educate his audiences at the annual conference of the Farmer's Union in Wellington. He had been invited to give two speeches. The first was called 'Agricultural Education in Japan', in which he stressed his appreciation of the simple rural Japanese life and the strength of the family.[1] His comments include such gems as 'the strength of the Japanese nation was in the sacrifice of the women to their families' since children were breast-fed until they were twelve to eighteen months of age. He slipped in a strong condemnation of Anglo-Saxon women for their failure to breast-feed, and their adoption of artificial foods. (The fashion for New Zealand women of the time was against breast-feeding babies, certainly not to the degree or duration King had seen in Japan.) His Seacliff work had convinced him that early nutritional problems were at the root of mental disorders and he knew that infant mortality had declined in France by 40 per cent during the Franco-Prussian war of 1871, when women were unable to farm out babies and had to resort to breast-feeding. What the Farmer's Union made of this is not reported, but Truby continued on day two of the conference with a description of Rotch's method of 'humanising' cow's milk for the feeding of infants. He began his talk with a homily on infant feeding:

> If it is necessary to be guided by the laws of nature, and to be

A PROTOTYPE FOR PLUNKET

systematic and accurate in the feeding of plants and lower animals, such care is surely incumbent on us in the rearing of human beings. Yet what do we find in practice? In spite of the fact that suckling is the only perfect method of feeding any young mammal, it has become the exception and not the rule . . . Nutrition given by the mother in the natural way is always the best . . . for the most part she the mother who rears her child by means of a bottle is densely ignorant of the duties of maternity, and does not realise the injustice she is doing to herself and her offspring. She has no knowledge of or respect for the laws of Nature, and imagine, the advertising charlatans have superceded Providence in the feeding of babies.

The vision of an assembly of farmers at a national conference willingly listening to diatribes on breast-feeding is hardly credible, but given Truby's undoubted powers of oratory, we must assume that they did listen. He probably won over the farmers with analogies they more readily accepted relating to Nature's laws of the nurture of plants and animals. Little did the farmers realise that they were experiencing the first public outpourings of King's 'To help the mothers and save the babies'. This was not the last time they would hear it.

Shortly after the conference, King was approached by Chief Justice Sir Robert Stout, who had been impressed with the presentation. He gave Stout a summary which incorporated a précis of the 'humanising' of cow's milk. Stout's response was to request the editor of Wellington's *Evening Post* to publish the address. The *Post* acceded to Stout's request: 'The information ought to be widely disseminated . . . if medical experts like Dr Truby King say that one of the causes [of infant mortality] is improper food, it is surely necessary that the mothers of children should know how to preserve the lives of their infants.' Truby King's address followed. Soon after this, King published *The Feeding of Children,* and then an expanded version, *The Feeding of Plants and Animals.*

Stout had been prompted by his patriotic desire to prevent 'infant loss'. This was a familiar theme to King. From his reading he knew that the British feared that unless the Colonies were occupied by people of British stock, they would be invaded by foreigners, especially 'Asiatics'. Britain in the twentieth century was experiencing a more humanitarian trend, echoing growing concern for people at risk, especially children, resulting in the Factory Acts of 1879 and 1887 and the Prevention of Cruelty to Children Act of 1889. The prevalent belief was that 'hand fed' infants thrived better than breast-fed. Baby foods like Benges, Allen & Hanburys and Nestlés were becoming convenient and widely accepted.

America, too, was grappling with infant feeding. The 'humanisation' of cow's milk, to make it more approximate to the constituents of breast milk, was being investigated. By 1893 New York had its first milk pasteurisation depot.

In France the great fear was depopulation; it was noted that the natural population increase (births minus deaths) had declined nearly sixfold during the nineteenth century. Of real concern to the French was Germany, whose natural population increase in the same period was positive. Despite exhortations to 'increase and multiply', the decline continued. Fears that the young French republic would be dwarfed and overwhelmed by Germany stimulated improvements in neo-natal care and education. Healthy, educated children were seen as the future of France.

Infant mortality had therefore come under scrutiny. In Paris, more than a quarter of infants died in their first year. In the last decade of the nineteenth century, over a million infant French lives had been lost. This prompted investigation into infant diseases and care, especially feeding. As early as 1876 investigators had concluded that the major killers gastroenteritis and diarrhoea could be prevented by proper infant care, suitable food and feeding. Pierre Budin, Professor of Obstetrics in Paris, became aware that his women patients were returning 'because the previous infant had died'.[2] He embarked on a study of infant health and established France's first infant clinic in 1892. A visiting foreign doctor remarked, 'Your clinic is not very interesting, all the infants are doing very well.'[3] Under Budin's care, the infant mortality rate was cut significantly. Records showed that the rate of death per thousand births in Paris averaged 178, while for infants attending his clinic the rate was reduced to forty-six. This was achieved by many of the principles that Truby King would adopt: home visits, dispensaries for the supply of milk, supervision of infants in foster homes and emphasis on breast-feeding. The work of Budin and others was greatly admired in Britain and Europe, where infant mortality rates were just as worrying as in France. Budin's influential book, *The Nursling*, published in 1900, became a standard tome on infant care. He died in 1907, just after the English translation of his book was published. In the foreword, Professor Simpson of Edinburgh University noted, 'With a dwindling birth rate, it becomes a matter of urgent necessity to discover and develop means of reducing infant mortality.'[4] King had been one of Simpson's better students and, with a good reading knowledge of French, would have been aware of Budin's work.

By contrast, early New Zealand was 'healthier' than Britain, with its favourable climate, lack of real poverty and primary production focus. The birthrate was increasing, and the infant mortality rates were already the lowest in the Western world, half that of England and Wales. Socially, New Zealand was not lagging behind. The Women's Christian Temperance Union was founded in 1885, being instrumental in the Infant Life Protection Act in 1893, the year Truby's father died. The same year another group, the Society for the Protection of Women and Children, was formed and by 1900 had branches in the main cities. In 1904, to popular acclaim, Richard Seddon initiated the Child Life Preservation Memorandum. This resulted in the registration of midwives and the establishment of a training school, a world first. By 1907 the four cities had St Helen's maternity hospitals, with services freely available to all.

The New Zealand of the early twentieth century already had established voluntary women's groups and state maternity hospitals. All it lacked was a source of authoritative advice for mothers. Truby seized the opportunity. Capitalising on the concerns espoused by Stout, he neatly dovetailed the infant mortality issue with his pro-breast-feeding ideas. He was building up a considerable head of steam, and by 1906 was confidently asserting it was every child's birthright to be breast-fed. He was vociferous in his attacks on the prevalent practice of artificial feeding. Never afraid to pander to nationalistic fears, he would use jingoistic phrases in support of 'the English race'.[5] Some of his more extreme utterings were taken to be Eugenist in their stance. His supporters Stout and MacGregor were vocal advocates of the Eugenic movement, and King certainly paid more than lip service to it. He cleverly incorporated Eugenic ideas into his crusades, but remained focused on his main theme of a sound mind in a sound body.

By this time, Mary King was 'the most beautiful baby, fat, rosy and strong',[6] all apparently due to the power of correct feeding with humanised milk. Truby resolved to take the Mary King experiment out to the people. He had discussed the lofty ideas of reducing New Zealand's infant loss and improving the general health of babies with the medical fraternity. Their lukewarm response did not deter him. His practical response was to carry on the experiment in the village of Seacliff. He reasoned that if a nurse could show families in their own homes how to care for infants, she could communicate to the mothers the principles of proper feeding and care.

After discussion with Miss Beswick, matron of Seacliff Asylum, King chose as his prototype community nurse a 'noble little highlander',[7] staff member Miss Joanna MacKinnon. Joanna was not a registered nurse, nor did she have any training in infant care, but doubtless her Scottish origins, her fondness for children and her personality shone through. Paid by and equipped with careful instruction from Truby King she began work in Seacliff village, teaching mothers how to modify cow's milk in their homes. The first baby to receive humanised milk was a boy of three months. He had been fed on a patent food and was 'thin and feeble and suffering from indigestion'.[8] Miss MacKinnon showed his mother how to prepare the milk and with this changed diet he was soon strong and healthy. The mothers of the Seacliff village were hardly going to argue with the dictates of their Dr King.

Miss MacKinnon's success in the village encouraged Truby King to extend the experiment. She was boarded in Dunedin with the

Murray family, working under his close supervision. He made sure her work was widely known, and that 'Nurse' MacKinnon would, on request, visit the home to give demonstrations of the method of home modification of milk and advice on infant care.

Before Christmas 1905 Truby King was publishing instructions in the *Evening Star* on 'The guidance of mothers in the feeding of infants'.[9] With the co-operation and support of the press, the message was getting out.

King and Miss MacKinnon were astute enough to enlist pillars of the church in their educational crusade. Sister Alice of the Wesleyan Church and Sister Evelyn of the Presbyterian Church were both trained by Miss MacKinnon in Truby King's methods. Eighteen months later Sister Evelyn established the first Presbyterian orphanage in New Zealand. By April of 1906 Miss MacKinnon had become known as Nurse MacKinnon and had fifty babies under her direct care. King was working on the provision of fresh milk. At the time, milk was poured into 'billies' of dubious hygiene from cans on delivery lorries. Infected milk resulted in gastroenteritis, one of the major causes of infant mortality at the time. Aided by Dr Falconer, he approached the Taieri and Peninsula Dairy Company to see whether they would modify cow's milk for infant use. The company agreed to supply the facilities for refrigeration and bottling and to deliver chilled milk to the mothers if Truby King supplied a nurse and an assistant specially trained in its preparation. The ubiquitous Nurse MacKinnon supervised the scheme, and an assistant was recruited, trained at King's expense and put to work at the dairy company. The venture was a total success.

Next, King addressed the question of sugar content in humanised milk. He contended that lactose (sugar of milk) was superior to cane sugar, being natural and more easily digested, resisting fermentation in infants' stomachs. He was partially correct, in that breast milk has a much higher lactose content than cow's milk, but his accusations against cane sugar were hardly proven. He went further to identify cane sugar as 'the leading cause of indigestion and diarrhoea in infants'.[10] Members of the medical profession who did not support

King's extravagant statements were charged with 'overlooking the fundamental principle of biological chemistry'.[11] The scorn that King could pour on dissenters was considerable, but his adherents increased, with assistance from the ever supportive press.

King then sought to lower the price of imported lactose. The only source of lactose was chemists who were unwilling to reduce their margins. With the grocers onside, he took the simple, if bold approach of importing a ton of lactose of 'the highest quality procurable'.[12] The cost to him was two months' salary, but he shrugged off the risk. The exercise was a success, and in a year lactose consumption in Otago had soared 2000 per cent and through his lobbying the import duty had been removed.

His crusade to lower infant mortality by feeding hygienic humanised milk where mothers could not or chose not to breast-feed was paying off. His profile was increasing, as was that of Nurse MacKinnon and her team. King, who never lost an opportunity to push his latest theory, thundered in his annual report to the Inspector-General of Mental Hospitals in 1906, 'I have devoted much practical attention during the year to questions bearing on prophylaxis in regard to the rising generation.'[13] One assumes he was making a connection between the improvement in infant care and the potential decline in numbers of future mental patients? MacGregor continued in his unhesitating support.

CHAPTER ELEVEN

The Plunket movement

'IT is wiser to erect a fence at the top of a precipice than to maintain an ambulance at the bottom' is a common saying that was adopted by Truby King as motto for his weekly 'Hygeia' newspaper column.

One of King's more notable successors at Plunket, Dr Neil Begg, made the profound observation that 'the *treatment* of disease is very different to the *prevention* of disease'. Both the medical profession and the government, in Begg's opinion, were slow to recognise this. King, he believed, was one of the first to appreciate the difference and to formulate a solution. This was to involve women in the promotion of their own health. The involvement of women signals the beginning of the Plunket movement.

By 1906 King's public utterances in Dunedin were coming thick and fast. 'An Appeal to Mothers' was published in May, followed by

'The Training of the Human Plant' in July. The work of Nurse MacKinnon and her assistants (still funded entirely by King) was becoming widely recognised. He lost no opportunity to address public meetings, often with Nurse MacKinnon, or Miss Beswick, his Matron at Seacliff, following up with a practical demonstration. King often managed to emphasise that the need for reforms in infant feeding and education were part of what he described as the 'prevention of mental illness'.

He had less success with the conservative medical profession, who were not always keen to embrace change or new ideas. Doctors also criticised King in his role as a government doctor, believing he had no right to encroach on their practices. While the majority of the profession was unprepared to embrace the outspoken and publicity-seeking asylum doctor's ideas, chinks in the professional armour were beginning to appear, and at least three Dunedin doctors were sufficiently impressed with the work of Nurse MacKinnon and team in ministering to their own wives, that they publicly endorsed King's work. One of them was Dr Louis Barnett, later Sir Louis, distinguished Professor of Surgery.

By mid-year King was finding the increasing workload as propagandist for the infant-welfare movement was deflecting him from his mental health duties at Seacliff. He raised the profile of Nurse MacKinnon, letting her take over the answering of letters to the newspaper. 'I feel the time has come to leave matters entirely in her hands,' he wrote, 'though I am willing to accept a general responsibility for any advice she may give.'[1]

At the beginning of the following year the system of infant care as demonstrated by Nurse MacKinnon had become accepted in the Dunedin community. Together with sisters of various churches, she was providing a valuable service. Production of humanised milk for mothers had reached 200 pints per day. King was not wasting his time, either. Realising the importance of propaganda, he was busy bending the ears of any politician, businessman or person of influence. Shrewdly, he reasoned that the upper- and middle-class women were the key to its continued success, and spent as much time as he could preaching to them his messages of 'saving infant lives'.

The influenza epidemic of 1907 claimed the lives of many babies, but served as a focus for King's mission. With the support of a number of influential Dunedin people, an enthusiastic public meeting was held in the Dunedin Town Hall on 17 May 1907. This was his most significant speech. The big hall was abuzz with interest. With co-operation from the newspapers, he was assured that the meeting would be well attended. The stooped, slightly dishevelled character took the podium and launched into his address. He called on all the persuasive powers and emotive tricks he knew, conjuring up the spectre of the Yellow Peril, declining birth rates, insanity resulting from poor infant nutrition, and the shocking infant mortality rate, especially among illegitimate babies. He offered them solutions, ones that they could implement and control themselves. He had pitched his talk at women, stressing humanitarian issues with which they could empathise.

The outcome of the meeting was the decision to form a Society to continue the work begun by Truby King. The Society was soberly named the Society for the Promotion of Health among Women and Children. The steering committee comprised Truby King, his wife Bella, and five influential women who had helped Truby in the initial experimental period.

A week later he had approached all the women he wanted to make up the committee. They all accepted. As Nurse MacKinnon said, 'There were few who grudge time or effort for Truby King.'[2]

The committee comprised twenty-four members, all with influence and commitment to the cause. King had covered his bases well. There were wives of four lawyers, six prominent businessmen, a member of parliament and eleven members of the medical or nursing professions. Their religious affiliations included Presbyterians, Jews, Anglicans, Methodist and Wesleyan. Even the Salvation Army was conscripted. Mrs Hosking was elected president. Her husband was a noted lawyer who would shortly take silk and eventually become an influential judge, and had collaborated on the drawing up of the

Society's constitution, which was a formalisation of King's aims and objectives and is reproduced in Appendix Two.

In the three years since Truby and Bella had adopted Mary, Truby King had gone from an outspoken holistic farmer and asylum superintendent to leader of a movement that would sweep him on to bigger and better schemes 'to save the babies'.

Soon after the Society was formed, the indefatigable Nurse MacKinnon uncovered the scandal of licensed foster homes for babies. This was to drive Truby King in yet another direction, which would lead to the formation of Karitane hospitals.

Illegitimacy was a problem that the Edwardians didn't want to acknowledge. Babies born out of wedlock found their way into licensed homes, created by the Infant Life Protection Act of 1896, administered grudgingly by the police. The system did not work well, allowing unscrupulous women known as 'baby-farmers' to profit from looking after babies in dubious conditions and with little regulation. At the time, there were only four 'police matrons' responsible for all licensed baby homes in the country.

Nurse MacKinnon found three babies in an 'ill-treated, starved condition'[3] in a stable adjoining a Dunedin house. King, never one to worry about rules or protocols, shipped two of them off to his home at Seacliff to be cared for. The police did not share Truby's horror and declined to close the home.

On 23 May 1907 the inaugural meeting of the Society for the Promotion of Health of Women and Children was treated to King reading an anonymous letter received by the Mayor of Dunedin: 'The women of this city should go a little further . . . it is no use adopting precautions . . . if a child's future during the helpless period of its existence is not also provided for . . . The State cares for the stock of the colony by providing veterinary surgeons. The welfare of the mother is provided for by maternity homes – but what of the child?'[4]

King suggested a licensed home should be set up to care for infants. He offered the Society his Karitane cottage for a six-month trial period. Naturally the Society accepted, passing a remit: 'To ensure to all infants in the community of the type now lodged in licensed homes that they should be well fed and well clothed; that they should have plenty of air and sunlight; that they should be kept clean and be kindly treated, and that they should not be placed in homes where they would be the sole source of livelihood.'[5]

And so the Karitane cottage was licensed as a home, pressed into service to look after the first two customers – Lilian (5½ months) and Cecil (4½ months). They began their recuperation at Seacliff but after two months moved to the newly prepared cottage at Karitane. Lizzie Hughes, the nurse who had brought up Mary King, was put in charge, with the assistance of two nurses from Seacliff. Truby King supervised the babies' feeding regime, and so began the first 'Karitane' hospital. King equipped the cottage, Society ladies donated baby clothes. Within months thirteen babies were in the care of four nurses. Milk was provided gratis by the dairy company, sent by train packed in ice, collected at the station by locals and ferried by horse and trap to Karitane. Truby King had conscripted not only the ladies, but the community to his cause.

King went back on the campaign trail in mid-1907. After a run-in with Dunedin sceptics, he set forth to Wellington with some of the committee in tow. Their lobbying of the Minister of Justice did not succeed, but King won considerable praise and respect from the politicians. Another trip to Wellington followed to lobby members of parliament debating the Infant Life Protection Act. The reported debates have a curiously familiar ring to them, suggesting a number of members had come under his influence. It appears that sometimes it was easier to fall into step with King than to oppose him. The Society's campaigning had succeeded on many fronts. The Act was passed, the Dunedin Society acknowledged, and the name of Truby King reached a wider audience.

Enter Lady Victoria Plunket, wife of the Governor-General and mother of eight children, already well aware of the problems of infant feeding. She met Truby King and was immediately won over. The ability to influence the rich, famous and privileged is a testament to his persuasive skills as a communicator. With enthusiasm she accepted his invitation to become Patroness of the Dunedin Society.

This was a coup that he would later regret.

Meanwhile, at Karitane the staff and facilities were stretched beyond their limits. King had another room added to accommodate more babies, the stables were converted for the staff to sleep in, and babies slept on the verandah under a canvas awning. Lizzie Hughes worked six months without respite, a fact unnoticed by the totally dedicated but blinkered Dr King. A neighbour was co-opted to do the washing. Miss Beswick, matron of Seacliff, walked the five kilometres from Seacliff to assist the exhausted staff on her days off. As ever, King was at his best when under self-imposed pressure.

At the October meeting of the Society, it was decided the 'experiment' had been successful. By that time the home had cared for as many as twenty malnourished infants, who had, with the benefit of scientific feeding, fresh air, sunlight and clean clothing, put on condition and blossomed. Once babies were considered 'recovered', they were returned to their homes or adopted.

A sub-committee of Society ladies was formed to find a suitable home in Dunedin to continue the work. Mrs Leslie Harris, daughter-in-law of philanthropist Wolf Harris, headed the group. She arranged for the Society to lease one of the family's homes in Anderson's Bay. Founder of the importing firm Bing Harris, Wolf became a life member of the Society, and would continue to support it handsomely, eventually gifting the property to the Society. After he moved to London, his wife would play an important part in supporting Truby King's work at 'Home'.

Within months the Dunedin home was ready for occupation and the babies were transferred from Karitane. The six-roomed villa, set in three and a half acres of grounds, was an ideal baby hospital, with all the sunshine and fresh air that King insisted babies needed. Nurses lived in the converted stables. The Karitane Home for Babies was officially opened in December 1907, to a blaze of publicity. The 'Karitane' name would be used for all baby-care hospitals from this point on. Notable guests included four members of parliament, six doctors, several clergy and many leading citizens. The motto 'Save the Babies' was adopted for the home, with the grand mission 'to give a chance for a healthy life to babies who are brought into the world either without a home at all or under conditions that would not allow their being properly nurtured and cared for'.[6] On his return to Wellington, Cabinet Minister J. A. Millar announced a grant of £100 to assist the Society. The next year this subsidy would be increased to £500.

At first there was no resident doctor and the home lacked the facilities to care for 'serious' medical cases. Initially, the staff were unqualified, but later were registered midwives after Mrs Gordon joined as Matron. The ever-reliable Nurse MacKinnon was also present. In the first year thirty-four babies were treated. Success was mixed, as many babies were seriously ill and beyond the level of care the home could provide. The system of care was the same as devised by Truby King at Karitane: humanised milk, regular feeding and plenty of fresh air, sunshine and exercise. Accurate records of weight and fluid intake were kept. King's fanaticism for regular weighing, measuring and recording would become a cornerstone of Plunket dogma.

Despite their grand ideals, the first year was less than fully patronised. Public acceptance was not total. Three infant deaths cast a pall over the project. King's ambitions were clear and the project was not allowed to fail. With his clarity of vision, single-mindedness and ability to communicate and motivate, he kept the concept on track.

Training was one of the major goals. King's vision was to impart the message to everyone. This started with trainee nurses, extended to mothers and then to the general public. He held lectures wherever he found an audience. His now-enlarged pamphlet, *The Feeding and Care of the Baby*, was heading towards 100 pages, printed at his expense, with profits going to the Society. He articulated the message of breast-feeding wherever possible, supported by feeding with humanised milk for infants that could not be breast-fed. Large fat babies that had been fed on patent foods were not necessarily healthy, he told his audiences. They should be aiming for 'firm, bright, clear skin and fresh complexion like breast-fed babies'.[7]

Not content to stick to the knitting, King could not resist the temptation to stray into dubious territory. He had an aversion to dummies or comforters. Woe betide an infant that was so pacified. A baby admitted to the home was quickly broken of the habit. King believed that it was important not to separate the infant from its mother, contrary to the view then current that a baby didn't need 'mothering'. His concept of 'mother and baby' saw the extension of the Karitane home to encompass 'mothering' which allowed the mother to be admitted to the home along with their baby. In 1909 it was decided to admit a mother who needed help with weaning her infant who was not thriving on breast milk. She was to be the first of many.

The Society did not rest with the Karitane home. Lizzie Hughes was employed to contact families having infants under six months old. Obtaining details from the Registrar of Births, she would visit the family to give them information about the Society: those families who showed interest would then be visited by Nurse MacKinnon.

The Karitane home made the public welcome. In 1909 1600 people signed the visitors' book. Ever the visible target, Truby King continued to attract criticism in areas of the press: 'Dr King is a public servant and as such should devote his whole time to public duties,' grizzled a letter to the *Otago Daily Times* of 7 January 1908. The editor, a King acolyte, was having none of this, thundering that 'the work for the babies was part of the work for preventing insanity'. The Inspector of Mental Health duly weighed in with his support as well, and the King juggernaut thundered on.

With the formation of the Dunedin Society in 1907, King's fame was spreading. He could no longer be dismissed as the 'eccentric doctor from Seacliff'.[8] He had fashioned a name for himself as the spokesman for the Save the Babies movement and conscripted the influential ladies of Dunedin into a Society that was gathering momentum, a Society with the imprimatur of Vice-Regal patronage. King was beginning to get invitations from other groups, aware that something was happening and not wanting to miss out.

The Canterbury Mothers' Union had been the first. He talked at the monthly meeting on 'The Preservation of Infant Life' only a week after the Dunedin Society was formed, and next day to a public meeting. The Mothers' Union determined that if Dunedin could have a Society, so should they, and another public meeting resulted in the formation of The Canterbury Society for the Preservation of Infant Life. In a matter of months their first fundraising event had raised £125, and a nurse was recruited, trained by the ubiquitous Nurse MacKinnon, and set to work in the Canterbury community.

The Wellington ladies had already had a foretaste of Frederic Truby King when he and his entourage came to lobby parliament the previous year. The secretary of the Society for the Protection of Women and Children, Lady Stout, noted in a letter to the Dunedin group: 'I am much interested in your work in connection with the health of women and children . . . I shall bring the subject before the members . . . and see what can be done in forming a Society . . . I think it would be better if we could undertake the work in connection with our Society.'

As the Canterbury group was forming, a Wellington public meeting resolved that the SPWC would undertake similar work to the Dunedin Society. Funds were raised, and a nurse appointed. The Wellington branch of the Society for the Promotion of Health of Women and Children was inaugurated in March 1908, with an executive committee from the SPWC.

In Auckland Lady Plunket was preaching the gospel of Truby King. As was the fashion, the Vice-Regal couple were in their Auckland residence for the summer. Lady Plunket summoned the burghers of Auckland to Government House in January with a zeal approaching that of the good doctor, 'to form a branch of the Infant Life Protection Society'.[9] Nobody could refuse the invitation. The guest list included the Prime Minister, ladies, gentlemen, doctors, clergymen, nurses and mothers.

Lady Plunket's speech was down-to-earth. She said that the old idea that mothers knew instinctively how to care for their children was nonsense. While it was true that they tended to be touchy about advice, they had to be taught what was best for their babies. 'Yes, rightly or wrongly we are touchy, but I want to make it clear that this society will not interfere with mothers or force advice on them. The nurse will only visit where she is welcomed.'[10] Sharing the stage was

Lady Plunket presents the first Plunket medal to Miss MacKinnon.

Miss Beswick, Matron of Seacliff Hospital, and a long-term King supporter. She had been persuaded to 'holiday' at Government House in support of Lady Plunket's recruiting drive for the new society. King's message, delivered in Lady Plunket's rich upper-class tones, was well received.

Lady Plunket was instrumental in the formation of sister societies in New Plymouth, Napier and Christchurch. She was accompanied by Nurse MacKinnon on her promotional tour. There is no question that the social standing of Lady Plunket helped immeasurably in giving the society credibility and status in its formative period. Equally there is little doubt that it was Truby's magnetism and force of character that recruited Lady Plunket to the cause.

By the middle of the year there were five separate societies, varying slightly in titles and specific objectives. At Lady Plunket's request they became branches of the New Zealand Society for the Health of

Women and Children, with the Dunedin branch being the governing body. Then, in the tradition of Florence Nightingale, a nursing training system was implemented, but unlike the Nightingale system, which focused on the treatment of disease, the focus was on the maintenance of health and the prevention of disease. Instigated by Lord and Lady Plunket, the purpose was to train health visitors who would instruct mothers in infant care, free of charge. The training was to take place at the Karitane home in Dunedin under the supervision of Nurse MacKinnon. At the suggestion of a politician, the nurses were to be called 'Lady Plunket Nurses'.

This resulted in some opposition from the ranks of professional nurses, and resulted in the Society requiring a certificate in general nursing or midwifery as a prerequisite to training as a Plunket nurse. This comprised three months at the Karitane home in Dunedin. Nurses were not paid during their training period, which probably discouraged many younger or financially challenged nurses from being able to train as a Karitane nurse. Nurses worked with babies and attended lectures by Truby King and other doctors. Further Plunket nurse training involved spending time at the dairy company observing the modification of cow's milk, as well as community work visiting Dunedin homes with the Society's nurses. At the end of the training, nurses sat an oral and written examination. While all of this was happening, King was still in charge of Seacliff. There is no evidence in reports from his inspectors that exception was taken to his extracurricular activities.

Once qualified, nurses were provided with board and lodging and received a salary of £100–£150 per annum from the local branch. (By comparison, Truby King received a salary of £600 in his capacity as director of Seacliff.) Nurses worked six days a week and received one month's holiday a year. A bicycle and a uniform were supplied. Each nurse wore her Lady Plunket medal and a grey armband with the VP (Victoria Plunket) monogram in white. The role of the Plunket nurse was primarily educational. On application any mother could be visited by the nurse in her own home, with visits continuing for as long as necessary. The nurse reported monthly to the local committee.

When Lady Plunket and her husband returned to England in 1910, they left behind them a society run by women, dedicated to the health of the mother and child. Its acceptance by the medical profession had, not unexpectedly, been slow and frosty, but by the general public it was seen as a success.

By 1912 the Society's work was becoming more widely appreciated. The Department of Health endorsed King and Plunket to the point where the state issued every new parent with a copy of *Baby's First Month*. The infant death rate had declined measurably. King was notionally back at Seacliff, but he still seemed to be everywhere at once.

The Minister of Health sensed King's mission and requested that Truby undertake a nation-wide lecture tour, taking the message to all parts of the country. Officially granted three months' leave from Seacliff, Truby with Bella in tow set off to preach the Plunket message. Today there would be an entourage of officials, secretaries and support people. In 1910 it was just Truby King, with Bella to keep the show on the road. In a gruelling six months, double the original time allocated, from July until Christmas, they gave more than 100 public lectures, met countless thousands of notables, answered the same questions, inspired tens of thousands of women and gave of their very souls. The outcome was the formation of sixty new committees. That the Kings could achieve this unaided is a remarkable testament to Truby's persuasive powers and Bella's organising skills. How the perennially unwell Truby coped is not recorded. As usual, he seemed to thrive on self-imposed pressure.

Motor vehicles were still a rarity, so their travel was mostly by train. Bella King's prosaic diary is all we have to go by, as Truby was not one to record daily events. A typical day would involve 'Fred' going for a swim, breakfasting, travelling to the next town, meeting a group of women, viewing the hall, having dinner with local identities, delivering the speech, more meetings, more talking, then off to bed, exhausted.

Bella's diary of four days from 24 November records:

Glorious morning. Fred had a swim before breakfast. En route to Dannevirke. Reached D at 12. Mr Bickford and Mrs Knight met us and took us to lunch. Saw nurse and went to hall. Fred gave a lecture. Saw several mothers & babies – all much interested and asked many questions. Fred [had] a talk with several of the women then had afternoon tea & caught the train to Palmerston which we reached at 8.15 pm. Off to bed at 9, very tired.

November 25. Called at 5.45. Lovely morning. Left Palmerston at 7.10 and reached Marton at 9. Lucy met us with car and we drove to the Corbs and Coronation hall en route. At 11 met some members of committee and had a talk and an address. Walked back to Corbs for lunch, and left Marton by 2.30 train for Taihape. Heavy rain after address at Marton, showery later. Reached Taihape 5.22. Mrs & Mrs Arrowsmith and Studholme met us and motored us to the hotel where we met Dr McDiamid and Mr & Mrs Loughman at dinner. Had a talk about Society matters and arranged to return on the 14th Jan, going on to Auckland.

November 26. Reached Auckland before 7 am. Dr Beattie met us and drove us to Avondale. Lovely fresh morning. Went round gardens with Mrs Beattie while Fred developed photographs. In afternoon, Mrs Bloomfield and Miss Henderson came and we talked over matters until after 6, went to Tizards for supper.

November 27. 6 am on way to Hamilton, reached Hamilton 1.30. Saw mayor and several other men. Held meeting with some of the Hospital Board. Had tea then a walk around. Had a long rest after dinner. Dr ? called and we had a chat and then walked down town and then across the railway line to see Mrs ?, stayed about an hour.

November 28. Had a great sleep. Fred up at 6 and went off to get a swim – baths supposed to be open at 6, not open till 6.45. Met ladies at 11 and had a most excellent meeting. Mrs Bell was appointed Hon Sec and all ladies present formed themselves into a committee. Had lunch and then caught train to Rotorua.

Life on the road for Bella and Truby didn't leave a lot of time for relaxation, with Truby's lack of organisation often coming to the fore. There are several references to his absent-mindedness, as when he sent a telegram to his last hostess asking her to forward his forgotten pyjamas to the next town, only to find at bedtime that he was wearing them under his suit. Whether it was his hostess or Bella, Truby's unconscious reliance on his women was omnipresent.

Mary King's biography recalls:

> The hour of the meeting would draw increasingly nearer as they lingered over a discoursive dinner at the home of the host. The hall would fill up and then would come the frantic ringing on the phone. 'Has Dr. King left yet?' 'No, but I'm doing my best, I'll get him away as soon as I can.' With huge bundles of outsized diagrams, jugs, measuring spoons, etc, they would try to fit him in to the taxi, whose door he would have to hold open, arriving at the hall with half a yard of chart protruding and three-quarters of an hour late.
>
> Then he would electrify the audience, galvanising them into action on behalf of mother and child, and the following morning some worthy and hitherto unruffled house-wife would wake up to find herself the President of a local Branch of a Society which would absorb every fleeting moment for the rest of her life.[11]

Truby King recognised in all of this the crucial role played by women. He wanted to sell them a scheme that they could administer themselves; to mobilise them to form committees to promote infant health. He had to tell them about the importance of breast-feeding, fresh air, proper regular feeding and hygiene. Equally, he did not want to alienate the men. They too had to be mobilised to provide support for the women's committee. This he often achieved by fostering the setting up of 'advisory' groups of prominent businessmen, ensuring that he had covered all parts of the whole. Whether he was actively conscripting men to the cause, or simply being a clever manipulator, is unclear.

It would be wrong to conclude that every town received Truby and Bella with open arms. Suspicion, especially from the medical profession, was still a problem. While his charisma worked well with audiences of mothers, King's short fuse and intolerance of opposition often got him into trouble with his peers. Some were converted, some would wait . . .

At the end of the 1912 Truby and Bella were back at Seacliff and the Plunket Society's foundations were laid throughout the country. Truby had sold to women the role of preventing disease by taking responsibility for the feeding and care of children. He had promoted the Dunedin society's model of well-to-do women, mostly married to professional people, in charge of the voluntary Plunket organisation. This model was to endure for the best part of fifty years, as was the centralised control of Plunket from Dunedin.

One of the later presidents of Plunket recalled attending the annual Plunket conference in the Regent Theatre in Dunedin in the 1970s and recoiling in horror at the elderly 'fur coat' brigade who still ran the organisation.[12] However, these were influential ladies, born to administer a voluntary organisation, who had professional husbands with incomes substantial enough to keep their wives in twinsets, pearls and sensible shoes, but also the wherewithal to devote time and resources. Truby King, dead for forty years, would have been proud of them.

Chapter Twelve

The elusive Bella

The more I delved into the convoluted life of Truby King, the more I became aware of the paucity of information relating to his wife, Bella. It was only when trying to fully understand Truby's erratic behaviour and eventual mental decline that I realised the invisibility of his wife. Little was written of her, with attention always focusing on her charismatic husband. Bella appeared satisfied playing an invisible supportive role, leaving Truby the adulation and limelight. Adopted daughter Mary chose to downplay Bella's role, perhaps telling us indirectly about her own subjugation and the influence exerted by Truby. The puzzle of Bella King remains.

Isabella Cockburn Millar was bright and scholarly, the only daughter among six children. Her upbringing was Scottish liberal. It is recorded by her brother that 'All sorts of people met in our home and discussed the subjects of the time – politics, economics, literature, the sciences and the arts'.¹ The Millar family were educated, well read and enjoyed the privilege of travelling in Europe. Her brothers all joined the professions. Bella distinguished herself in German, French and Latin at school. She gained the Gold Medal as dux of her college, the Edinburgh Institution for Young Ladies.

In the words of her friend Mary Cairns, 'Her countenance had a delicate bloom, the skin sometimes transparent, and when she was animated her bright eyes sparkled, her cheeks were suffused with a soft pink that came and went delightfully.'² Another friend noted: 'Bella saw and brought out the best in people, and so she made them her friends and always lightened her intercourse with a touch of humour. After school days, Bella's love of literature and poetry developed under the inspiring lectures delivered in connection with the Edinburgh Association for the University Education of Women. Young women (and some not so young) filled the benches, and most sat the examinations. In the Tercentenary Year of the Edinburgh University (1884) Bella Millar took second place and a prize, with a First Class Honours Certificate, under the Professorship of the brilliant David Masson.'³ In those days women were barred from taking a degree.

Her adopted daughter, Mary, was less flattering. 'The attraction, from the start, on Fred's [Truby's] side was mental rather than physical. Bella had no claim to physical beauty. Her stature was too short, her brown hair too thin and her forehead too protruding. She was, moreover, a victim of rickets which manifested itself in her slightly bowed legs and retarded physical development. But her wit was quick, her temper even, her disposition sweetness itself and her mental capacity extraordinary.'⁴ Notwithstanding the strong bond between daughter Mary and her adoptive father Truby, it is apparent that Mary didn't enjoy quite the same relationship with Bella. She never forgave Truby and Bella for prohibiting any communication with her birth mother. In a more charitable moment, she credits Bella with being 'gentle, never cross. She never tried to curb Truby's enthusiasm. She was a meek wife, content to let him have his way.'⁵ In her oral history, recorded in her eighties, Mary observed that she

The moon gate in the Melrose garden.

Curious brickwork adjacent to the Truby King house, Melrose.

Above: *Ironwork surrounding the mausoleum at Melrose.* Below: *Karitane isthmus, from a watercolour by Mrs Charles Moore, painted from the Seacliff hill. Kingscliff is among the trees on the isthmus.*

Truby King's funeral cortège enters the Melrose garden.

THE ELUSIVE BELLA

never really accepted Bella as her mother, and I have always suspected elements of competition for Truby's attention.

Bella was Truby's soul-mate – intelligent, well read, quiet, devoted and placid. She too was hampered by ill-health. Was she a perfect match for the diminutive, quick-tempered, mercurial Truby? She was possibly his equal intellectually, and even at four feet ten inches, she was hardly dwarfed by him. (Comparatively, she would have towered over Queen Victoria.) Bella appeared content to play second fiddle, coping with Truby's absent-mindedness and disorganisation, steering him gently back on course.

Bella was a better than average landscape painter. Buried deep in the Hocken Library's Plunket files are examples of her watercolours that suggest she should have painted more.

History will always accord the success of Plunket to Sir Truby. Those who knew her would have it that Bella deserved at least as much applause for her role as minder, journalist, keeper of records, organiser, secretary, translator, friend and companion.

Bella is widely credited with much of the writing of the 'Hygeia' newspaper columns that Truby used to communicate with the mothers of New Zealand. Radio had yet to make its impact, and the power of the newspaper was dominant. The weekly 'Our Babies' column began in the *Otago Daily Times* in 1908, and was eventually syndicated in more than fifty newspapers throughout the country. Hygeia was the Greek goddess of health, daughter of Asclepius, god of medicine. To Hygeia is ascribed the power 'to take responsibility for our lives and take charge of our health'. The original columns were written by Truby King himself, while Bella is credited with the later columns. It is likely that she acted as secretary, editor, respondent and co-ordinator, with Truby providing input and editorial purview.

Public response was immediate, and by the end of the first year, 700 letters had been written to Hygeia. When a point was to be emphasised, Hygeia would fall back on answers to fictitious correspondents. 'Anxious Mother from the North Island' was frequently dispensed homely advice. Replete with nicely structured summaries and conclusions, Hygeia was a self-instruction course for worried mothers.

No topic was considered sacrosanct by Hygeia. As well as practical advice on colic, bedwetting, prevention of diarrhoea and bathing of baby, the column would not shirk advice on 'the unspeakable dummy', 'the high ideals of wifehood', 'cottage gardening' and control of the bladder. Pandering to xenophobia, Hygeia would occasionally tell us 'what London is thinking'. Many of Truby King's pet topics were well ventilated in the column: overfeeding, the care of teeth, the need for fresh air, constipation and regularity of bowel movements, not to mention regularity of feeding and weighing. Two Hygeia columns are reproduced in Appendix Three.

Truby would undoubtedly have had a strong editorial input to the Hygeia columns, but it is very likely that Bella was responsible for their production. Certainly she churned them out while Truby was away in England in 1918–19, but it's likely that the editorial oversight of Truby wouldn't have been too far removed. Her willingness to take a back seat, playing a supportive role to the dominant and assertive Truby was undoubtedly the key to his success, and perhaps a tribute to her skilful role within their partnership. Without Bella to pick up the pieces, provide the continuity and locate the missing parts of the whole, it is unlikely that the man would ever have succeeded as he did.

Bella herself gives the biographer little encouragement. Her diaries recording trips through the country with Truby are mere factual recordings of dates, times and events. Archival information dealing with Bella is more sparse than one might have expected. The only written evidence available are letters from Japan, written to her friend 'My Dearest C', Charlotte Beswick, matron of Seacliff. On Truby's instruction, Miss Beswick retained Bella's letters, which provide a commentary of the six-month tour of the Orient. In her biography, Mary King reproduced more than a dozen letters which show Bella to be a recorder of events without giving away much of her personality or innermost feelings.

Little else is written of Bella. Phillipa Mein Smith, in *The Book of New Zealand Women,* is generous in her assessment:

THE ELUSIVE BELLA

On all their travels she performed the role of tour manager; she knew that without her Truby King was soon hopelessly muddled. She travelled the length of the country with her husband on an official tour in 1912, answering innumerable letters and keeping him organised. She also wrote reports on his behalf, both on this tour and when at home. In 1913 she accompanied Truby King to England and helped him measure babies in London's slums in an effort to show that his feeding tables were better than those of an English rival, Dr Eric Pritchard, and that his schedules conformed to the laws of nature. In Europe, she acted as Truby King's interpreter and translated mothercraft pamphlets for him to read. As his personal secretary she spent much of her life answering his voluminous correspondence, writing individual replies to mothers and nurses who wrote from around the world; she would follow him round the house with a pencil, jotting down the points that he dictated, gently bringing him back to the subject when he side-tracked himself.

As Truby King's wife, Bella was expected to support her husband's quests, but, as a tertiary-educated woman was able to put people at ease. She played a crucial management role in her own right, as a link and liaison between her husband and the Plunket Society headquarters in Dunedin and the nurses and philanthropic women in local Plunket Society branches. It was Bella who wrote out the lists of instructions for nurses. These, like her newspaper columns, were checked by Truby King. Matrons of mothercraft homes and Plunket and Karitane nurses in New Zealand and overseas wrote to Bella for advice because they knew that Truby King was often too busy: and Bella was their friend. Bella King helped make her husband famous; in this partnership the joint contribution exceeded the sum of their individual effort.

In his dedication in *Feeding and Care of Baby* Truby King paid the following tribute to his wife: 'To the memory of a gracious little lady – my wife – without whose constant help and encouragement this book would never have been written.' His letters home, from his regular overseas sojourns always began 'My dearest wifie'. There is, however, no evidence of spontaneous affection, and this may well

Bella King.

have been the extent of his warmth. It remains a paradox that a couple without children of their own could play such a role in the foundation of Plunket. Mary King advances Bella's rickets as the reason for Truby and Bella being childless, but this is unsatisfactory. Truby's mother had rickets, a widespread condition of vitamin deficiency of the time, the consequence of which was bone formation without the necessary calcium or phosphorus uptake. It did not deter Truby's mother and many other Victorian women from having large families. There remains to me a degree of contradiction in Truby and Bella's ability to influence the Plunket organisation without themselves ever directly experiencing consanguineous parenting.

Bella died in January 1927 at the age of sixty-six, following a long illness. At her request she was buried in Porirua cemetery close to her great friend, Mrs Hassell. Truby had a friend photograph her grave and sent a print, together with a tiny spray of flowers, to every

THE ELUSIVE BELLA

Plunket nurse in New Zealand. This was a particularly touching gesture, as Bella would have met every nurse personally on her travels with Truby around the country. The gesture was widely appreciated. Eventually, on Truby's decease, Bella's remains were disinterred and reburied with Truby in the Melrose mausoleum.

Plunket researcher Lynne Giddings comments that 'the extent of the contribution made by his wife Bella to the [Plunket] society's success is now better recognised, though she herself may have accepted her relative invisibility as proper for a wife of her time.'

Only the *Otago Daily Times* bothered with an obituary, noting her work as Hygeia 'who for many years had been the guide and helper of thousands of mothers who read her articles in the press, was wonderful and beyond praise in its wise and balanced information about the health and welfare of children'.[6] The Plunket Society also honoured Bella posthumously with the announcement, shortly after her death, of the Lady King Scholarship, funded by public subscription and a government grant. The first recipient was Helen Easterfield, who as Dr Helen Deem became medical director of Plunket services.

CHAPTER THIRTEEN

Taking Plunket abroad

IN MID-1913 Truby King, with Bella and Mary, set sail for London to represent New Zealand at an infant welfare conference. After the conference, Truby and Bella worked with the poor in London, to demonstrate 'the New Zealand way'. With two nurses, babies were visited, weighed and the mothers instructed. Essentially they were preaching breast-feeding, regularity, measurement and fresh air. Staying until Christmas, they left behind mothers and babies flourishing under a common-sense regime. The Kings proceeded to Vienna and Berlin to confer with Europe's infant specialists before returning to New Zealand via London. Truby did not turn down the opportunity to preach the gospel of infant welfare and correct feeding, and probably managed to slip in some more blunt observations on over-pressure in schools and whatever bee currently lodged in his bonnet.

They all returned home to Seacliff. The Great War raged in Europe, but things were otherwise 'normal'. Plunket was consolidating and Truby found other outlets for his surplus energy, notably in the Catlins, where he further refined his farming ideas on his newly acquired acreage.

The relative calm was shattered in 1917 with a call from 'Home', in the form of a cable from Lady Plunket: WILL YOU COME AND START YOUR WORK IN LONDON STOP MARLBOROUGH SCHOOL OF MOTHERCRAFT PLACED AT YOUR DISPOSAL STOP PLEASE STATE SALARY STOP BRING MATRON STOP WILL FORM COMMITTEE ON NEW ZEALAND LINES STOP PLEASE CABLE REPLY STOP LADY VICTORIA PLUNKET AND MISS WINIFRIDE WRENCH STOP[1]

Sir Evelyn Wrench, founder of the Royal Overseas League, with his sister Winifride had visited New Zealand in 1913, and had been given the full Truby King VIP tour, being shown Seacliff, Karitane, Dunedin, Plunket hospitals and a bevy of bonny babies. They departed indoctrinated and impressed.

This was an invitation that King could not turn down. He wrote to the Minister:

> Sir
>
> Re the cable of the Marlborough School for Mothercraft requesting me to establish work at Home on our New Zealand lines, and placing the institution at my disposal as a teaching centre, under control of a matron to be selected from among our specially trained nurses, I have to report as follows: –
>
> If I were allowed to go Home in the course of a few months, my services would be of infinitely more value, from a broadly National and Patriotic point of view than if I were to be kept continuously in New Zealand. This opinion is founded on the deep conviction that the results of a practical campaign, properly organised on New Zealand lines so as to lead to the establishment of 'Plunket Committees' throughout the Old Country, with the centre at London, would result in the saving of from 5,000 to 10,000 lives a year in a

very short space of time, and a further progressive reduction afterwards.

Judging from an informal conference which took place last Tuesday between the Inspector-General of Mental Hospitals, the Civil Service Commissioners and myself, it appears that my services could be suitably provided for by arranging for the recall of some Senior Medical Officer of the Department now at the Front.

Provided you can approve and arrange for my absence for, say, fifteen months, without any breach in the continuity of my relationships to the Mental Hospitals Department and the Superannuation Fund, I am prepared to undertake the service required.

Regarding salary, I am not in a position to offer my services free, as I should like to do, but I should ensure that my total emoluments would be below rather than above what I receive in New Zealand.

Nurse Pattrick would be the ideal matron, and is willing to accept the Home position, provided it can be arranged for her to be spared from the Army.

Regarding the professional ability of the Marlborough School for Mothercraft, I may say that there are included on its list of Medical Officers Sir Betram Dawson, three leading London specialists on infancy and the care of young children, and Professor Kenwood, who is one of the most noted authorities on Hygiene in general. Benjamin Broadbent is, as you know, the leading spirit in England as regards reform in connection with the welfare of mother and child.

As I was asked to reply by cable, I shall be glad to be enabled to do so as soon as convenient.[2]

The Minister replied:

In accordance with the telegram I have despatched to you today, I have to inform you that your request for fifteen months' leave of absence was considered by cabinet yesterday. It was then resolved to grant you twelve months' leave without pay. I have no doubt that if you find it necessary to have the leave extended by three months in order to complete your work, a request to that effect later from Great Britain will receive the careful consideration of the Government.

I may add, as Minster of Internal Affairs, for your information, that it will not be possible for me to recommend His Excellency the Governor-General to issue a passport for Mrs King, if it is desired that she should accompany you to Great Britain. The Imperial Government have issued strict instructions that no women desirous of travelling through the danger zone should be allowed to leave New Zealand, excepting under circumstances of exceptional necessity and urgency.

Allow me to congratulate you upon having been invited to undertake this important work, and to wish you every success in it.

Yours faithfully

G.W. Russell

Minister in Charge of Mental Hospitals[3]

Lord Plunket cabled: YOUR FINANCIAL STIPULATIONS APPROVED STOP COMMITTEE PROPOSE OBTAINING HOSPITAL FOR MOTHERS OUTSKIRTS LONDON STOP PLUNKET[4]

Winifride Wrench wrote to Truby from the Marlborough School of Mothercraft in London:

> Your cable reached me yesterday, and I need not tell you how delighted I am to think that there is a chance of your coming here and starting your work in London. And it is splendid to think that you have the ideal Matron as well. Since my return in 1913 from travelling round the Empire with my brother, I have been working continuously in Infant Welfare work and have been in close touch with the people chiefly interested in this question in London.
>
> From what I know and what I have learnt, I am convinced that our greatest need in this country is a Training Centre on Karitane lines. In spite of all the excellent individual work being done in all parts of the United Kingdom, there is no training school for doctors and nurses

who wish to specialise in the care and feeding of babies – with the natural result that the standard of knowledge among the leaders of the movement is a low one.

You will find the nucleus of good work awaiting for you to expand and develop, and you will have an absolutely free hand so far as we are concerned. Our School of Mothercraft consists of two large private houses in Trebovir Road, Earl's Court, thrown into one. The rooms are lofty and airy and all have large French windows. We face north-east and we look out over gardens at the back.[5]

Truby King left New Zealand at the end of 1917 aboard the *Niagara*. Since Bella was not permitted to accompany him, she and Mary went to live in Nelson, where Bella had friends. Mary went to school at Nelson Girls' College.

Travelling via Honolulu, Truby spent five weeks in America, crossing the country, delivering lectures, meeting doctors and giving a first-class impersonation of a one-man tornado. He travelled down the Pacific coast from Vancouver to Portland, Seattle, San Francisco and Los Angeles, before crossing to Chicago and New York for a triumphant meeting as the guest speaker at the Academy of Medicine. The American trip was highly successful, with King benefiting from warm and indulgent receptions everywhere. America in 1918 was booming, largely unaffected by the European war. It could not but infect him with its brash confidence. He departed New York in March in high spirits, ready to continue his triumphant journey.

The contrast with wartime Britain was not good. Most commodities were subject to rationing; this, combined with the inevitable red tape, were harbingers of a difficult future. Truby was met by the loyal Miss Beswick, his old matron at Seacliff, who had retired to live on the south coast of England. She wrote to Bella that Truby had arrived 'looking wonderfully well, although he is too thin'.[6]

London in early spring, with bombers overhead at night, was not quite the same as America. Truby King was lonely, ensconced in the Waldorf Hotel, which, despite its exclusive reputation, he found unsuitable. The weather was cold and damp, his spirits bleak, his health not much better. Always inclined to hypochondria, and without Bella to buoy him up, he did not have an easy time. After weeks of suffering he wrote to Bella: 'I had been living at the Waldorf Hotel and was getting more and more sick of being a mere number. You know how neither of us has ever cared for hotel life for long, but nowadays every objectionable feature of such places is accentuated, owing to the incompetence and independence of the residential staffs, made up largely of amateurs and casual rejects.'[7] He moved into lodgings in Gypsy Hill, paying £1 a week for a front sitting-room and bedroom, with breakfast costing 2/- and dinner 2/6. This improved his spirits somewhat.

Professionally, things were patchy. In May he gave the first of four lectures at the ultra-prestigious St Thomas' Hospital, near parliament and Westminster Abbey, to a packed audience of doctors, nurses and medical students. His fame had preceded him, and the attention and flattery he was accorded were gratefully received. More flattery followed, with the prestigious American Paediatric Society making him an honorary fellow later that month. This he valued highly.

Miss Pattrick and two Kiwi nurses were established at Earl's Court, but they too found things difficult. Truby's letter to Bella tells the story:

> Marlborough School of Mothercraft
> 29/31 Trebovir Road, Earl's Court
> London, SW5
>
> July 15th 1918
>
> My Dearest Wifie
>
> You must wonder at my not having given you any account of the work here from the Society's point of view. Well the fact is that from the first moment of my arrival in London things have been more or less impossible to explain or describe, and while progress has not been satisfactory I have been overwhelmed with far more than anyone could overtake. If I wrote to you for a whole week I could scarcely convey the situation, and hitherto I have not felt that it was really desirable to

convey most of the intimate side as concerns the organisation which got me to England.

Never in my life have I been in so embarrassing and uncertain a position as I was in for some months after arrival. On the physical side I was far from well and yet I don't think that anyone supposed I was ill, but I had a cough which I could not throw off, and, living in the heart of London in a very heartless hotel without a vestige of bright sunlight by day and with groping darkness in the streets by night, one felt a bit spiritless and as near pessimistic as one's temperament would allow.

The splendid reception I had had throughout the U.S.A., and the warm friends I made everywhere, including the trip across the Atlantic, made London seem very dull, grey and depressing in the winter and early autumn. The contrast with London we had known was extraordinary, and you must remember that ever since I arrived we have had one long monotonous series of depressing messages as regards the war. A few days after arriving I got up early and intended to run out to Beckenham to see the Stillwells but found Victoria Station crowded with soldiers in khaki with their rusty iron helmets and their war-kits on their backs, blocking the line for some hours. It made the whole thing very real and near – and this is the daily state of matters. Not any pomp or circumstance of war but evidence everywhere of its cruel drudgery and ever present tale of hardship and suffering for those who are bearing the brunt of it. Day after day one would see the long line of motor ambulances stretching from Charing Cross station down Villiers Street, and of course this was only one of many such – especially after the big fights. On the other hand, the civilian population of London suffered practically nothing but trifling inconvenience, and is largely better off than it had ever been before and was spending money recklessly.

All this was not an exhilarating background, but such backgrounds alone do not dominate the individual life though they tend to render everything more or less sombre, especially after coming from the bright optimistic hustle and 'go' of America where I had been presented for the most part with the best and most progressive side of things. Of course I saw plenty of the seamy side of their great cities, but I saw it mainly with people who were working enthusiastically to bring about a better state of affairs and who were really doing very effective work.

I expected to get straight to work with the Marlborough School of Mothercraft and the other organisations which had been referred to in Lord Plunket's cablegrams. No enthusiastic Committee came to welcome me, but a rather prosaic secretary of the Overseas Club came to the Waldorf Hotel in the evening and said that both Lord Plunket and Miss Wrench were ill. There was no social welcome at all; and when I saw the New Zealanders – Miss Pattrick, Mrs Harris, Mrs Hosking and Miss Beswick – they disillusioned me very thoroughly. Miss Pattrick had been snubbed for every suggestion she made, and as they took no notice of her views and opinions and wanted her to back their utterly absurd proposals as regards developing and getting ready a place which Lord Leverhulme had offered to let the Committee have the use of for the term of the war, Miss Pattrick played a very masterful game by retiring back to the safe stronghold of her former position in the Army, pending my arrival.

All references to New Zealand were considered bad form, and as the New Zealanders were never consulted and had no say on the Committee, they had ceased to attend the meetings.

When I saw Lord and Lady Plunket they told me, to my amazement, that they wanted me to keep in the background for two months, while Sir Bertrand Dawson got me patronised and rendered acceptable as it were by the elite deadheads of the profession.

Meantime, letters were coming in from the provinces and elsewhere asking me to give addresses, etc. Then came the first meeting at which Lord Plunket introduced me to the Committee, the meeting taking place in their home in Sloane Square. I was to be very much the humble servant to carry out the instructions of the Committee. Lord Plunket said that he had cabled me that the Marlborough School had been placed at my disposal; but that they had decided that it ought to be at the Committee's disposal, etc. I was not to do anything without the consent of the Committee, and especially I was not to grant any interview or do any propaganda work without their leave. How I wished I were back among the real, earnest disinterested workers in New Zealand.

Poor Truby, betrayed by the very people he aspired to, neutered by the Committee, frustrated by the Establishment. How shattered he must have felt, adrift in the country he called 'Home', betrayed by the people he thought he understood and knew how to manipulate. But it was worse than that. It transpired that the Plunkets were at the heart of the conspiracy. On their return to England, they had redefined the concept of the Plunket movement from Truby's creation to their own, casting themselves as the saviours of babies, relegating King to a supporting role, merely the doctor who implemented their wonderful scheme.

King George V had just conferred the Companion of the Most Distinguished Order of Saint Michael and Saint George on Truby King, but that wasn't sufficient for him to defy Lord Plunket and his Committee of English aristocracy, and he knew he was in a tight spot.

In the end the Kiwis triumphed, with the resolute Miss Pattrick adding steel to Truby's resolve. She would go on to play a pivotal role in Plunket back in New Zealand at the end of her sojourn in London. Truby continued in a letter to Bella:

> Things have been pretty sultry sometimes at Committee meetings. Once I took the gloves clean off and denounced our erstwhile patrons and said it was disgraceful to have misrepresented matters – that I have been 'got Home under false pretences'. Their anxiety at the start was, of course, that I might give them away by letting out the fact it was the Committee and not the Plunkets who had made the society in New Zealand.[8]

In time the rift healed and Truby King finessed some more sympathetic people onto the Committee. The Chairman, said Truby, 'is a Sir Alexander Roger who has, if anything, too much faith in me and is too sanguine of success.' He also conscripted Mrs Harris, wife of philanthropist Wolf, who had played such a supportive role of the Plunket Society when they lived in Dunedin. Eventually King came to terms with the British way of doing things and progress was achieved. In the end, his antipathy towards the Plunkets subsided. When Lord Plunket died in 1920, Truby King sent a warm letter of sympathy, as did the Plunket Society. Lady Plunket reverted to Lady Victoria Braithwaite and continued her interest, eventually revisiting New Zealand. On her ninetieth birthday the Society recognised her with a presentation.

Professionally, things were looking up for Truby King. He went to Downing Street. He was in demand for speaking engagements; visited Ireland and travelled widely in England. He was appalled at Ireland's infant mortality, much higher than New Zealand; he noted that the rate in the country, where despite poverty, healthy outdoor living and breast-feeding were the norm, was three times lower. His rationalisation of the high infant mortality in the cities was the poor housing and drunkenness.

With the end of the Great War in sight, King was given a military rank so that he could participate in advice on post-war rehabilitation. Major Truby King was an unlikely sight. There are stories of the slight, uniformed gent walking out of Trebovir Road incongruously clad in khaki with a trilby hat, with Miss Pattrick in pursuit to exchange it for military headgear. Truby King would not have struck fear into the heart of the Hun.

In September 1918 King went to France. The American Red Cross bent over backwards to help him, remembering his visit to the States and the impact that he had made. The contrast between the laid-back American organisation and the chaos he had endured at Home was once more highlighted. Returning to France in October, he persuaded the Army authorities that, with his mental health expertise, he should visit the front. Despite his poor health and slight physique, he was never one to shirk a challenge. His descriptions are poignant.

Instead of hedgerows and avenues of trees, there were merely splintered and shattered trunks, or stumps a few feet high. The solid earth had been riven and hurled into the air, leaving a jumble of deep craters and mounds, without a trace of fields, plantations or buildings of any kind, save here and there a few stones where some cottage must have stood. Here and there were remains of a horse; and sometimes we passed a trooper trudging his way back towards the fighting front. The whole impression was one of sad, grey desolation, infinitely pitiable and depressing.

The losses and sufferings of the French peasantry give some idea of the guilt and cruelty of unprovoked war waged in a peaceful country. As for our troops, their endurance and heroism, living in mud and filth, passes all understanding.[9]

Having glimpsed the horrors and stupidity of war, King went to the American Red Cross Conference on Infant Welfare in Toulouse, then back to England, where his year's secondment was up. The New Zealand government granted Truby an extension 'to carry on the work and render it permanent and progressive', whatever that meant. The British infant mortality rate was 103 per 1000 live births, compared to forty-eight in New Zealand. At an important post-war medical conference, valuable resolutions were passed on the need for thorough and consistent teaching of the medical profession, nurses, midwives and the general public on the promotion of health and fitness of mother and child. King felt some progress was at last being made. *Feeding and the Care of Baby* was becoming widely available, and was even being translated into foreign languages. The message was finally getting out.

Early in 1919 Truby King was appointed as one of three representatives of the British Empire at the Child Welfare section of the three-week-long Red Cross conference in Cannes, on the French Riviera. The big issues were famine, starvation and typhus, but for King the greatest impact was the collegiality of it all, being able to confer with many of the top names in child medicine. He took particular interest in the Rollier Institute in Switzerland, and the pioneering work they were doing on solar therapy, especially for sufferers of tuberculosis. This accorded with his holistic 'fresh air and healthy living' philosophy he had developed at Seacliff. Later, he would refer a Wellington society friend suffering from bovine TB to the Rollier clinic. Leaving France, King visited Austria, Switzerland and Poland, seeing the effects of war-induced malnutrition and poor diets, before returning to London.

The frustration of working with the British soon told on Truby. He deplored the waste and the bureaucracy, and missed the devotion of his New Zealand Committee. Bottle-feeding was rife, with strong preference from the medical profession towards artificial feeding. A depressed Truby wrote to Bella:

> You know, dearest, how I long to be back with you, but I can no more turn my back on all this and the appalling conditions on the Continent 'than I could turn my back upon a well into which my children had fallen'. It touches the fate of millions – indeed the density of humanity – and nothing can prevent my probing it to the depths, and getting at the back of things so far as lies in my power. I can no more fail to make use of what has become built up in me, and further perfect my knowledge and powers in this connection than you could give up writing the weekly baby Column. It is all one story.[10]

King seized the opportunity to capture the 1000 post-war wives and babies bound for Australia. He saw the five sailings per week as laboratories where his rapidly trained apostles could spread the gospel of 'saving the babies'. Truby, Miss Pattrick and her team turned young ships' doctors into their missionaries in quick time.

By the autumn of 1919 Truby King had had enough. His secondment was finished and the English were beginning to embrace his ideas, although not as fast as he would have liked. He was under pressure to spread the gospel as he returned. The Governor-General of South Africa requested he return via the Cape. The wife of the Governor of Victoria insisted he come to Melbourne. He compromised, delegating the South African trip to his trusty Scottish nurse Miss Paterson, who had worked with him in Warsaw. On her

TAKING PLUNKET ABROAD

arrival in New Zealand she would become the bane of Truby's existence, trying unsuccessfully to get him to finish his book on infant feeding and care for the medical profession. He never did.

He arrived in Melbourne at the end of November to be greeted by a civic reception from the Lord Mayor. His speech, 'Key to the Future of Australia', is worth examining for what he had absorbed in two dismal years in England without Bella.

> You want to keep Australia white; but if you find the Eastern nations more moral, nobler and more willing to make sacrifices for the continuity of the race, you know the results must be the same as has been the case with great civilisations of the past. Greece and Rome went down, not through any failure in the valour and courage of their young men, but because of the increase of luxury, the repugnance to rearing families, followed by decadence and sterility and eventual extinction. If the population of Australia does not do its duty to the race then there cannot be any resistance to other races coming in and populating this fair land.
>
> To produce a hardy virile race, it is necessary that the young womanhood of Australia be re-taught lessons which have come to be regarded as old-fashioned. Mothers must be taught the nature of the education which they must give to their children. Every girl ought to be brought up with the realisation that she cannot afford to live for herself alone; that she is part of an infinite past and an infinite future. She should be taught how to safeguard that which has been given her – a miraculous body with the power to reproduce – so that the next generation might be better than the one that has gone before. A woman should be safer, happier and healthier in pregnancy than at any other period of her life.
>
> Education is, for instance, vitally necessary with regard to the care of the teeth. Few people realise that when an infant is born its first set of teeth are already formed in the gums and that the state of those teeth depends very much on the health of the mother during pregnancy. There is hardly a person today who is not deficient to some extent with

regard to teeth, jaws, palate or nasal region – the whole region by which our bodies must be nourished. Decay of the teeth is one of the gravest diseases of mankind.

The happiest children, [he pointed at a chart of infant death-rates] are those born into large families, and there is something radically wrong where we find that families of the present generation are so much smaller than those of the past. If girls were properly instructed, they would acquire the right ideals and be proud to become mothers. Neglect on the part of mothers today arises mostly through thoughtlessness, and lack of imagination regarding life's true values. There is nothing worse for our girls than going night after night to picture shows. A certain amount of recreation in this way is beneficial, but the confirmed 'picture fan' does not make for her own future happiness nor for the future greatness of her State.[11]

What the audience in Melbourne thought of that is not recorded. Here we find two new themes entering the King lexicon: the care of teeth, and the obsession with picture shows. 'Teeth' came about via King's meeting at Cannes with Dr Wells of the British Lister Institute, who were leaders in nutritional research. How Truby became agitated about the influence of movies on children is unclear. In 1921 he published under the Plunket banner a fifteen-page pamphlet 'Picture Shows – Their Evil Effects on Children and the Need for Reform, Regulation and Control'. This purported to be a discussion of resolutions passed at the 1920 Plunket conference, but was in essence Truby's stage-managed crusade against moving pictures, featuring 'An open letter by Dr Truby King'. It is presented in Appendix Six.

On a more sane note, Truby King's addresses around Australia resulted in the setting up of committees with the 'Welfare of Mother and Child' as their motto.

CHAPTER FOURTEEN

The later years of Plunket

In 1921 Truby King was appointed Director-General of Child Welfare, and had moved to Wellington. Plunket continued to survive as a voluntary organisation independent of government control, offering mothers free advice. By 1931 the infant death rate, at thirty-two per 1000, was the lowest in the world; there were 129 Plunket nurses, making nearly 200,000 calls to mothers and babies in the home, at the mother's request. Over 623,000 mothers and babies visited the Plunket rooms in that year. New Zealand was an acknowledged leader in infant care. The name of Truby King was still on everyone's lips, despite the fact that he had relinquished the position of Medical Director of Plunket and was approaching the twilight of his life.

In the New Year's Honours of 1925 King was knighted 'for services to the Empire'. The Post Office complained that there had never been such a rush of letters, telegrams and cables from all round the world. Sir Truby wrote to all Plunket nurses:

> Dear Co-Workers, My wife and I wish to convey to you our great appreciation of your kind congratulations. Though the honour comes in name to us, it is the Society as a whole that has won the distinction; and as long as our nurses continue to play their part as devotedly as they have done in the past, the Society will deserve well of the State and the Throne. Our own is not the first title graciously granted to the Society. Recognition of good work faithfully carried out came years ago when the title 'Royal' was conferred by their Majesties on the New Zealand Society for the Health of Women and Children. This ought to act as a perpetual inspiration and incentive to each of us to give our best and to do our best at all times, for the sake of women and children, for the advancement of the Dominion and for the honour of the Empire.[1]

Not every aspect of Plunket met with total acceptance. The delightfully forthright Dr G. M. Smith wrote:

> The Plunket Society for many years underfed babies. Sir Truby King's work was magnificent, much of the baby technique was splendid, and many infants survived that but for him would have died. For the first time a simple technique of cleanliness in infants' food and general care was energetically taught to the mothers and nurses of New Zealand. That is the reason for the great success. It was not due to their ideas of feeding; that part of it was all wrong, and known to be wrong 30 years ago. (But note a healthy baby is tough. He can usually survive in spite of a healthy diet.)[2]

Dr Smith railed against Truby King's Plunket dogma and Plunket's independence of the state and the medical profession.

Dr Helen Deem had succeeded Dr Tweed just before the war as medical advisor to the Society and acted in a way Truby King would have strongly approved, despite her gender. She was a human dynamo, every bit as committed as the Great Founder. After four years of marriage and one child her husband died. Deem flung herself

THE LATER YEARS OF PLUNKET

wholeheartedly into Plunket and its activities, working seven days a week. Perhaps her most ambitious work was a massive statistical study of nearly 9000 infants from all over New Zealand. They were measured, weighed and had their nutrition recorded. From this emerged growth curves for the first year of a baby's life that were hailed as being the most significant work since Truby King. Helen Deem paid tribute to him thus:

> Sir Truby King visualised the ways and means of reducing this young country's infant loss, but his efforts were also directed towards fostering the all-round health of the babies who survived. He was a pioneer in the field of Health Education, believing 'that as far as motherhood and babyhood were concerned there was as much need for practical reform and "going to school" on the part of the cultured and well-to-do as there was on the part of the "so-called poor and ignorant".' To this end he envisaged an Infant Welfare service, and, accordingly, established a Training School for qualified nurses (Plunket Nurses), who would eventually teach 'Health' to mothers in their own homes and at Plunket Rooms. The society was started inter alia as a league for mutual helpfulness; the fact that the great majority of our mothers today seek Plunket advice proves conclusively that the service which was designed to 'Help the Mothers' is fulfilling its objectives.[3]

After the Second World War the Society had to come to terms with the maternity hospital crisis, with the state system and the six Karitane hospitals unable to cope with the 'baby boom'. Plunket rose to the occasion, helped advise the government, and kept their sanity and independence. By 1947 85 per cent of all babies were seen by one of the 190 Plunket nurses, who made over 220,000 home visits, with more than half a million mother-and-children visits to Plunket rooms. By now there were over 100 Plunket branches, still ruled from Dunedin by the fur-coat brigade.

The post-war challenges of the polio epidemic were met by Plunket, when the Society ensured that the children of New Zealand were immunised. Plunket Mothers' clubs were formed, introducing another layer of women volunteer helpers. Plunket work was seen as a respectable and respected activity within the community; it provided an opportunity for women to meet away from the traditional environs of church and family, and increased their confidence and self-esteem. Plunket still received 'state assistance without state interference' despite governments of varying persuasions. The Society's iconic status could not be undermined. In the future, the issue of accidents in the home would become a cause that Plunket would take up and work hard to resolve.

Helen Deem retired and in 1956 she was succeeded by Dr Neil Begg, a pediatrician by training and a Truby King admirer. Begg continued the good work in the King mould, albeit with greater conciliation and restraint, but less fire and brimstone. In 1957 the vermilion Truby King stamp was issued. It was the first New Zealand stamp to depict a private citizen. Begg carried on the King tradition in the fight to eradicate hydatids, a child-killer that had its origins on the farm and had been a notifiable disease since 1873. Just as King had conscripted the mothers to take ownership of their children's health, Begg conscripted the farming community to attack hydatids. The Plunket Society and Federated Farmers accepted the challenge of self-help in disease eradication, culminating in dog owners agreeing to an annual levy of £1 per dog towards hydatids eradication. Truby King would have thoroughly approved of this successful campaign.

By the 1960s there were 109 Plunket branches, with 230 Plunket nurses. Breast-feeding was again in decline, from 80 per cent in 1938 down to a more modest 43 per cent, perhaps reflecting the increase in solo mothers, working mothers and differing pressures from a changing society. This was the era of Dr Spock, whose permissiveness contrasted with the Victorian rigidity advocated by Truby King. Modern mothercraft was pushed into the background. Neil Begg in 1970 published *The Child and his Family* to reflect changing beliefs in child care, and signal a more permissive approach to bringing up infants. Plunket became more liberal, more democratic. With 75 per cent of the branches now in the North Island, the Society could no longer resist the move north. The ladies of the fur-coat brigade in

Dunedin accepted the end of their dominance of Plunket affairs, and the head office moved to Wellington.

The issues concerning Plunket were coming thick and fast. Maori had never been represented in the Plunket movement. The statistics didn't recognise them, nor did the Dunedin ladies. Early King writings had been translated into several languages, but never into Maori until Maui Pomare took action in 1916. The increase in Polynesian mothers in the greater Auckland area became an issue. Also there was the difficult question of battered babies, which led to a focus on child safety in general. The Society's relationship with Maori and Polynesian mothers has never been strong. Plunket would argue that volunteer work was not easily encouraged across racial barriers. The health system provided further impediments, with different treatment of Maori babies. In the last two decades, some improvement has been noted, with Kaiwhina Plunket nurses working on the marae. A recent historical document from Otaki records poignantly the uneasy relationship between Plunket and iwi:

> Our mother was one of the first Maori Plunket nurses, having completed her three year general nursing training at Palmerston North hospital, followed by a year of maternity training (in Gisborne during the war) and finally a year in Dunedin completing her Plunket training. When she became a 'patient' at Otaki Maternity, the Plunket nurse arrived to 'do her rounds' but when she and Matron got to Mum's ward they talked to the woman next to Mum, glanced at Mum and commented as they walked past that 'of course you'll have the District nurse'. At that time Plunket was for Pakeha and the District nurse visited Maori families. When we asked our mother why we didn't have the Plunket nurse for our little sisters, she always said we didn't need one as she was our Plunket nurse. When I was admitted to Otaki maternity 30 years later, I opted for the Plunket nurse!'[4]

By the 1970s the six Karitane hospitals had run their course. Successive annual meetings grappled with the spiralling costs, declining usage, bed occupancy and changing times. Plunket had to recognise that the cost of running such hospitals was too high and that the service was no longer appropriate. Karitane had become a 'dumping ground' for Social Welfare children. Each hospital was 'owned' by Plunket, with strong local emotions associated with any suggestion of closure. Invercargill threatened court action, capitulating only after a bitter public fight. The five other hospitals (Dunedin, Christchurch, Wanganui, Wellington and Auckland) gave way, amidst protracted and bitter recrimination. In the Melrose mausoleum, Truby would have experienced difficulty in remaining at rest.

Later, Plunket would have to contend with government meddling with the health system. With the advent of Health Boards and with a nervous eye on its funding requirements, Plunket found it necessary to realign its boundaries to suit the sixteen new entities. Then when the Health Boards were scrapped and four regional health areas instituted, Plunket restructured again. Every time a new health reform was announced, Plunket needed to be sure that they were not disadvantaged or marginalised. Lobbying became a necessity, and Plunket were forced to become more politically astute. Unsurprisingly, they found little support from other agencies who were also at the mercy of government health policy like IHC, CCS and Family Planning. A continued strong support for Plunket was demonstrated in 1992 when rallies and marches were held in all main centres, culminating in a petition of over 100,000 signatures to parliament demanding support and adequate funding for Plunket services.

Lynne Giddings in her 1993 assessment of the Plunket Society noted:

> The Truby King system, as espoused by the society, emphasised a regular routine of feeding, sleeping and excreting for babies. Weight gain became the measure of success. To many women then and since, this authoritative advice was possibly a relief. Over time, however, the focus on routine became formalised into a rigid set of rules thoroughly taught to Plunket and Karitane nurses in their training, and the nurses became authority figures in their own right.
>
> For the most part, Plunket nurses had to reflect the dominant ideology of the society to gain acceptance with the women on

their branch committee. If a nurse disagreed with the ideology or teaching of the medical director, the women on the committee did at times support the Plunket authorities rather than their local nurse. This rigidity of approach to infant care has received much critical attention in recent years; historians have linked it with paternalistic attitudes prevalent in New Zealand towards women and children.

Since the 1980s, the society has worked to dispel the view that all the Plunket nurses do is 'weigh babies', encouraging nurses to work with mothers in ensuring the care and safety of their babies. Home visits have remained a high priority, and have been a life-saver for many women. The early mothers' groups have been revamped and formalised as the invaluable New Mothers' Support Groups, which began in the 1970s. Since then, too, an increasing number of Plunket nurses have been mothers.[5]

Plunket in the twenty-first century has a thoroughly modern look. Its website proudly boasts its direction: 'To ensure that New Zealand children are among the healthiest in the world' (though statistics would suggest they have been that way since time began). The 'Purpose Statement' says 'Plunket believes in supporting the development of healthy families'. Both statements are accompanied by their Maori translation.[6]

The document confirms Plunket's accord with the principles of the Treaty of Waitangi and notes proudly that over 90 per cent of all babies born in New Zealand are enrolled with Plunket services. The identified health goals include:

- Reduction in Sudden Infant Death Syndrome (cot death) rates
- Reduction in unintentional injuries to children
- Increase in breast-feeding rates
- Reduction in the incidence of child abuse and neglect
- Increase in immunisation coverage
- Improvement in parenting skills and social support for families
- Reduction in rates of hearing loss in children

- Reduction in the incidence of asthma in children
- Promotion of child and family nutrition.

Plunket views itself as 'a community-based organisation which employs qualified staff working in partnership with a team of volunteers. Plunket services are partially funded by the government. The remaining costs are covered by volunteer fundraising, enabling Plunket to offer a range of programmes and facilities in local communities.'

An informed source who wished to remain anonymous observed that it was fascinating how little Plunket had changed since its inception. The volunteers were still white, middle-class women who retained authority over the professional nursing staff, via their fundraising. 'We own the clinics, the cars, pens & pencils' remains the attitude of the ruling class of Plunket.

How Truby King would view the Plunket of today is uncertain. He might find the jargon as perplexing as we find his Victorian terminology. He might disapprove of the more modern, relaxed and consultative Plunket nurses, who had lost the 'battleaxe' authoritarian demeanour of his day. Or he might feel that Plunket has been extremely successful in implementing his 'community care' strategies, having adapted to changing times without giving away its precious independence. He would see how little has changed from his initial prescription and might well be proud of the Plunket of the new millennium.

CHAPTER FIFTEEN

A mausoleum in Melrose

In 1921 Truby King was appointed Director of Child Welfare. This signalled the end of his time at Seacliff and a transfer to Wellington, after thirty-two years at the asylum. In essence, this was a vote of confidence in both Truby King and the Plunket Society. For King, now sixty-two, it represented a chance to work with central government, closer to the seat of power, something that he'd not experienced before. To accommodate him, the Health Department had been divided into two: Public Health and Child Welfare. King's empire now extended from the time before birth to the end of a child's schooling. Notwithstanding his other positions and titles, the wheel had come full circle with his additional appointment as Inspector of Mental Asylums.

In April the family moved to 25 Tinakori Road, once Frances Hodgkins' house. As ever, Truby King was in debt, but this still did not deter him. Bella was seriously unwell and would only live for another six years. Mary King was now sixteen, had finished high school and was about to embark on a two-year kindergarten teacher training course, doubtless with Truby's fulsome approval, as he would have seen this as a 'suitable' occupation for a woman.

King had sold the Catlins farms but kept the cottage at Karitane. Scorning the advice of friends and colleagues, he bought ten acres of exposed gorse-covered hilltop at Melrose, in the extreme south of Wellington, near the Zoo, overlooking Evans and Lyall Bays, with a view north to the Hutt Valley. Today it overlooks the busy airport; in Truby's day it was a very long tram-ride from the centre of town, and by those who didn't understand Wellington's capricious weather was considered one of the finest building sites in the capital. On a bad day it might have been considered one of the windiest, most frightfully exposed hilltops in the country.

In 1923 a Plunket Mothercraft Home was opened in Wellington in the same premises as the Plunket Rooms. The capital lagged behind New Zealand's other cities without its own Karitane Hospital. Truby King would soon rectify that. Meanwhile, in his new position he was always on the move, talking to whoever would listen, visiting Health Camps, preaching the Plunket cause, or even ranting about the evils of forceps delivery of babies. Relations with his department were less than cordial. He had grown used to the autocracy of his fiefdom at Seacliff, where he was in sole command with little reporting responsibility or monitoring from his masters. Directing an empire in Wellington was significantly different, and King had to adjust his approach from the mentally disturbed to the more easily disturbed. His civil servants would find him difficult in the extreme, and he suffered a myriad of frustrations. Appointments to bodies including the Prisons Board and Mental Degeneracy and Sexual Perversion Committee began to weigh him down. His workload did not diminish, but his output began to slow. As Inspector-General of Mental Health, appointed in 1924, King's profligacy was famous. One year he was reported to have run up £900 in taxi fares; on other occasions, he was reported to have cashed valueless cheques at hospitals that he visited. Whether this was arrogance or absent-mindedness is not known.

The Rotary Club of Wellington was formed in the year after King's return to Wellington. An American creation, based on service to the community, Rotary has slowly permeated the western world, and in the new millennium has even found its way to Russia, Moldova and beyond. Some of its achievements are impressive, including a major role in the worldwide eradication of polio. The membership of the

Byron Brown and Truby King at the Otaki Health Camp, c. 1926. Health Camps proliferated in New Zealand from the 1920s, coming under King's influence as Director of Child Welfare in 1927. His relationship with Health Camp people was frequently strained.

fledgling Wellington club read like a *Who's Who*: Ewen, Gray Young, Harcourt, Kirkcaldie, Marsden, Myers, Norwood, Odlin, Parker, Roberts, Stewart, Vickery and Whitcombe were familiar names among the inaugural luminaries. The club sought speakers to inform, challenge and stimulate the members at their weekly meeting. Who better in their first year than Frederic Truby King?

King had not long been appointed Director of Child Welfare and was a frail and stooped figure, but his ability to win over an audience, honed by years of selling his 'save the babies' message, was as good as ever. The Rotary Club was an easy audience for him to flatter, challenge and win over. In his address, he convinced the assembled members that they should undertake a project of magnitude and importance: the funding of Wellington's own Karitane Hospital and Mothercraft Training Centre. No doubt Wellington's rich and influential went home that evening full of the wonders of Truby King and the need to build a hospital to serve the capital's mothers and babies. Their wives would have been impressed, if perhaps a little bemused at their husbands' apparent enthusiasm.

Gray Young, who would also design King's house, was to be the architect. The Rotary Club undertook to raise the money. Rotary is very good at fundraising, but this was a mammoth undertaking that would take fourteen years to complete. Truby's contribution was to donate one quarter of his four-hectare Melrose property for the Karitane Hospital. Of the £25,000 raised, the club contributed £2000, the balance coming from Rotary-organised public fundraising projects. Rotary would never undertake anything quite like this again.

The foundation stone was eventually laid by her excellency, Lady Alice Ferguson, on 28 July 1926. The Queen Mother opened the home nine years later. Meanwhile, King had commissioned Gray Young to design him a house and the adjacent Karitane Products factory at Melrose. Gray Young was born in Oamaru in 1885 and educated in Wellington. He was articled to Wellington architects Crighton and McKay straight from school. At the age of eighteen, Young had designed his first house, a home for his father in Kelburn. At twenty-one he won a competition for the design of Knox College,

Dunedin, and shortly thereafter began practice on his own account.

His domestic buildings were in various styles including English domestic revival, Californian bungalow, colonial revival and neo-Georgian. He died in 1962, a partner in the influential practice of Gray Young, Morton, Young, Calder and Fowler (the practice lives on as Calder Fowler). In a career that spanned sixty years, Young designed over 500 buildings, the best-known being Scots College (1919), Wellesley Club (1925), Wellington Railway Station (1936), AMP Chambers (1950), Christchurch Railway Station (1954), and various parts of Victoria University – Stout (1930), Kirk (1938) and Easterfield (1957). One of his nicest buildings is the first Georgian-style house he designed, the 1913 Elliot House at 43 Kent Terrace, Wellington. This was the residence and consulting rooms of Sir James Elliott, physician to the Governor-General. Naturally Truby King chose to consult the Vice-Regal Doctor Elliott as his own physician, and through him he would have gained an appreciation of Gray Young's work.

The Karitane Maternity Hospital was appropriately scheduled to take nine months from conception to completion. The hospital was premature, but delivered without fuss, thanks to efficiency on the part of architect and builders. Gray Young saw the design as 'simplicity . . . coupled with dignity and repose . . . to afford rest and relief to the mind and to the eye, as well as the body'.[1] Truby King had envisaged 'a temple to motherhood, built with an intangible sense of refreshment, regeneration and recreation'.[2] Young used architectural features akin to those of the Wellesley Club as well as the Truby King house. Situated on a knoll at the southern end of the Melrose property, the hospital is a long rectangular building with two right-angled wings projecting eastwards at each end, enclosing a grassed court. The nursery wing comprised three 'heating' zones: a warm ward for incubating premature babies, a cooler 'weakling' ward and a large nursery. Wide, north-facing folding doors opened onto a roofed verandah, where babies would get their fresh air, sunshine and other King-stipulated essentials. The mothercraft wing comprised a series of six bedrooms connected to a wide balcony. Nurses and staff accommodation made up the remainder. Later, after Truby King died, Gray Young would design extensions to the Karitane Hospital, adding a three-storey accommodation block in 1941. Then, with the Second World War imminent, the hospital and King's house were commandeered by the Army as a training establishment. Army huts were erected near the tennis court and the nurses' quarters became barracks. Had Truby King lived to see such sacrilege he would have undoubtedly had something sharp to say. The hospital finally closed in 1978, along with its five sister establishments. This building has since been used as budget accommodation, a 'new age' centre, and now, under the name Capital House, it functions as a conference facility.

The Karitane Products factory, designed by Gray Young, was built at the same time as King's house (total cost for house and factory was given as £5600,[3] all coming from his perpetually empty pocket). How Truby existed in a state of financial disarray speaks volumes for his mana, and for the tolerance of his bankers. It was well known that all his published writings were produced at his own expense, with any income going to Plunket. He appeared to survive in a constantly mortgaged state, hardly bothered by it all, until periodically taken to task by the bank. The Karitane factory occupied a lower position on the side of the hill, approximately 100 metres from the hilltop residence. While King's house bore an uncomfortable resemblance to a state house, the Karitane factory was delightfully art deco. Gray Young had taken advantage of the sloping hillside to design a three-storey factory so the manufacturing process could make use of gravity. He incorporated parts of the bungalow style of King's house in the reinforced concrete design but it is likely the art deco appearance was the result of substantial extensions in 1938, doubling the floor area.

In its heyday the factory employed four men, with eight women involved in packaging the Karitane products Karilac, Kariol and Karil. At the top of the stairs was a photo of Truby King, along with members of the Karitane Products board. Out the back was the 'tin plant', a separate factory run by Mr Ritchie, making metal containers for Karil and Kariol, which because of their oil content required more

A MAUSOLEUM IN MELROSE

robust packaging. An extended account of Karitane Products appears in Appendix Four.

The King house at Melrose is described by some as 'American colonial character, modest and unpretentious, plain, weatherboarded structure with casement windows and low-pitched galvanised iron roof'.[4] That its horizontal weatherboards have strong connotations of a State house is, perhaps, not surprising since Gray Young was responsible for a number of State house designs. Commentators agree on a 'skilful exploitation of the dramatic qualities of the site, particularly with the design of the verandah, porches and windows'.[5]

The house occupies the crest of the hill, with ground falling away on all sides. It comprised four bedrooms, two bathrooms, two toilets, formal living and dining room, library and kitchen. The south-facing library features a unique sliding sash window with a lowering mechanism that allowed Truby to indulge in his hobby of astronomy. This feature was added later, not appearing on the original plans, but has all the hallmarks of a King-inspired idea.

A feature of the interior was the jarrah flooring in the living-room and study, which King admired in 'Olveston', the Theomin residence in Dunedin. A Gray Young trademark is the wooden panelling in most rooms. The living-room featured a handsome inglenook with built-in sofas alongside. The long verandah had French doors opening into several rooms. The doors and windows give views of the harbour, hills and open seas. Originally the property was terribly exposed, so one of Truby and Mary's first tasks was the planting of pine trees on the lower slopes at the property's extremities. They now partially obscure what would once have been breathtaking, if well-ventilated, views.

The house was completed in 1924 when King was sixty-six. Truby and Mary moved in before the builders had completed their work, having lost yet another servant at Tinakori Road. This time the reason for departure was quoted by Mary as insanity.[6] It is not recorded who fell victim, but presumably it was the servant. Bella, in the meantime, had been in hospital for several months. She arrived at Melrose in time to make and hang curtains.

In an attempt to minimise the wind's intrusion, Truby devised an

Melrose – The House of Windows, facing East.

ingenious set of sliding metal screens to protect against the prevailing wind without impairing the view. Borrowing the idea of expanded steel mesh, used with reinforced concrete, he positioned similar panels of mesh so that the wind was deflected, but the view through the holes in the mesh was not substantially reduced. These screens are no longer at the house.

Wellington's reputation for extremes of weather is thoroughly deserved, and Melrose on a bad day would have been the last place a sane person would want to be. Not King, who staunchly insisted that 'there was always one side of the building that was totally sheltered'.[7] Many people wryly recall visitors arriving with umbrellas that had been blown inside-out. On a good day the Melrose property would have been spectacular, with panoramic views in air clear enough to see forever. The rest of the time only King's insouciance would mitigate against the elements. When hosting the New Zealand Institute of Architects in 1925, he praised Gray Young 'for securing the maximum amount of fresh air and sunshine without inconvenience from the various winds'.[8] Whether he had to shout this into a howling gale was not recorded.

With the house complete, there remained a nagging problem, but for Truby King not an insoluble one: an unsightly neighbouring property. Where lesser people might have positioned a tree to obscure the perceived eyesore, he purchased the house, rectified the elements he found objectionable, had it painted, split it into three flats and let them out. It is questionable whether the rentals received justified the outlay in expense, but Truby was satisfied.

In January 1925 Truby King received his knighthood, Bella King was ailing and Mary King had completed her kindergarten training. Truby, meanwhile, received plants ordered from all over the world for his garden. Rhododendrons came in quantity from the Hutt Valley, from Taranaki, from Dunedin, from Australia, England and Holland. Dan Russell, the full-time gardener, was kept busy planting under Sir Truby's direction. (His gardening exploits are detailed in the

King and Plunket acolytes on the Melrose verandah.

following chapter.) Truby dispatched Mary to accompany a woman with a sick baby to South America, which had dire consequences for Mary's health, causing her to break her return journey in Scotland to recover from a tubercular attack.

Two years later Isabella King died of a cerebral haemorrhage. She had been unwell for the past five years or more. Truby buried her in Porirua Cemetery alongside an old friend. He immersed himself in work, but it was apparent that he was severely diminished by Bella's death. Mary reported: 'He showed little sign of outward sorrow, but he was a broken man. Only those who knew him well realised what he was suffering.'[9]

CHAPTER SIXTEEN

The manic gardener

The main purpose of good gardening is the perfect rearing and growth of our fellow-beings, called plants, with a view to direct utility or beauty, or both – and always with a definite plan and purpose, carefully thought out well in advance.

Seeing that plants are living beings with daily and hourly needs similar to our own, the gardener should make an absolute rule to attend to the living before the dead. Of all the faults and mistakes of the gardener, the commonest is forgetfulness or neglect of the needs of the plants themselves in his preoccupation with some particular garden work on which he has entered and which is not absolutely urgent at the moment.

The claims of living plants should always take precedence over any other works in connection with the garden, whether the question is one of the care of seedlings while in the nursery-bed, or when being lifted out and replanted, or in the immediate care and safeguarding of cuttings, or prompt attention to heeling-in, or planting out of new arrivals from public nurseries or elsewhere.

One of the profoundest and most widely applicable sayings of Socrates was, 'In every work the beginning is the most important part, especially when dealing with anything young and tender', this saying applies with equal force and truth to the Nursery for Plants as it does to the Nursery for Babies; and in both cases, lack of attention at the start and consequent impairment of strength and vitality is never completely made up for in after life.[1]

When told by his daughter Mary that she was going to write his biography, Truby King expressed pleasure. Would he have been pleased with the result? Mary presented us with a picture sympathetic to her adoptive father, being eulogistic, one-dimensional and devoid of balance. Before her research material was lodged, she is believed to have expunged the archives of anything that presented him in an unfavourable light. But buried in correspondence, lists, instructions to gardeners and plant orders, we find evidence of attitudes, obsessions and behaviour that are fascinating and apparently overlooked.

As noted in the introduction to this book, I encountered Truby's work while researching the Barbier nursery in Orléans, which existed before 1900, eventually being overtaken in 1970 by the pressure of land development in the town of Olivet, just over the river Loire. The Barbier family are best known for their wonderful rambling roses Albéric Barbier and Albertine, but they also ran a large general nursery, growing everything from asparagus to grapes, berries, ornamentals, trees and shrubs. Their 1931 catalogue of 194 pages devotes a third of its space to roses of all shapes and sizes. But while King had visited the nursery in the course of his trips to France, it is interesting that his huge plant orders for Melrose from this master rose-grower did not include a single plant of their specialist product. How he managed to overlook sixty pages of the world's best roses suggests either blinkers or a man on a determined mission.

King's earliest influence in the garden would have been his father Thomas, who was something of a plantsman and, according to his biographer Margot Fry, an importer of seeds and plants.[2] His father's fluency in French may account for Truby's Gallic importations. Mary King's first mention of his gardening interests relate to the time he was working for the bank in Masterton, aged twenty.

In Edinburgh, while heading his university classes in medicine, Truby found time to take Botany papers and would have enjoyed the highly reputed Edinburgh Botanic Gardens, which had large collections of plants, including hundreds of species of rhododendron collected from China at that time. These were the exciting times for the Victorian plant collector, bringing new and exotic species back to the mother country, and Truby would have been caught up in the revived interest in botany and the fascination with new species.

The first-hand evidence of King the plantsman is at Seacliff. Unimpeded and unconstrained, King was able to indulge himself in the creation of grounds to soften and civilise the forbidding asylum. With an army of 'willing' workers, he could undertake grand schemes of earthworks, landscaping and planting. The results were impressive. Even today, with the asylum gone, Seacliff as a municipal park has a decrepit haunting majesty. Then before his Karitane house could be built, the problem of coastal erosion had to be confronted, lest the peninsula become disconnected from the mainland by tidal and river interaction. But Melrose was the time he could indulge himself in planting his own garden. In 1923, at the age of sixty-five, he could begin. Was there a plan? Emphatically not. King liked, above all, for things to be natural, and the prospect of a carefully considered, well-designed garden did not accord with this. Mary King, in a 1992 reply to a letter of inquiry from the landscape architects responsible for the garden's conservation, confirmed this: 'I do not think there was ever a written Plan or Document of the planting to be done in and around "Mount Melrose". Any planning was in the mind of Truby King . . . like Topsy, the garden "just grew".' The comprehensive 1993 analysis of the garden provided by consultants Boffa Miskell was at a loss to explain much of the garden design: 'The layout of the garden does not reflect a particular garden style, nor is it based on traditional garden design layouts'.[3]

The ten-acre exposed hillside provided King with an impressive challenge. Undeterred by the steep slopes, Truby and his team of gardeners began building paths, retaining walls, steps and access ways. He wrote of his intention that 'mother and baby should walk through the gardens'.[4] Early pictures show the house perched on a hilltop with a few pergolas and surrounding bush. The development of the garden would have taken place over about ten years, from 1924, on completion of the house. Although it has been suggested in an unpublished thesis that Gray Young was responsible for the garden design, I am convinced that it was all the work of Truby King.[5]

His idiosyncratic use of bricks in the Melrose garden must be seen as a major feature. As well as the more usual bricked paths and walls, we have piers, pergolas, posts and porticos constructed of bricks. In

The Melrose garden, 1934.

The Melrose garden at its best, c. 1943.

total, hundreds of thousands of terracotta bricks have gone into the construction of elaborate and eccentric features, none more so than the 'moon gate', a circular feature in a tall brick wall. On a relatively steep section, his use of brick retaining walls to create a number of terraced areas is sensible. It is the extent and the complexity of these bricked features that take the eye. While the paths provide functional access, many of the other brick constructions have less utility value. Some of the walls adjacent to the house are out of place and ill-conceived.

The brick walls alongside the house may well have housed Truby King's strawberries. Whereas a keen gardener might consider a dozen plants, Truby's ambitions were considerably greater. He ordered a total of 355 strawberry plants from Barbier alone. There are thirty-five recorded varieties, the majority bearing such exotic names as Belle de la Perraudiere, Reine des Perpetuelles and Mervielle de France. He ordered six of most varieties, sometimes a dozen. To his brother-in-law he commented how well the strawberries had travelled from France, so it is likely that many Plunket mums and babies ate well on exotic *fraises*. The walls adjacent to the house have systematic voids, where half-bricks have been omitted. It appears that King utilised these for planting his strawberries, to grow in pockets of soil in bricks warmed by the sun. The archives show correspondence concerning Truby's planting of 'a hundred runners of Bradley's Seedling', supplied by Dr Jeffries of Nelson, and planted 'upon the front face of the brick wall, looking north'. To supplement the foreign strawberry importation, Truby also purchased 125 unspecified varieties from Bennetts in Dunedin, and in 1933 correspondence shows Truby was still seeking more. An order to Duncan & Davies requested 'two dozen well-rooted runners of the Strawberry which you will believe will be most suitable for my conditions in Wellington'.[6] What became of the profusion of these berried treasures is not recorded.

Not satisfied with extensive strawberry plantings, he managed to find room for forty-eight imported gooseberry plants and fourteen blackberries.

Spurning the winds for which Wellington is renowned, Truby King planted maples, those most beautiful but wind-intolerant trees, on his exposed Melrose slopes. He ordered over eighty specimens, many of which were catalogued as growing to fifty feet, while a smaller number may have been destined for growing in pots. He propagated Norway maples from seed, which he wrote of 'doing for over thirty years'.[7] Unsurprisingly, there is no evidence of the survival of these tender treasures.

Broom (*Cytisus*, *Genista*) was an unlikely prospect for him to consider planting in mass. But from 1924 to 1929 he ordered nearly 300 *Cytisus*, comprising nineteen varieties. If that wasn't enough, he added 475 *Genista*, in twenty-seven different varieties. Most came from France, although some came from Dublin, Edinburgh and Dunedin. Not one for understatement, he noted to another gardener in 1925:

> I really think I have a complete collection of everything desirable . . . my feeling is that the brooms are going to be just as important for us here as the rhododendrons on which we have been specialising. I cannot imagine that anywhere in the world there are hillsides in Nature more suitable as the habitat of the whole broom family. Kipling did not fail to notice the wonderful effect of the common broom when in flower as the background of the city of Wellington when one looks up at the hills from the harbour.

There is no evidence that Kipling and King met, but their paths are very likely to have crossed. Kipling dedicated this verse to Wellington:

> *Broom behind the windy town, pollen o' the pine –*
> *Bell-bird in the leafy deep where the Ratas twine*
> *Fern above the saddle-bow, flax upon the plain –*
> *Take the flower and turn the hour, and kiss your love again!*[8]

If Kipling, a xenophobe Empire loyalist, could eulogise about broom, then it was good enough for Truby King.

> Our idea is to plant the nor-eastern and nor-western slopes of the hill almost entirely with a collection of broom ranging in colour from yellow, brown, red, pink, cream colour to pure white, and in height, from a few inches up to 10 or 15 feet.[9]

What happened to the broom? Today there is no evidence of the hundreds of plants. Were the mothers and babies in the hospital consumed by hay fever, or did the plantings just prove unsuitable?

As the garden developed and the shrubs grew up round the house, Truby would get a saw and go out before breakfast to cut away branches that were obscuring the view of harbour and hills beyond. He would tie his handkerchief round a certain branch, retire to the dining room to see if it was really the offending limb, go back and saw it off and then tie his handkerchief round another one! Mary King said he regarded it as a crime to cut off even a single twig unnecessarily.

In 1925 Truby King was appointed Vice President of the

Wellington Horticultural Society, with the observation: 'Your life's interest in horticulture is known all over New Zealand. The Melrose Garden, 1934.'[10] Not content with his planting at Melrose, King wanted to beautify the environs of the city. Finding a kindred spirit in Mr McKenzie, Director of Parks and Reserves, he set about the planting of open spaces around Melrose. He would think nothing of organising a horse-drawn plough to prepare the ground, then seeding it with oats and red clover, and finally planting with trees and shrubs. He was also fond of conscripting his 'keen cottagers' to planting schemes. There are tales of King knocking on doors in suburbs adjacent to Melrose, leaving instructions for the man of the house to attend on Saturday morning with a spade and a barrow of topsoil.

There were two substantial greenhouses adjacent to the Karitane Products factory, where Truby and his staff propagated large numbers of plants. To supplement his own production, he imposed heavily on his friend Victor Davies, founder of New Plymouth's famous Duncan and Davies plant nurseries. His correspondence beginning 'My Dear Davies . . .' alternated between advice to Davies on what he should be doing and requests for assistance in propagating plants, and included requests for donations of plants for municipal planting. King recognised Davies' superior plantsmanship, and lost no opportunity to exploit the relationship. Any nurseryman who wished to supply Sir Truby with plants would need to steel himself against the requests for plants for 'beautifying the district'.

In a letter to McKenzie in 1925 he wrote:

> And now I want to take the opportunity to thank you most heartily on behalf of myself and our co-workers at Melrose for the helpful and encouraging way in which you have met our every wish for beautifying the district . . . If you happen to be passing up Manchester St, I am sure you will be greatly pleased to see how exceedingly well the hydrangeas, buddleias, rhododendrons, tamarisks and other plants are doing. This makes a great impression on everyone, because they begin to realise what a very great difference it will make to the district if we

get all the suitable positions along the road well planted with good flowering shrubs.

A letter to the Victor Davies in 1933 gives an insight to many of Truby King's attitudes (the underlining is his):

> All the plants that I am wanting from you will come under the jurisdiction of the Mayor and Corporation of Wellington; and will be supervised and directed by Mr McKenzie (the Director and Curator of Parks and Gardens) working in conjunction with myself. This means, as you can well understand, that I supply the brains, science and practical knowledge. But McKenzie and the Council give me every assistance they can in the form of '<u>unemployeds</u>' who are mostly useless <u>unemployables</u>. However, the Council and McKenzie heartily appreciate the fact that for every pound that they spend throughout this whole District, I contribute more than £10. Of course, I derive no personal benefit whatever, which is not shared equally by everyone – rich and poor alike. I have pursued this policy for the last 13 years, and the plants and plantings have been provided solely by myself. But for this, the whole area below Sutherland Crescent would still be merely a wind-swept, steeply sloping valley, scourged by Nor'westerly gales which render gardening of any sort impossible without sheltering trees and shrubs.
>
> Nearly all the cottages below Sutherland Crescent have been put up in the course of the last 8 years by working-men who were tempted by the Government's kind offer (or <u>political bribe</u>) to provide 90% of the money needed. You may be interested to know that in this District alone the political job in question has cost half a million sterling to our long suffering little Dominion !

King thought nothing of hiring armies of gardeners. He commented to his Dunedin supplier Perrett in 1924: 'I have a first rate man for a few hours a day who was at Kew and served his time with Veitches . . . now I have a team of four first-class young men working steadily under Mr Barnett (my expert).' Never one to miss the opportunity to drop names, he acknowledged Kew and Veitch nurseries as the training ground of 'Chinese Wilson', one of the world's great plant collectors, whom he would have met when the famous man visited New Zealand.

Mainstay of the Melrose garden was the Scot, Dan Russell, who joined Truby King in the early days and carried on when he donated the property to the Plunket Society in 1932. Russell remained at Melrose until retiring at the end of the war. His wages in 1930 were £5 10/- a week, while his 'boys' received one pound a week, and a 'really good lad' thirty shillings. By contrast, King's salary on retirement would have been at least four times Russell's. On his last trip to England with Mary in 1930, King despatched an eight-page typed letter to Russell. He apologised for his hasty departure, then informed Russell that 'times are hard' and that he would have to take a pay cut and dismiss one of the other garden staff. Russell was ordered to sell some of the surplus rhododendrons to a Lower Hutt nursery, and be frugal with other matters. Whether King was not sufficiently organised to confront Russell before departure, or couldn't bring himself to deliver the news personally, is not recorded.

The Melrose garden was at its best in the 1940s, twenty years after Truby began planting. A 1943 picture (showing clearly the mausoleum) illustrates the density of planting and high level of care. By 1950, with the retirement of Dan Russell, drastic modification had taken place, with much of the verdant growth removed in the interest of decreased maintenance by the Plunket Society. At its peak, Truby King's Melrose garden would have been an interesting place to visit.

In addition to purchasing massive numbers of trees, plants, flowers, shrubs, fruits and vegetables from Barbier, he imported plants from Australia, England, Ireland, Japan, Holland and Scotland. He also purchased a large number of plants from Otago nurseries that he would have known from the Seacliff days. Domestic orders from Taranaki, Wellington and Hutt nurseries are commented on, but not documented, although records from Bennetts nursery in Dunedin show over 840 trees and shrubs were supplied. The majority of plants were ordered between 1922 and 1929. Despite his donation of plants

THE MANIC GARDENER

to local beautification projects, it has been speculated that Truby King could not have planted all these thousands of plants in his ten-acre property alone, and that he was probably trading in plants.[11] Certainly he was generous with his plants, especially to people of title or status, but I found little evidence that he was trading, certainly not profitably. While continual lack of money may have been annoying, it did not appear to deflect Truby from his goals.

From what I gleaned from the archives, I have assembled a summary of King's foreign plant purchases, although there would be many more from domestic sources.

No.	Plant	Different varieties
86	Acer	3
64	Amelanchier	5
125	Ampelopsis	4
41	Azalea	13
374	Begonia	various
834	Berberis	13
14	Blackberry	3
58	Ceanothus	4
25	Cerasus	4
19	Chamoecerasus	9
20	Clematis	4
16	Cordyline	7
150	Cornus	8
232	Cotoneaster	22
25	Cydonia	5
292	Cytisus	19
15	Erica	3
12	Erigeron	4
350	Escallonia	5
12	Fagus	5
4	Fig	4
35	Fuchsia	2
475	Genista	27
175	Gladiolus	3
48	Gooseberry	2
74	Gypsophila	6
12	Helenium	6

No.	Plant	Different varieties
9	Helianthus	3
20	Hibiscus	10
65	Hydrangea	19
25	Hypericum	4
41	Japonica	4
16	Jasminum	3
32	Laburnum	3
82	Lonicera	9
125	Mahonia	2
52	Malus	8
57	Olearia	14
54	Paeonia	18
12	Penstemon	2
9	Perowskia	2
101	Philadelphus	13
18	Phlox	2
300	Pinus	2
344 lbs	Potato	3
10	Prunus	4
19	Senicio	7
86	Sidonia	8
12	Solidago	3
32	Spirea	10
355	Strawberry	36
47	Syringa	19
28	Veronica	9
36	Viburnum	2
11	Weigelia	2

6094 plants in total

Truby King's greatest gardening obsession was with rhododendrons.

> I have nearly 400 of the finest Rhododendrons in the world, visible from one point: and they vary in height from 5 to 10 or 12 feet, and will be perfect domes of flowers, in succession, throughout the coming eight months. Besides, I shall be only too glad to give you as many cuttings and plants as you like, of the finest and best specimens from everywhere – including the pick of the Dutch

Rhododendrons, many of which are already six feet high and doing splendidly.[12]

From the Greek *rhodos* (rose) and *dendron* (tree), the rhododendron was discovered in the sixteenth century, coming to Britain in 1656. Rhododendrons exist in all shapes and sizes, from tiny miniatures to very large trees. Shallow-rooting, they prefer semi-shade and acidic, free-draining soils. That they enjoy high rainfall is testified by some of Taranaki's great rhododendron dells. Evergreen, they flower from autumn through to spring.

Linneaeus brought order to botanical names and established the genus Rhododendron in his book published in 1753. By 1800 there were twelve species known in cultivation. The next hundred years, with increased travel and better communications, saw plant collectors searching the world for new, novel and interesting botanical specimens. China opened its borders in the middle of the nineteenth century, with the signing of the Treaty of Nanking and the ending of the opium wars. Botanical adventurers in large numbers sought to supply the old world with exciting plants, shrubs and trees, and rhododendrons from the remote Chinese mountains were among the most publicised treasures.

What started Truby off on his relentless quest for rhododendrons? Edinburgh is undoubtedly the clue. In his six years there, he could not have failed to grasp the botanical fever present with Edinburgh-trained botanists almost daily bringing back new plants. While his birthplace, Taranaki, now enjoys an international reputation for the rhododendron, it did not really become established there until the twentieth century. Newton King became infected with brother Truby's rhododendron fascination, and is known on his advice to have planted a number of different varieties on his Taranaki property in the 1920s. Pukeiti, the garden flagship of Taranaki, was not established until the second half of the twentieth century.

It is unlikely that the archives are complete, but from what is available we know that King purchased at least 600 rhododendrons, from a variety of disparate sources:

Bennetts, Dunedin	1922 until 1932
Silberrad & Son, London	1923
Waugh, Hutt Valley	1923
Seton, Fairfield, Otago	1924
Perrett, Dunedin	1924
Dicksons, Edinburgh	1924
Taylor & Sangster, Victoria, Australia	1924
Wallace, Tunbridge Wells, UK	1924, 1926
Van Houtte, Holland	1924
B Van Nes & Sons, Holland	1926
M Koster & Sons, Holland	1926[13]

His rhododendron orders were often typed on Department of Health notepaper and contained elaborate instructions as to their packing and despatch. For example, his instructions to Silberrad & Son of London in 1923: 'I want you to make sure that they are despatched to New Zealand by the New Zealand Shipping Company's Steamer "Tekoa". I have a special introduction to the captain, and shall see him about having special care taken to place the plants in the best part of the ship.' Or to Wallace in Tunbridge Wells: 'Special arrangements have been made with the Chief Steward for the plants to be carried in the store for vegetables, etc. where the temperature is maintained between 40–60° Fahrenheit.'[14]

He went to great lengths to describe the boxes in which they should be packed, including with his instructions a sketch of the desired containers and packaging materials. His elaborate, detailed requirements point to a knowledgeable gardener who was determined to acquire every last specimen in the finest condition. How he collected them appeared not to matter. It was said of Truby that 'whenever he saw a Rhododendron that he did not have, he would not rest until he was able to get it, even to the point of keeping a spade in the boot of the car so that his driver could steal, if necessary, the prize'.[15]

There are some aspects of his rhododendron collection that are curious, for example his passion for making multiple orders. He often ordered the same variety several times. Nobleanum, for instance, was ordered from his Australian supplier in 1924, and in the same year from his English supplier. Then in 1926 he ordered three more plants from the Dutch firm, Van Nes. It has been suggested that he had determined that they *would* grow for him, and was doggedly asserting his right to have them perform. There are over thirty examples of multiple orders of the same rhododendron, generally from different suppliers.

The second point of contention is the suitability of rhododendrons to the Melrose site. It is noted that they are one of the longest-suffering of garden plants, and can frequently be seen cheerfully growing in an abandoned garden with a few fruit trees, many years after all else has gone. The few remaining remnants at Melrose give the lie to this observation. The 1992 inventory lists only five of the six hundred rhododendrons that might have been planted by Truby King. This begs the question of King's dogged determination that Melrose would become his national collection of rhododendrons, despite the site's unsuitability. Discussions with contemporary gardening historians support this contention, and confirm the unsuitability of rhododendrons to the site.

King's correspondence with Bledisloe shows that he raised a number of rhododendrons in large tubs, and would often supply them to Government House. The fact that they grew so well in tubs (as well as in the garden, said Truby) may more be a judgement of how poorly they grew in the garden rather than how well they grew in tubs! An interesting aside to Truby's obsession with the famous and the titled, is his reported fancy for installing potted specimens in the garden just before an important visit, to create the effect of a permanent garden display. He wouldn't be the first to operate this deception.

His rhododendron correspondence with Lord Bledisloe and Edgar Stead can be found in Appendix Eight.

Truby King's garden wisdom can be summarised from a typed note in the Hocken archives:

IN A STRANGE GARDEN

1. Attend to the Living before the Dead.
2. One year's Seeding means seven years Weeding. By means of the leaves and roots plants are fed and nourished; but 'flower-formation' tends to impede growth, and 'seed-formation' often kills outright.
3. Leaves and roots feed and nourish the plant; flowers impede growth more or less: Seeding always tends to arrest growth, and may kill it outright. Hence the Golden Rule:
'Pick fading border-flowers; and cut back most free-flowering shrubs, climbers, etc. directly their season's beauty has nearly passed off.'
Never delay the clipping for weeks, or even days; and never hesitate to sacrifice a few belated flower buds.
4. Go down on your knees every night and thank God* for the gentle hoe and the devil for the cruel root-cutting spade.
5. God* being thrifty, taught us how to 'mulch'; and the devil, being a 'waster', taught us how to waste water.
Superficial watering is ineffective and even injurious. Either habituate the plants not to expect any drink except from the heavens, or else water deeply when over-dry. Let the roots depend for moisture on prevention of evaporation, hoeing and surface mulching, rather than on watering.
6. Seed-beds are almost always sewn far too thickly. The result is drawn-up, spindly plants which starve and strangle one another. Such weaklings are not worth transplanting; better dig them in and sow thin next season.
7. Plant a rose in *May* and it *must* live; in any other month it *may*. With few exceptions, early autumn is the best season for transplanting in general, and for propagating by cuttings, layers, etc: this applies largely to seed-sowing also.

The asterisk * note contains the only religious reference that I have found in King's writing. It is believed he never attended church but a reference in the archives notes 'a deeply religious attitude to life'.[16]

CHAPTER SEVENTEEN

The end

ON HER return from South Africa, Mary King became Truby's secretary, available at all hours for dictation, the typing of letters or notation of yet another scheme that he was hatching. She would regularly work until midnight, and it is unlikely that she had any life of her own.

In 1930, with Mary in tow, Truby King set off to London for the last time. Reports of his presentations at the Conference on Maternity and Child Welfare tell of a forgetful, repetitive, irascible old man. Mary King noted: 'He was growing more and more intolerant of all ideas which did not exactly coincide with his own, and it was a pathetic fact that many who had not known him in the old days failed to realise that it was but the gradual disintegration of a great mind, which was long outlived by a feeble but tenacious body.'[1] Perhaps fortunately, his intention of establishing a Karitane

Products factory in London was not realised.

After an abortive attempt to establish a residence adjacent to the Australian baby food factory, Truby King was finished in Sydney. He had been unwell, and had slipped on the bathroom floor and sustained a spinal injury. Prescribed morphine and constant nursing attention, he dismissed the nurse after two weeks, threw away his orthopaedic brace, determined that he was recovered and carried on, albeit with a body more terribly bent than usual. He returned to Wellington where the Melrose house had been rented, so he stayed in hotels. Stories abound of Truby insisting his rooms were not dusted, writing himself messages in dust on windows and mirrors and speaking interminably in corridor telephones, impervious to fellow guests. Unperturbed by his weakened state, he continued travelling, lecturing and preaching what he could recall of the Plunket message. At the 1931 Plunket conference in Dunedin, the contrast between Sir Truby and the old Truby King was marked. His mental powers were substantially in decline.

Declining powers or not, he still managed another trip to Melbourne, intending to sort out some imagined deficiency in child feeding. Again, the visit was less than successful.

Although Mary King makes elliptical reference to his mental decline, she does not come to grips with the reality of her father's condition. The recorded recollections of some of the staff of Kingseat Hospital are less equivocal. Mr Moss discussed how he personally handled the committal papers for Sir Truby. He mentioned how Truby was committed but never hospitalised, the implication being that a previous Director of Mental Health should not, if at all possible, be interred in one of his own hospitals.[2] Mr Tibble, who worked at Seacliff noted that Dr Gray, a King acolyte who succeeded Truby as Director-General, blocked an application to have Truby committed to Porirua asylum, and seconded staff to care for King.[3] Truby's affairs were taken over by the Public Trustee and Truby in effect became a prisoner in his own house, under full-time care.

Dr Neil Begg's summation was kindly: '. . . in his later years he forgot to listen and would brook no argument, his correspondence

THE END

Truby King in the 1930s, an old man.

becoming testy as he lapsed into autocratic ways. It is sad that too often we remember in a person the rigidities of old age while forgetting the brilliance and sensitivity of their earlier life.'[4]

In July 1932, at the annual meeting of the Wellington branch of Plunket, Truby King formally handed over his home to the Society. He moved to one of his rented properties in Sutherland Crescent, adjacent to Melrose, with a housekeeper and 'nursing care'. The following month he fell down the steps at the Karitane Hospital, cracked two ribs, and suffered a substantial blow to the head and serious bruising. His body was beginning to succumb.

The final straw may well have been his unique disease of 'red neuralgia', which caused exquisite pain to the soles of his feet. Mary tells the story:

> Like Bernard Shaw, Sir Truby, in his advancing years, became practically a vegetarian. This was, in part, necessitated by the development of erythromelalgia (red neuralgia). This disease, from which Sir Truby suffered throughout the last four years of his life, was discovered by Dr Weir Mitchell. It is an extremely rare malady, and in no case seemed to have been met with in New Zealand until Sir Truby's family physician diagnosed the painful condition of his feet as such.

Naturally, Truby would not succumb to an ordinary common disease!

Fading, he would not give up. He demanded a daily glass of parsley juice from fresh parsley grown in the flower-beds near the drive. He had Mr Ritchie construct an ingenious cooling contraption that involved a tank at the end of the bed, and circulated water around his painfully heated feet. By 1934 walking caused such exaggerated pain that Truby was confined to bed. He would have constant nursing care to the end.

On 10 February 1938 Truby King died in his sleep, in his eightieth year.

The *Otago Daily Times*, always an ardent supporter, featured a large picture of a younger Truby, together with forty column inches of reflection on the great man's work. The Plunket Society's president, Mrs James Begg, was reported to say:

> This society mourns the loss of its great founder, Sir Truby King. The society of which he was the head, owes its being to his spiritual and moral leadership, which inspired thousands of men and women to enlist in the cause which was so dear to his heart, the welfare of women and children. Sir Truby King began the crusade which was to have such wonderful success when in the prime of his life, and even when waning physical powers deprived the society of his immediate direction, it remained his chief interest. The sympathy of the society is extended to Miss Mary King, relatives and intimate friends in their bereavement. Sir Truby King's memory will remain an inspiration to the society,

enabling it to continue his great work for women and children as its best tribute to its beloved leader.[5]

The *Dominion*, in an editorial entitled 'A Great Humanitarian', recalled with remarkable restraint and prescience:

> Sir Truby's passionate life-work was the saving and the very remoulding of the physical and mental lives of born and unborn armies of children. Our elders may recall the social losses of a previous era through lack of ordinary understanding of the laws of hygiene and nutrition, a state of ignorance that today seems inexplicable.[6]

The *Evening Post* was more fulsome, reporting eulogies from all sides. Prime Minister M. J. Savage's tribute to 'The Greatest Friend of Little Children' painted a picture of King as a New Zealander leading the world in motherhood and child welfare. He characterised him as a medical scientist and a zealous humanitarian. Not to be outdone, Peter Fraser, Minister of Health, remembered Truby's 'almost fanatical zeal', and New Zealand's leadership in lowering infant mortality. Dr Watt, Director-General of Health, paid tribute to Truby's work as Director of Child Welfare, noting generously:

> It can be said the movement of which Sir Truby was the founder originated in his mind, was animated by his energy and enthusiasm and spread and developed through the co-operation of the many supporters he was able to interest in the scheme.[7]

The Wellington Plunket Nurses were not to be outdone:

> Stronger of heart and richer in mind are the Plunket nurses through having been associated with Sir Truby King and his life interest for parents and babies. The light that he lit is ever bright to carry on his great work for the love of humanity. The Plunket nurses feel honoured to interpret his teachings which will live throughout the ages, and in many countries in the world.[8]

The *New Zealand Medical Journal*'s obituary was generous in its view of a man who had often been at odds with the profession.

Sir Truby met with a great amount of opposition. Prejudice and ignorance had to be overcome. He himself was regarded by many as a crank and eccentric. Many of his friends and professional contemporaries would run round corners, rather than meet him in the street, for fear he would draw them into interminable discussions, and then force them to do something against their will.

His personality was a unique combination of scholar, bookman, artist, actor, author and producer, as well as agriculturist and physician. To those who were fortunate enough to share any of his interests he was able to reveal a fascinating charm, an erudition that was never ponderous.[9]

Under Mickey Savage's direction the cabinet decreed that Truby King should be accorded a state funeral, the first for a private citizen. His body lay in state in St Paul's Cathedral, guarded by eight Plunket nurses. The *Evening Post* featured a macabre picture of the coffin in

Nurses keeping guard beside the coffin in St Paul's Cathedral.

THE END

Funeral procession, Wellington.

front of the altar, with severely dressed women standing at each corner, hands defiantly crossed. The Plunket nurses were making their last sombre stand. There is considerable irony in this, given Truby King's opinions and treatment of women.

On Saturday afternoon the Bishop of Wellington conducted the funeral service before the coffin was carried through the streets of Wellington to Melrose, where he performed the interment.

Crowds lined Lambton Quay while the funeral procession wound by, led by the Port Nicolson Silver Band, the coffin attended by pallbearers who comprised politicians Peter Fraser and Walter Nash, Mr Justice Blair, Dr Watt, Dr Tweed, Dr Gray, Sir William Hunt, Sir Alexander Roberts, Mr Pattrick and Mr Scott.

The order of the cortège was as follows:

1	Representative of his Excellency, the Governor-General
2	The Bishop of Wellington
3, 4	Pallbearers
5–9	Ministers of the Crown

10	Speaker of the House of Representatives
11	His Worship the Mayor of Wellington
12, 13	Members of the Legislative Council
14–19	Members of the House of Representatives
20–24	Representatives of the Plunket Society and Karitane Products
25–27	Representatives of the British Medical Association
28–31	Representatives of Health and Mental Hospital Departments
32	Representatives of New Zealand Nurses' Association
33	Representatives of residential and day nurseries
34	Chief of Staff, New Zealand Military Forces
35	Second member, New Zealand Naval Board
36	Chief of Air Staff
37–39	Representatives of Wellington City Council
40–42	Chairman and members, Wellington Harbour Board
43–45	Chairman and members, Wellington Hospital Board
46	Chairman and representatives, Wellington Education Board
47	Magistrates
48–50	Representatives of religious denominations
51, 52	Suburban mayors and county chairmen
53–60	Heads of government departments
61	Representatives of St. John Ambulance Association
62	Representatives of New Zealand Red Cross Society
63	Representatives of New Zealand Educational Institute
64	Representatives of Trades and Labour Council
65	Representatives of Associated and Wellington Chambers of Commerce
66	Representatives of New Zealand Manufacturers' Association
67, 68	Private Secretaries
69, 70	Representatives of trading banks
71	Representatives of the press
72	Representatives of the Rotary Movement

As the funeral procession wound its way round the Basin Reserve, cricketers stopped playing and spectators stood until the cortège was out of sight.

THE END

At Melrose the anticipated parking chaos resulting from the difficult access eventuated. Loudspeakers carried the Bishop's words to the large crowd as Truby King's casket was interred in his tomb. Special legislation had been enacted two years earlier to enable Truby to be buried in his garden. Later, Bella's remains would join him.

Mary King was absent, recuperating from illness in Adelaide.

The mausoleum occupies a promontory below the house and is enclosed by paths and garden. In their 1992 management plan, Boffa Miskell noted: 'It is likely that Sir Truby King planned and directed the construction of the mausoleum and the associated modifications to the garden above and about it, prior to his death and interment in 1938. The monument and the associated plantings appear to have been well planned and integrated into the original garden setting.' (The special legislation authorising Truby's burial in his garden was enacted in October 1936.)

In 1990 the Wellington City Council, at the urging of the director of Parks and Recreation, Richard Nanson, acquired the remaining 1.9 hectares of the property, comprising Truby's house and garden

The unveiling of the Melrose commemorative plaque.

The Karitane Hospital at Melrose.

adjoining the town belt. Council have acted on many of the recommendations of the management plan devised for Truby King Park, with restoration of pathways, repairs to brickwork and substantial replanting of the dell with rhododendrons relevant to Truby King's time. Despite difficulties of access to the property, it is hoped that the house and garden, with public support, will become a national monument.

Today, Truby's house is subject to a heritage order under the Council's District Plan. It also has a Historic Places Trust 'B' classification, which means 'it merits permanent preservation because of its great historical significance or architectural quality'. The mausoleum in the garden in which Truby and Bella are interred has an 'A' classification, which means it has 'such historical significance that its permanent preservation is regarded as essential'.

Why did Truby King choose to die in Wellington? He had travelled widely and would have glimpsed many places better suited to retirement. Wise people plan their retirement. Doctors reputedly

THE END

retire and spend their wealth in their perception of refinement, while clever people choose a climate and environment suited to their desires. Many people retire close to their family, but Truby didn't really have one. Adopted daughter Mary had fled to Australia, perhaps to escape his increasingly irascible demands. Today, elderly people migrate to Australia's Gold Coast, or to the retirement havens of Tauranga or Waikanae, or to somewhere where they can indulge themselves in golf, bowls, bridge and booze. Truby could have chosen from many such places. But he detested sport, did not drink and remained focused on his goals. Taranaki, where he grew up and where his brother was established, might have been considered, but his difficult childhood, lack of empathy with Maori and the Taranaki climate may have mitigated against this choice. The Catlins, where he farmed successfully while at Seacliff, might have held some appeal, with its high natural and wilderness rankings, but may have been considered too remote and backward. Karitane, where he retained the seaside house and where he and Bella spent the most productive years of their lives was, however, too remote from power and influence. Dunedin, his Edinburgh palindrome, where Robbie Burns and Plunket ruled, must have been a serious candidate. This was the centre of medical learning, but then Truby King wasn't an establishment doctor.

He was perpetually broke, but able nevertheless to finance any scheme he dreamed up, so we can discount a financial explanation. The truth is, he never retired. He couldn't relinquish his obsession with influence. It was the failure of mind and body that wrought his eventual end. He stayed in Wellington because that was the seat of power, that was where Bella was buried, and that was where he would end his days. He and Bella would be buried in the strange garden on the windy hilltop.

Appendix One

The Feeding of Plants and Animals

The Feeding of Plants and Animals is a delightful seven-page booklet published by Truby King in 1905. He did not lose the opportunity to lace his prose with homilies directed at various perceived social ills and his proposals for their solution. Sifting through this, one cannot but be impressed by his grasp of the scientific method and his lucid explanations. While some of the terms are quaint, the message is obvious.

This is the section on The Feeding of Plants:

> I am asked to write on the broad subject of feeding plants and animals, but, to convey any precise ideas at all, I must employ the alphabet of science.
>
> My A B C must be, on the one hand, Phosphates, Alkalies, and Nitrogenous salts; and, on the other hand, Proteids, Carbon-hydrates

and Fats. Take the simple case first. What food does a plant need? Mainly air and water. Given these, an ordinary plant, with reasonable protection, will grow and flourish in the presence of sunshine, provided it has a suitable medium in which to push out its root system and to serve as a basis from which to rear the stem and leaves. Air, water and sunshine are common property; and mere land, apart from the question of quality, is cheap enough. What, then, is left for the farmer to supply when he has given his plant a suitable mechanical basis of support? What does a plant need to take out of the soil that land should vary so much in price? The common notion is that a plant builds most of its solid structure out of the solids it absorbs from the soil, though a moment's reflection over what remains after the burning of a tree or field of ripe corn would point to the true conclusion, namely, that the whole plant – root, stem, leaves and seed – is made out of mere air and water, with a trace only of solid mineral matter. But it is just this trace which is important for the farmer to know about, because, while Nature has been liberal enough to supply him without a charge with an inexhaustible stock of air and water, she has left it largely to himself to keep stored up in the soil with his own labour and money the proper proportion of mineral matter and nitrogen needed by the crops which he elects to grow.

Much can be done by systematic rotation and through tillage to keep the land in good heart – in other words, to induce Nature by means of sunshine, frost, rain, bacteria, etc., to keep on liberating from the upturned soil and subsoil year after year a sufficiency of the special salts needed for each succeeding crop. Proper rotation and tillage forms the basis of all good agriculture, and really constitute the best means of manuring the land; but, when we desire to make specially paying crops take their turn more rapidly than Nature is able to renew her supplies, we must be prepared to make up the deficiency ourselves. In one soil the potash will tend to run short, in another the phosphates, in another the nitrogen; and this result will be much affected by the nature of the crops grown.

APPENDIX ONE

The purpose of the science of economic manuring is to learn to add each season for the particular crop we intend to grow just what is lacking in our soil, and nothing more. It requires no thought or knowledge to buy a manure labelled "Potato Manure" or "Turnip Manure", as the case may be; but this is mere wasteful empiricism, because such compounds can be specially adapted only for a particular soil in a particular condition. They contain all the manurial constituents, where, perhaps only one is markedly lacking. Attentive, accurate observation and experiment alone can determine what is really needed, and every farmer can find out this for himself without expense if he will take a little trouble.

Consider the case of a particular crop – the potato. At the present time this is specially important, on account of the "blight", which is nature's messenger warning us that, if we do not keep our crops in robust health and vigour, she is going to back a lower form of life to destroy them. Our only response in the face of the enemy is the expensive one of arming ourselves with spraying pumps and poisons to kill the organisms as they come on year after year. The precaution is a proper one, but more essential things to do are

(1) to grow only the hardiest and most resistive types of potatoes;
(2) to procure good medium-sized seed from vigorous crops in other localities;
(3) to keep the seed properly, so that it may not use up its strength by loss of first growth before planting; and, finally
(4) to plant early in well-tilled ground containing the proper manurial constituents.

We are fortunate if we happen to have a new bush clearing or a lea paddock which has not borne a potato crop for many years, but in the best potato districts such conditions are becoming rare. At Oamaru, for instance, I find farmers engaged in growing potatoes over and over again, almost without intermission, and with the addition of little or nothing in the way of manure. The steady decrease in the quantity and quality of the crops, which the farmers all admit and deplore, is inevitable.

DIAGRAM OF POTATO SHOWING SOURCES OF ULTIMATE COMPONENTS. THE SHADED AREA BELOW INDICATES THE ONE PER CENT. DERIVED FROM NITROGEN AND MINERAL MATTER ABSORBED FROM THE SOIL.

Surely it would be worthwhile to find out precisely what is lacking. Nature contributes free everywhere at least 99 lbs of the weight of every 100 lbs of potatoes grown. We are called upon to supply only what she fails to make up, viz., at most, about one percent of the weight of our crop. In other words, if we manage to increase a five-ton crop to a ten-ton crop by manuring, we shall have contributed to the tubers only about one cwt per acre of pure phosphoric acid, potash, and nitrogen, at a cost of about £2 8s 6d. This sum would provide a quarter of a ton of manure made up of 3 cwt superphosphate, 1¼ cwt of sulphate of potash, and ¾ cwt of sulphate of ammonia, which allows a margin for impurity of commercial manures, for what is carried away by drainage, for what the plants fail to absorb, and for what they employ in building their roots, stems, and leaves. It will have cost us thus £2 8s 6d for the yield of an extra five tons of superior potatoes, and we shall have done much to render our crop vigorous and to save

APPENDIX ONE

it from the ravages of disease. Such a compound manure as I have indicated would tend to largely increase the yield of potatoes on any land impoverished by cropping because it contains all the necessary manurial constituents and is rich in potash, which is a special requirement of all the solanum tribe-potatoes, cape gooseberries, tomatoes, native poro-poro (bull-a-bull), etc., – which we know to revel in our bush clearings, rich in the potash of fallen leaves and burnt trees.

Some soils lack little but potash. In such cases why should we incur great expense in providing full proportions of nitrogen and phosphates? Usually all three constituents are beneficial, but they need to be supplied in proportions varying widely according to the soil. The problem of economic manuring can be solved in one way only, and it can be approximately solved very simply. When drilling a paddock for potatoes, mark out a small even-looking patch for testing. Say the rows are 31 inches apart: select 10 drills and put pegs 15 feet apart in each drill. Each short row between the pegs will then represent 1/1120th of an acre, and will serve for 10 potatoes placed 18 inches apart. A quarter of a pound of manure to 15 feet is, then, equivalent to $2\frac{1}{2}$ cwt per acre. Treat the patch as follows: –

At the end of a single season a farmer who carefully carries out this simple experiment with an equal sample of potatoes will have learned more about the science of economic manuring in relation to his own farm than any books or professors can tell him. I have supplied sets of weighed packets of manures with directions, to two schools and to a number of persons interested in progressive farming both in the North and South, this year, and shall be glad to do the same next season. Our object is to try to stimulate interest in farming as a profession, and to acquire and diffuse reliable and practical information as to the special manurial requirements of various parts of the economy. We hope also to enforce attention to the great truth that the highest wisdom lies in sparing no pains to maintain the young organism throughout in the best possible condition. In plants, just as in the case of animals, the inroads of disease are best prevented by keeping the organism well nourished, vigorous and healthy. It is better to be prepared to fight one's enemies than to poison their wells. The potato plants which suffer most from various blights are those which have the least vital energy and resistiveness – the turnips attacked by aphides in a field are not, as one might expect, the healthiest and most appetising, but the weakest and least resistive; so also with human beings and consumption or any other disease. The broader principles of life apply equally to plants and animals. Such laws and principles ought to be conveyed to the rising generation, could be easily illustrated to children in schools, and would be appreciated by them.'

Was Truby King a first-class scientist? Probably not. But he was able to understand science, to harness it for his own ends. He was a borrower of scientific principles, a user of the more superficial and obvious consequences of science. His communication of scientific principles in simple, understandable ways was probably his major achievement.

APPENDIX TWO

Constitution and Rules of the Plunket Society 1907

Name

The name of the Society is
The Society for the Promotion of Health of Women and Children
(Registered)

Objects

The objects of the Society are indicated by its name, and include the following: –

1. To take over the existing scheme of work carried on by Dr. Truby King during the last two years in the promotion of the health of women and children.
2. To disseminate accurate information on matters affecting the

health of mothers and children by means of lectures, pamphlets, correspondence, and otherwise.
3. To provide for the preparation of humanised milk for issue to the public.
4. To provide for the analysis of milk.
5. To provide and employ nurses ready at any time to give advice and instruction to mothers in the home or elsewhere, with a view to conserving the health and strength of the rising generation, and rendering both mother and offspring hardy and healthy and resistive to disease.
6. To promote legislative reform in matters pertaining to the health of women and children and thereby in particular: –
    a) To ensure prompt registration of births.
    b) To ensure prevention of work inimical to health and vitality in factories, etc., on the part of women for given times, before and after childbirth.
    c) To improve the provisions for the care of waifs and strays, and especially of children in licensed houses or boarded out.
    d) Removal of duty from sugar of milk.
    e) Free access by members of the Committee of this Society to Registrar's records.
    f) Examination by a doctor before children are committed to licensed houses.
7. To co-operate with any present or future organisations which are working for any of the foregoing or cognate objects, such as: –
    The Sisters of the various Church Organisations and Religious Orders.
    St. John Ambulance Society.
    The Salvation Army.
    The Free Kindergarten.
    The Society for the Protection of Women and Children.
8. To investigate the conditions under which waifs and strays are at present kept, especially during the first twelve months of

APPENDIX TWO

life, and so far as possible to make provision for their proper care where they are found to be improperly housed or treated: –

a) By getting them placed in suitable private houses under the care of women not dependent solely upon fees received.

b) In cases where proper provision cannot be made as above indicated, to provide suitable accommodation and nursing at the Society's expense in special homes.

Membership

9. All persons who subscribe the sum of 5s a year to the funds of the Society shall be deemed members of the Society. The Society's year commences on the 1st day of May. Any member who is in arrears after the close of the year shall be liable to be struck off the list of members by the Committee.

10. A past or future donor of a contribution of not less than £50 shall be a life member of the Society without being bound to pay the annual subscription. Anyone desirous of becoming a member must send in his or her name to the secretary, accompanied by one year's subscription, unless he or she is already a life member or becomes such on joining the Society.

Committee

11. The Society and its operations, its funds and property, shall – subject, however to the control in all things by general meetings of the members – be governed, managed, and disposed of by a Committee of the members of the Society, consisting of the following: –

President: Mrs J. H. Hosking.
Vice-presidents: Mrs J. M. Ritchie, Mrs G. Joachim.
Secretary: Mrs Carew.
Treasurer: Mrs M. Cohen.

Mrs James Allen.	Mrs Sale.
Mrs Keith S. Ramsay.	Mrs J. Loudon.

Mrs T. Nisbet.
Mrs A. Jackson.
Dr. E. Siedberg.
Mrs E. O'Neill.
Adjutant M. Duff.
Mrs J. F. M. Fraser.
Nurse A. Holford (St Helen's).
Miss Fraser (Hospital).
Mrs Stilling.
Mrs Edwards.
Sister Ernestine.
Mrs J. M. Gallaway.
Mrs G. L. Denniston.
Mrs D. E. Theomin.
Dr. Agatha Adams.
Miss C. M. Beswick.
Mrs Leslie Harris.
Mrs Truby King.
Mrs W. S. Roberts.
Mrs R. Donald.

12. The officers and other Members of Committee shall continue in office until the election of their successors at an Annual meeting. Retiring members shall be eligible for re-election. Any vacancy occurring in the Committee during the year may be filled up by the Committee.
13. The Secretary, or in her absence any of the other officers, shall be the Convenor of the Committee, and a meeting of the Committee shall be bound to be convened whenever the President or Vice-president or any two other members of the Committee desire a meeting to be called.
14. Any three Members of the Committee shall form a quorum.
15. The Treasurer or Secretary shall have power to receive subscriptions and donations.

Appendix Three

Hygeia columns

Marriage should not be a woman's only profession, but it should be her highest hope. Every girl should try and make herself worthy of it, both in body and mind, and this attitude will not make a girl grow into a less sensible old maid if she has to be one.

On the contrary it is of course quite obvious to anyone who will look beyond schooldays that the healthy normal all-round development that will make the best of a girl for marriage will also make her in the long run most fit to earn her own living, and most inclined to earn it in ways that will satisfy her higher nature as a woman which should crave all things for life in a home, whether her own or mother's or failing this in some calling such as nursing, which will satisfy the natural tendency of all good women to offer some sacrifices of herself for others.

Occasionally Truby would make use of Hygeia to communicate 'messages from headquarters'. This Hygeia column, from 22 June 1926 is an interesting restatement of the Plunket Society's aims and objectives, in King's best prose:

OUR BABIES

-

BY HYGEIA

-

Published under the auspices of the Royal New Zealand Society for the Health of Women and Children (Plunket Society)

"It is wiser to put up a fence at the top of a precipice than to maintain an ambulance at the bottom"

-

THE AIMS AND OBJECTS OF THE ROYAL NEW ZEALAND SOCIETY FOR THE HEALTH OF WOMEN AND CHILDREN

(As set forth in the Annual Report of the Wellington Branch for the year Ending 31st March 1926)

1. TO UPHOLD THE SACREDNESS OF THE BODY AND THE DUTY OF HEALTH: to inculcate a lofty view of the responsibilities of maternity and the duty of every mother to fit herself for the perfect fulfilment of the natural calls of motherhood, both before and after childbirth, and especially to advocate and promote the breast-feeding of infants.

2. TO ACQUIRE INFORMATION AND KNOWLEDGE ON MATTERS AFFECTING THE HEALTH OF WOMEN AND CHILDREN, AND TO DISSEMINATE SUCH KNOWLEDGE: through the agency of its members, nurses, and others, by means of the natural handing on from one recipient or beneficiary to another,

and the use of such agencies as periodical meetings at members' houses or elsewhere, demonstrations, lectures, correspondence, newspaper articles, pamphlets, books, etc.

3. TO TRAIN SPECIALLY AND TO EMPLOY QUALIFIED NURSES, TO BE CALLED PLUNKET NURSES, WHOSE DUTY IT WILL BE TO GIVE SOUND, RELIABLE INSTRUCTION, ADVICE AND ASSISTANCE GRATIS TO ANY MEMBER OF THE COMMUNITY REQUIRING SUCH SERVICES, on matters affecting the health and well-being of women, especially during pregnancy and while nursing infants, and on matters affecting the health and well-being of their children: and also to endeavour to educate and help parents and others in a practical way in domestic hygiene in general – all these things being done with a view to conserving the health and strength of the rising generation, and rendering both mother and offspring hardy, healthy and resistive to disease.

4. To co-operate with any present or future organisation which are working for any of the foregoing or cognate objects.
N. B. THE SOCIETY WAS STARTED AS A LEAGUE FOR MUTUAL HELPFULNESS AND MUTUAL EDUCATION, WITH A FULL RECOGNITION OF THE FACT THAT, SO FAR AS MOTHERHOOD AND BABYHOOD WERE CONCERNED, THERE WAS AS MUCH NEED FOR PRACTICAL REFORM AND 'GOING TO SCHOOL' ON THE PART OF THE CULTURED AND WELL-TO-DO AS THERE WAS ON THE PART OF THE SO-CALLED 'POOR AND IGNORANT'.

Our society was founded 19 years ago, and a new generation has arisen in the meanwhile. Children who were not in their teens at the start are now heads of families, and many of them play an important part in directing or influencing the course of the Society's work in various ways. We, therefore, think it desirable to reaffirm our 'AIMS AND OBJECTS', as printed at the beginning of every Annual Report, and which have never varied since first drafted in 1907.

There is one 'AIM' to which our attention is called from time to time by adverse criticism on the part of some of the new generation of our supporters. They recognise the amazing success of the Society and its great and growing value in the life and health of the community: but they think it unreasonable to ask anyone who does not profit immediately, directly, and personally by its teaching, training, and help to subscribe to its upkeep. They say, 'Let those pay who make use of the Society.'

The spread, success, and ever-widening influence of our work have been admittedly phenomenal, and we ought all of us to try and realise and understand the reason for this, and not regard it as due to mere chance or accident. We know, on the contrary, that the success of our Health Mission to parents has been due to the intrinsic value of the sound, well-thought-out instruction and practical training given by our nurses and conveyed in our books, etc.; and also to the ease with which this instruction can be had 'just for the asking'. The argument that people do not value what costs them nothing is entirely refuted in this case by the very large number of subscribers to the Society among our ranks of those it has helped, and by the wonderful response from 'Plunket Parents' whenever we ask them to help us in any special effort. That is the experience of every branch of the Plunket Society.

Our work is primarily educational and humanitarian – our aim being to teach the mothers the rules of hygiene applying to their own health and that of their children. This object can only be attained by the co-operation of the mothers themselves, and as many of them have to be educated into understanding that they need the knowledge we can supply, we on our part have to maintain an organisation to give this instruction – and to give it freely and gladly to whoever comes seeking the necessary information or help.

The essential work of the Plunket Society is on the same footing as the educational system of the Dominion. The Government does not wait for children to ask it to educate them: it provides and organises schools for their instruction-indeed, it goes one step further and OBLIGES the

APPENDIX THREE

children to attend its schools whether the parents are convinced of the benefit or necessity of their doing so or not. In other words, the Government compels the children to be educated for the good of the whole community. We say the mothers must also be educated for the same reason: otherwise, we shall all suffer by the increase in the number of costly institutions needed to provide for the unfit members of the population.

In support of our scheme for the education, care, and safeguarding of mother and child we appeal to the community to take the place of the Government by enabling us to continue to provide a better and more acceptable means of voluntary (but State-subsidised) education than any Government Department in the world can supply.

The object of the Plunket Society's scheme of education is to raise the standard of health in the home and in the nursery, and thus assure a race of capable, efficient children – strong, healthy and RESISTIVE to disease. We feel that this is the only way to prevent the increase and accumulation of the unfit and the submerged and diseased who have become a drag and handicap in the Old World. In order to attain our object we must look to the willing and hearty co-operation of the self-reliant adults of New Zealand. Selfish individuality and a narrow outlook would prevent anything really effective being done in a matter of this kind. We need the broad-minded enlightened and generous support of the whole community. Our nurses ought to be looked upon in their true light as friends and advisers, not as collectors of fees. The Education Department does not ask its teachers to collect fees from the children of their parents. However, we are fully alive to the fact that all those who avail themselves of the services of the Plunket Nurses or the Karitane Hospitals should feel doubly bound to support the Society by becoming members, and by making such other contributions to the building and working funds as they can afford.

Everyone is now waking up to the fact that untrained ignorant parents are a source of great danger and distress, and that they impose a very serious expense on all taxpayers – direct and indirect – in the building and the upkeep of hospitals, asylums, gaols and various charitable institutions. We are satisfied that in New Zealand, at least, the best way to overcome this cruel and expensive form of ignorance – parental ignorance – is to support the organisation which has been working steadily and consistently towards that end for nearly 20 years along lines that are becoming more and more widely recognised and appreciated throughout the whole world. But we must bear in mind that good education is always expensive in the first instance, though the yield of its harvest is a thousandfold.

APPENDIX FOUR

Karitane products

Truby King's contribution to the decline in infant mortality relates to the reduction in deaths due to diarrhoea, attributable mainly to correcting the constituents of artificial feeding. Mothers who followed fashion and chose not to breast-feed were giving their babies a variety of foods, none of which came close to approximating human breast milk. Truby King's genius was in the simple adjustment of cow's milk to mimic the composition of human milk.

His justification was eloquent. He quoted the protein make-up of human, calf and rabbit milk noting that a human takes 26 weeks to double its body weight, while a calf takes 6–8 weeks, and a rabbit a week. The protein proportions for human milk are 1.5 per cent, for calf 3.5 per cent, and for rabbit 15 per cent. King was quick to realise that the growth rates balanced exactly the available protein. Similarly with fat. A baby whale living in water needs more than 12 times the fat of a calf or human baby, because of its heat requirements. The fat ratios are: human 3.5 per cent, calf 3.5 per cent, whale 45 per cent. King concluded that the milk of one mammal is suited to its needs alone, and that cow's milk would need modification, or 'humanising', before it would suit the needs of a baby. Other researchers had found different techniques for humanising cow's milk. In France, Budin made it palatable by super-heating, but did not address the problems of protein or fat imbalance. Budin reduced infant mortality due to diarrhoea, but did not address weight gain from fat and protein imbalance. King's ideas were technically sound, but had the added advantage of being easily implemented in the home, by adding Karitane products to cow's milk to produce a breast-milk equivalent, with correct sugar, fat and protein balances. He proved this while living at Seacliff and getting Plunket started in Dunedin, and demonstrated its utility by being able to impart the techniques to Plunket nurses who were then able to teach it successfully to mothers. While King's contribution could be seen simply as a reduction in the infant mortality rate, a more significant, if subtle contribution was doubtless in the improvement in the overall health of infants due to better nutrition. He was achieving his goal of prevention of disease.

On moving to Wellington, Truby King was removed from the focus of Plunket affairs and needed another project to occupy his mind. He decided on a factory to produce the necessary humanising additives for the nation's baby foods. The Karitane Products Society was established in 1927 as an adjunct to the Plunket Society. King was 69 years old, had just lost Bella and was in the twilight of his life. It was said that advancing years made him more irascible, dogmatic and difficult. However, he still had a lot to achieve.

The original (unpaid) Directors of the Karitane Products Society (KPS) were Sir Truby King, Mr Justice Blair, Sir William Hunt (Managing Director, Wright Stephenson), Mrs Henry Hall (President, Wellington Plunket Society), Dr T. Derrick (Medical Director, Plunket Society), Mrs Derrick, Dr T. Gray (Director General, Mental Hospitals), Mrs Gray, Miss A. Pattrick (Director,

APPENDIX FOUR

Plunket Nursing), Mr P. Pattrick (Public Accountant), Dr M. Tweed (Medical Practitioner, later to succeed Derrick), Miss Mary King (Truby and Bella's adopted daughter, aged 22).

The Society's mission was 'the manufacture, at the lowest practical rates, of the best and highest grades of pure food materials for use in the ideal rearing of infants'. The motto 'Delays are soon forgotten – bad work, never' was the stern admonition on the factory wall.

The foundation deed required that all profits be spent in the advancement of the Mothercraft movement in New Zealand or elsewhere.

The factory, in the four-hectare grounds at Melrose, was within walking distance of Truby King's house and the Karitane Hospital. Emphasis was placed on sterility, cleanliness and order (three cornerstones of Plunket). King, with his hands-on supervision, ensured that his high standards were maintained. Most of the original equipment came from his cowbyre at Seacliff, where he first concocted his emulsion and 'humanised' milk.

Three 'K' products were made at the Karitane Products factory: Karilac, Kariol and Karil.

Karilac met the 'humanising' requirements – a question of adjusting cow's milk to have the same proportions of protein, fat and sugar as breast milk. King had correctly determined that lactose or 'sugar of milk' was preferable to cane sugar and had gone to some lengths to ensure its availability, and to convince the medical profession and public of its benefits. Interestingly, his work was eventually responsible for New Zealand's lactose industry, which is now an important export earner. Initially he decided to import lactose himself, to teach the local high-priced producers a lesson. They responded by securing a tariff on his imported product. King responded by adding small amounts of dextrin and maltose to avoid the duty. A bitter commercial battle ensued, but as usual King was right, even if he made enemies along the way.

He had called on pioneering work in the United States and France for the humanising of milk, but was himself responsible for the practical development work to formulate a range of appropriate

IN A STRANGE GARDEN

The Karitane Products factory.

supplements to cow's milk that were easily used by mothers. Karilac was sold in powdered form, in three different strengths, a set of graduated sugar mixtures to suit a baby's age and development. Each Karilac formulation contained 5 per cent gelatin, and varied only in the proportions of lactose to dextrose. A packet would last a fortnight.

Kariol was the answer King conceived to the need for supplementing cream with vegetable oils, butterfat and fish oils, to increase the fat content of cow's milk. It was mixed to form an emulsion and sold in tins. The original homogenising plant at Seacliff was an

APPENDIX FOUR

adapted stonecrusher. Kariol, sometimes known as New Zealand Emulsion, originally comprised peanut oil, but later King recognised the superior qualities of fish oil. Before the war, Karitane Products consumed 45,000 litres of cod liver oil annually.

Karil was an emulsion comprising cod liver oil and malt extract, and was designed for children over one year as a general-purpose dietary supplement, and sold in tins. Gordon Parry, in his history of Plunket, tells the story of King and Karil:

> When King was about to sail for England in 1928 he had worked out the ingredients for this preparation but had not overcome the problem of the oil content rising and floating on the surface. So he had a case of jars of Karil put in his cabin to determine whether the technique he had been trying was going to work. After 10 days at sea he opened the jars – calling in some independent witnesses – and found that each contained a perfect white emulsion with no signs of oil on the surface.

King initially restricted sales of Karilac and Kariol to be available only through Plunket nurses. This allowed him control of the mothers via the nurse, but got him offside with the chemists and just about brought the enterprise to its knees. Mothers who lived distant from Plunket Rooms and presented a note signed by a Plunket nurse were then allowed to purchase K products from selected chemists. This arrangement caused some practical difficulties, almost resulted in financial ruin, and was eventually resolved by setting up a more practical marketing approach, administered by a more pragmatic board of directors. By the early 1930s chemists were stocking Karitane products and nurses were released from marketing.

Products from the Melrose factory were shipped all over the world. The pre-war brochure of the Karitane Products Society noted: 'Regular shipments of our preparations are dispatched to different parts of the world, including the United Kingdom, Australia, South Africa, East Africa and Canada. In addition to the above regular exports, the Society sends from time to time supplies for individual babies to parents or nurses living in many different parts of the world.

For example supplies are forwarded to China, India, Ceylon, Straits Settlements, etc.' With the exception of China, it is noteworthy that these were all countries that would have been coloured red on the school map of the world, members of Truby's British Empire.

With the affairs of Karitane Products being profitably managed, King was seized with the idea of 'doing it all over again'. Australia had observed Plunket's successes but had been slow to take up King's ideas. He made numerous visits across the Tasman, aware of the uneasy jealousy that he engendered with some people. Doubtless he made more enemies in Australia than elsewhere, but this did not deter him, especially as advancing age had strengthened his resolve against non-believers.

Riled by a 40 per cent import duty on Karitane products and the authorities' refusal of relief, King determined he should build an Australian factory to manufacture his Karitane products. This was not to be one of his more astute decisions.

In 1928 he leased a building in Surry Street, Sydney, in a slum area close to the central railway station. In a speech to Sydney businessmen he hoped to recruit as directors for the project he launched into a stirring address: 'You *shall* listen to me. I am an old man, and only have a little longer to live in this world. You *shall* hear my message.' The factory was equipped and began production of Karilac, Kariol and Karil. From the outset it was not a success. King, in his seventies, without the support of Bella, had lost his incisive focus and was rapidly losing the plot.

The directors of KPS in Wellington were not of a mind to indulge his profligacy, and when in 1930 he proposed to go to London to investigate the building of an English factory, they tried to dissuade him, eventually only agreeing to his trip if he took Mary with him. To his request from London for money to build a factory, their response was resoundingly negative, calling him home to account for the continued losses incurred by the Sydney factory.

Truby dispatched Mary to Sydney to furnish the house he had acquired next to the factory. Mary's disgust at the tiny unsuitable cottage was plain. She capitulated, however, realising sadly that the

APPENDIX FOUR

father she idolised was showing signs of being human, frail and very old. They took up residence in Surry Street at Christmas. It didn't last long, for the heat, the slum location and Truby's poor health compelled his return to Wellington.

The directors of KPS shut down the Sydney factory shortly thereafter. Bill Scott was dispatched to close the operation and bring the equipment back to Melrose. Truby was not amused.

The Karitane Products Society continued to prosper with more practical, but still voluntary directors. Their baby products and fish-oil production ensured substantial profits that provided much-needed cashflow to an always needy and poverty-stricken Plunket Society. In 1948 the successful fish-oil factory in Timaru, which was producing over 60, 000 litres of high-quality fish oil annually, was sold to Glaxo.

Kariol ceased being produced in 1970, a victim perhaps of its own success. Breast-feeding was back in vogue and infant nutrition was no longer concerned with the feeding of fats.

In 1986 the Karitane Products factory closed its doors. Bill Scott, son of Bill Scott, the original Scottish manager, retired. The ghost of Truby King shuddered. Kariol and Karil were no longer in demand. Plunket sold the Karilac brand to Douglas Pharmaceuticals in Auckland, continuing to derive royalty income. The art deco factory building lives on cheerfully as apartments. The factory machinery is dispersed, the author being the proud owner of a set of its huge industrial scales.

Truby King was indirectly responsible for New Zealand's fish oil industry, which arose to meet wartime shortages of imported fish oil. Analysis of the domestically produced oil showed it to be markedly superior to its imported equivalent.

APPENDIX FIVE

Truby King's library

The south-facing library at Melrose housed Truby's book collection. Central on the southern wall is a large window, fitted with a device to allow it to be lowered, for unobstructed viewing of the night sky. The manual lowering mechanism, comprising a crank handle and ratchet device in a cupboard below, does not appear in the original architect's plans, and would have been fitted at a later date. Around the panelled walls are bookshelves that in Truby's day would have overflowed.

The handwritten library catalogue in the Hocken Library tells of the contents of the library on Truby's death. It comprises many fragile A5 pages and thousands of books. His extensive collection of medical books was donated to the BMA, childcare books to Plunket, and the rest otherwise dispersed. Archival material shows he ordered books from Foyles bookshop in London, often with the admonition 'second-

The Melrose library, 1939.

hand preferred, but new copies acceptable'. His daughter noted that Truby would often buy books in quantity, to give away to people whom he believed worthy of education.

Almost every topic is represented, from opera to classical mythology, all the great authors, many travel books, one New Testament and a child's Bible. There is no 'light' reading. The only novels are serious classics, and there are no books on sport.

The gardening library is an aid to the resurrection of the Melrose garden. As a snapshot of Edwardian gardening, it is remarkably complete and comprehensive:

Title	Author
A Book of Gardening for Sub-Tropics	Stout
A Book of Gardens	Waterford
A Book of Old-World Gardens	Hyatt
A Tour Round My Garden	Karr
Alpine Flowers and Gardens	Flemwell
Alpine Plants	Mansell
Annuals and Biennials	Jekyll

APPENDIX FIVE

Title	Author
Blacks Gardening Dictionary	Ellis
Bricklaying	Forbes
Bulb Gardening	Hampden
Bulb Gardening	Macself
California Fruits	Wickson
Carnations and Pinks	Fletcher
Chemistry of the Garden	Cousins
Colour Schemes for Flower Gardens	Jekyll
Cultivation of New Zealand Plants	Cockayne
Decorative Plants and Trees	Fletcher
Design in Landscape Gardening	Root
Dry-Wall Gardens	Smith
Elementary Chemistry of Agriculture	Woodhead
Elements of Farming	McConnell
Everyman's Book of Garden Flowers	Halsham
Evolution of Plants	Scott
Farm and Garden Rule Book	Brierley
Farm Crops	Baskett
Flower Culture	Hampden
Flowering Trees and Shrubs	Macself
French Gardening	Smith
French Market Gardens	Weathers
Fruit Trees and Grape Vine Pruning	Quinn
Fundamentals of Fruit Production	Bradford & Hooker
Fungus Pests of Fruit Trees	
Garden Development	Henslow
Garden Talks	Cram
Garden Trees and Shrubs	Wright
Gardening Don'ts	M. A.
Gardening for the Ignorant	
Gardens in the Making	
Gladioli	Macself
Greenhouse and Window Plants	Collins
Greenhouse Construction	Taft
Greenhouses, their Construction and Equipment	Wright
Key to Australian Gardening	Searle
Land Draining	Miles
Lawns and Greens	Sanders
Making a Bulb Garden	Tabor
Making a Garden of Perennials	Egan
Manual of Forestry	Schlich
Manual of Practical Farming	McLennan
Modern Culture of Sweet Peas	Stevenson
My Garden of the Red Rose	Aitken

237

Title	Author
New Rhubarb Culture	Morse
Perpetual Carnations Illustrated	Cooke
Planning and Planting of Little Gardens	Dillistone
Plant Propagation	Kain
Plants from Seed	Macself
Practical Bricklaying	Briggs & Carwen
Practical Bricklaying	Hammond
Principles of Agriculture	Harrison
Principles of Fruit Growing	Bailey
Productive Vegetable Growing	Lloyd
Propagation and Improvement of Cultivated Plants	Burbridge
Rational Fruit Culture	Davidson
Rock Gardening	Tannock
Rock Gardens	Jenkins
Saturday in the Garden	Farthing
Saxifrages	Jeremy & Malby
Seeding and Planting in Forestry	Townley
Select Extra-Tropical Plants	Mueller
Shrubs for Amateurs	Bean
Soils and Fertilisers	Macself
Soils and Manures in New Zealand	Wilde
Spirit of the Soil	Knox
Spraying Crops	Spraying Crops
Story of Plants	Duncan
Strawberry Growing	Fletcher
Sweet Peas	Junwin
Sweet Peas	Wright
Textbook of Pomology	Gourlay
The Book of Asparagus	Ilott
The Book of Bulbs	Arnott
The Book of Hardy Flowers	Thomas
The Book of the Scented Garden	Burbridge
The Book of the Strawberry	
The Bulb Book	Weathers
The Children's Book of Gardening	Paynter
The Complete Gardener	Thomas
The Garden Library	Vines
The Garden Under Glass	
The Herbaceous Garden	Martineau
The Potato	Grubb & Guildford
The Secrets of Many Gardens	Macfarlane
Tomato Culture	Tracy
Tropical Agriculture	Wilcox
Vegetable Gardening	Chisholm

APPENDIX FIVE

Title	Author
Wayside and Woodland Trees	Step
Wild Flowers at Home	Gowans and Gray
Wood and Garden	Jekyll

APPENDIX SIX

The evils of picture shows

At the 1920 conference of the Royal New Zealand Society for the Health of Women and Children in Wellington, Truby King stage-managed a discussion on his latest 'pet' subject. It went like this:

Mrs Johnstone (Gisborne): I move the following remit from the Gisborne Branch:
1) That moving pictures as at present shown are injurious to children and young persons
2) That censorship of pictures should be stricter
3) That pictures for children should be controlled by Government, through the Education Department. That picture programmes should be classified into:
   a) Adult programmes
   b) Schoolchildren's programmes

Mrs Comyns (Wanganui): I second the motion, and I am quite in sympathy with the desire for controlling moving pictures. I am a member of a school committee, and I know that the results are very injurious to children. It is about time something was done to prevent certain pictures being shown to the children. The educational pictures that we used to have some years ago seem to have completely gone out of use.

Dr Truby King: I should like to speak on this subject, because I think some of the picture shows are the most degrading things of our age, and have the most damaging influence imaginable. They require to be absolutely censored with regard to children. Children ought not to be allowed to see degrading pictures. There is no question about it that children have evil things indelibly printed on their minds, and they will never get them eradicated. I cannot understand why it is permitted. Of course, I know the difficulties of censorship. I was asked recently by a branch of the Educational Institute what my opinion was, because the Institute was going into the matter, and it was desired to know my views on the subject. This is what I wrote: —

> Dear Sir,
> Re your request for my opinion as to the Influence of Moving Pictures on Children.
>
> I am in entire sympathy with the New Zealand Educational Institute to safeguard and protect children from the pernicious influence of the prevailing type of moving pictures.
>
> Of course, these shows may prove almost as degrading to adolescents, beyond the ordinary school age, and even to young adults; but the protection of minors by special enactments, referring only to young persons under a certain age, would present comparatively little difficulty to the legislature, whereas there is always a strong feeling against interference in the case of adults.
>
> Furthermore, even if the picture shows were purged of all the indecency of suggestion, innuendo and conduct which makes up a

large proportion of the average programme, the exhibition, which would be suitable for adults, would often be quite unsuitable for children. Therefore, I am in entire accord with the idea of a stricter regulation of the attendance of children at picture shows – regulation as to the nature and quality of the pictures that may be presented to them, and regulation of the hours within which they may be allowed to attend.

No one questions that the cinematograph affords a most valuable means of education, instruction and recreation, if used fairly and rationally. The presentation of films illustrating travel, scenery, science, industry, animal and vegetable life, sports, games and every kind of show and pageant may be made suitable and attractive for all ages, but the depiction of a play or even what goes by the name of history, may be utterly unfit for children.

It should always be borne in mind that sexual precocity and sexual irregularity present the greatest difficulties of any civilisation which regards self-control and continence as essential in early life. Every conscientious master or mistress of a school – especially of a boarding school – recognises this as the greatest of their cares and responsibilities. Every physician burdened with the charge of a mental hospital has before him every day the disastrous results of sexual precocity and sexual irregularities. Speaking of the studious boy or girl and the risks they run of shipwreck before fully entering on life, Dr Savage, the leading authority on Insanity in London, said many years ago, that every such boy or girl is dangling between Eros and Psyche. It was the knowledge of this fact that lead our foremost teachers – men who were broad-minded humanitarians, and more than mere pedagogues – men such as Arnold of Rugby, and Almond of Loretto – to found and establish institutions where the trend of thought and feeling would be diverted from undesirable channels by the full measure of healthy outdoor recreation – bathing, swimming, games, and interesting occupations provided.

The special tendencies and risks of puberty and adolescence are too well-known to need insisting on; but, outside the medical profession few people realise that long before puberty thoughts, feelings, tendencies and habits may be formed which will disturb more or less seriously the proper balance and control of the organism, and impair future growth and development – physical, mental and moral. Nothing tends to sap, undermine and stunt individual and racial development and progress more than precocious sexuality and sensual irregularities and perversions . . .

King's letter continued for seven more pages, confronting the issues of sex education, venereal disease, moral training and character-building, and the wonderfully delicate phrasing of 'the universally-recognised delicacy, intimacy and sacredness of the functions and feelings concerned in the handing of the lamp of life from generation to generation', and the 'golden age of happiness and pleasure in life as a normal attitude in the matters of sex: the worries and doubts and broodings imposed on boys and girls of the adolescent period'.

To illustrate he was a man of the world, he gave instances of visits to the movies that had aroused his indignation. He spoke of observing 'well-dressed boys of good class' watching 'sensual, half-drunken looking blackguards', 'gilded scoundrels', 'flashy, attractive villains', and perhaps worst of all, he noted: 'The piano was played by a negro who had an extraordinary long tumbler beside him which was repeatedly filled with stout.' What a contemporary psychiatrist would make of that, we will not speculate. Truby appeared convinced that every moving picture repeatedly portrayed criminals, prostitutes, blackguards and negroes.

He concluded: 'The only way to protect the children is to keep them away from picture theatres as long as possible, or to have stringent regulations and special censorship so as to ensure that no child shall be allowed to attend picture shows which are undesirable and unfit for their age, and that they will be prevented from attending at unsuitable times.'

Predictably, the meeting endorsed Truby King's views and passed the following:

APPENDIX SIX

1. That moving pictures at present shown are injurious to children and young persons.
2. That this Conference represent to the Government its very strong feeling as to the utter inadequacy of the present provision in the way of regulation by censorship to safeguard the children of the Dominion.
3. That attendance of children at picture shows and the nature of the pictures allowed to be shown to children should be regulated through the Education Department.
4. That the nature of the programmes should be classified into (a) adult programmes: (b) children's programmes.
5. That this Conference unreservedly endorses and heartily supports everything read by Dr Truby King in his letter to the Educational Institute, copy of which is forwarded herewith.

Plunket published the booklet *Picture Shows – their Evil Effects on Children and the Need for Reform, Regulation and Control* in 1921. Of the fifteen pages, more than half were devoted to Truby King.

Appendix Seven

Publications by Truby King

Truby King was an inveterate writer; his style often verged on the instructional. Aside from his medical writings as a government doctor, these are his most accessible works:

Tree Culture in New Zealand
Published by the State Forest Service, following his 1902 lecture.

Feeding of Plants and Animals
Important seven-page pamphlet produced in 1905, reproduced in part in Appendix One.

The Evils of Cram
Published in 1906 by the *Evening Star* company: ninety-three pages of argument against over-pressure in schools. One of Truby's more extreme and odd documents, discussed in Chapter Seven.

Feeding and Care of Baby
The standard textbook. Printed by Truby King in 1908, reprinted, reprinted, revised, rehashed, reprinted. The first edition was a slender thirty-two pages; by 1946 it had grown to 257 pages. It was reprinted by Oxford University Press in London, then annually, sometimes twice in the same year. New Zealand editions were revised and reprinted every year or so. Truby paid for the printing and donated the profits to Plunket, partly explaining his precarious finances.

Translated into Polish and published in many countries of the British Empire.

Baby's First Month – Hints to Fathers and Mothers
Pamphlet of forty-six pages produced by the Department of Health in 1913. By 1916 it was enlarged to *The Expectant Mother and Baby's First Month*, with every applicant for a marriage licence receiving a copy.

It was also printed in London by MacMillan.

Natural Feeding of Infants
Produced in 1917 as a thirty-five page booklet by the New Zealand Society for the Health of Women and Children, eventually published in London during the First World War; 10,000 copies printed, sold at 1/- each.

The Evils of Picture Shows
In 1920 Truby produced a strange, twenty-page pamphlet detailing his views on movies, which was endorsed by the Plunket Society. Parts are reproduced in Appendix Six.

The Story of Teeth
Fifteen pages, published in New Zealand, Australia and London in 1935.
  Foreword: *Dedicated to my wife/To whom I owe everything*.
  Truby King's last homily.

Mothercraft Manual
Published in various countries under various guises, with different

editors. *Mothercraft* was a 241-page tome, produced in Australia by Mary King in 1941, while the manual was edited by Mabel Liddiard in London. Essentially they were simplified versions of *Feeding and Care of Baby*.

Hygeia
Newspaper columns beginning in 1908, syndicated throughout the land, offering sage advice to mothers. While they were often organised and edited by his wife, they bear the unmistakable imprimatur of Truby King.

From the Pen of F. Truby King
Published in 1947 by the Truby King Booklet Committee. 141 pages of Truby's writings. An accessible little book.

APPENDIX EIGHT

Truby King's rhododendron correspondence

Truby King's letter to Edgar Stead, Christchurch plantsman, is redolent with clues to King's character. Stead was a well-known naturalist and biologist, and King was highly respectful of his reputation.

42 Sutherland Crescent
Melrose
Wellington
21st July 1933

Dear Mr. Stead,
When you were away in England, your 'Locum-tenens' was infinitely kind and courteous to me, and I only wish I had had more time available for your ideal Rhododendron garden. He very kindly gave me a copy of a previous year's classified catalogue and description of all the most

important Species and Hybrids. Of course, I realised, by the list of responsible names, from Royalty downwards, that the intention was to make, the Capital of the Empire, the world-centre (or perhaps one should rather say the British Empire centre) for this typically English Genus – in the same way that Kew is for the whole range of plants.

I feel very strongly that New Zealand (with its infinite variety of climate and soil, within a comparatively small compass) is naturally more suited for the whole wide range of Rhododendrons than any other country in the world.

Christchurch would, of course, be an ideal centre; but my impression is that the British cult of Rhododendrons, for the Southern Hemisphere, should be centred in Wellington – as the Capital of our country and the seat of Viceroyalty.

I have not spoken to Lord Bledisloe about the matter; but I have often talked to him about Rhododendrons, and found he is not only a Rhododendron enthusiast, but that he has (at his place in Wales) most of the Hybrids I have established myself, besides a good many of the Species.

Both during the present Regime and that of their predecessor's (the Fergusons) I have kept Government House supplied for 8 to 9 months in the year with occasional clothes-baskets full of choice of Rhododendrons; and last year we let them have a good specimen of 'Charles Lawson' for the front hall. In my opinion, 'White Pearl' is equally beautiful, though not quite identical.

I know Tannock contends 'Charles Lawson' is markedly superior, and all New Zealand nurserymen charge a higher price for this Rhodo: than any other, except for the 'Marquis of Lothian', which is, I think, universally admitted to be quite the finest Rhodo: in the world. I don't know whether you are aware of the fact that there is now a considerable demand for 'Charles Lawson' in Australia, on the part of wealthy people who can afford to buy it. Probably Tannock's view is the 'raison d'etre' of this – because they rightly esteem Tannock very

APPENDIX EIGHT

highly; and Sir Heaton Rhodes' brother-in-law (Alister Clark) did his best to secure Tannock for Melbourne, at more than twice his N.Z. salary. [Tannock was a noted plantsman from Dunedin's Botanic Gardens whom Truby deeply respected.]

There is not a single month in the year in which we cannot gather a good basketful of Rhododendrons. A good example of this is 'Christmas Cheer' which has been in absolute perfection for the last few weeks. The secret is not far to seek: on our Southern slopes it is arctic and icy-cold in Winter; but on our steep terraced Northern slopes, facing the Harbour, there is never a trace of frost even in mid-winter.

<u>Compare this with Europe</u>. Away back in 1896 I knew snow to fall in the Riviera, even at Monaco and Monte Carlo; and continue unmelted for a week, while ice remained on the ground for several days.

The Winter of 1896 was the coldest experienced in Europe for several centuries. Indeed, <u>some months spent that Winter in dreary, smoky Edinburgh, inflicted on me a grave recurrence of active Phthisis with spitting of blood, to which I have been subject from time to time from infancy onwards</u>. This drove my Wife and me post-haste to the south of France. We halted for a few days in Marseilles; but ice was banked up there, even in the broad spacious and splendid main street ('Cannebiers') on both sides of the road for several feet high. This completely obliterated the footpaths, and compelled both vehicles and foot passengers to use the middle of the road, which alone was kept clear.

However, as you will realise (from what I said above) it was nearly as cold at Monaco and Monte Carlo: and my authoritative English Physician, who was living temporarily at Monte Carlo, insisted on my going straight to Egypt. But, even so, we had to spend the whole of the following Winter in Queensland, and my health was gravely impaired for years.

The point I want to specially emphasise is this: under no circumstances whatever could anything of the kind take place on the Northern slopes of my terraced hillside facing Wellington Harbour. Indeed it could not be '<u>paralleled</u>' anywhere in New Zealand. After all, we live in three small islands nearly 12 miles [I presume he meant 12 hundred] from the Australian Continent; while Europe and Asia constitute one vast, colossal Continent, with its lofty central 'Massif', from which we are getting all our new Rhododendrons blood, through men of the type of Wilson, Forrest, Kingdon Ward, and Farrer besides a number of younger enthusiastic collectors.

<u>My sheet-anchor for everything concerning Rhododendrons has been for the last 9 years Cox's masterful little book</u>, which no doubt you have found equally informative and useful. Indeed, in my opinion it is worth far more than all the other books put together; including Millais' two costly volumes to which I have been much indebted – in spite of their having not even the semblance of an Index, such as any hack drudge would have supplied at a cost of a few pounds.

Directly Cox's book was published, Sir Isaac Bayley Balfour, Regius Professor at Edinburgh University, posted me a copy in which he spoke of it with unbounded admiration; and another copy reached me by the same mail from my Wife's brother who was President of the Society of Chartered Accountants, and Honorary Auditor to the Botanic Gardens. He said that they were all wildly excited about the new book.

On the next page is a proposal for the formation of a 'Royal New Zealand Rhododendron Society' on similar lines to the English Society. I have drawn it up quite crudely, without consulting anyone, simply because it depends entirely upon yourself, and I should like you to knock it into shape, if you approve, because you know far more about the whole subject than I do.

Yours sincerely

(Signed) <u>F. Truby King</u>.

This letter, albeit written later in life when his mental powers were deteriorating, reveals many aspects of King's character: his snobbish name-dropping and apparent hypochondria, not to mention his wide knowledge of rhododendrons.

The proposal attached to Stead's letter for the formation of a Rhododendron Society was speculative, and apparently met with little favour:

THE ROYAL NEW ZEALAND RHODODENDRON SOCIETY

For Popularising Rhododendrons, and Promoting their Appreciation and Growth, by All Classes – especially Amateurs and Home-gardeners, as our Royal New Zealand Flowering-plant.

Patrons.–	The Governor-General of New Zealand, Lord Bledisloe, and Lady Bledisloe.
President. –	Edgar Stead.
Vice-Presidents. –	Mr Justice Blair.
	Sir Truby King.
and Executive Committee: –	Dr. Cockayne.
	Hope Gibbons.
	Keen Cottager.

The reaction of his proposed executive is not recorded, but Lord Bledisloe declined immediately, to King's chagrin. His letter to Bledisloe's Secretary, Sir Cecil Day, is interesting if only for the fawning tone:

Dear Sir Cecil,

I quite understand the Governor General's decision that at the present time it would be <u>inexpedient</u> to form a Rhododendron Society for New Zealand, in view of the need of money to aid the Unemployed. Indeed, I am relieved rather than otherwise by the proposal of a year's respite from active work myself in connection with the proposed Society.

As for my continuing to supply Rhodos: from the Estate at Melrose (as I have done so for the last 9 or 10 years) let me say that as a New Zealander I regard it as a privilege and pleasure to do so. The Plunket Society was very proud when eventually they were graciously authorised to incorporate the word 'Royal' in the official designation of their Society. We, New Zealanders, regard Vice-Royalty as equivalent to Royalty in this Dominion, and I hope that when the money market mends, and 'Frozen-Credit' no longer dominates and paralyses the world, Lord and Lady Bledisloe will honour us by becoming Joint Patrons of the proposed Society.

I knew that Lord and Lady Bledisloe had a charming home in Wales, and I knew also (by their warm welcome to some trusses of Rhodo: Loderi) that they were Rhodo-Lovers and connoisseurs; but had no idea, until Lord Bledisloe wrote me yesterday, that they had a complete, up-to-date collection of all the best Dutch varieties.

For my part, I have imported nothing new from Holland for the last 9 years. With the exception of a few, which I have planted permanently in the grounds, my plants are still easily movable, being in tubs, and provided with ideal soil and repeated mulchings. This causes them to grow almost as well, and to flower as freely as if planted out.

We have about 20 such Dutch Rhodos: (embracing say 6 or 7 varieties) asking to display themselves; and I hope the Governor and Lady Bledisloe will humour their vanity!

Sending the plants both ways, to and fro, is not the slightest trouble; because it only entails the lorryman calling at Government House in passing, both for the delivery and return. This he would have to do say 6 times, to and fro, in the course of six months. Embracing only a third of our tubbed plants.

In the spring of 1924 Truby King wrote to a number of his fellow rhododendron aficionados, seeking their co-operation in defining characteristics of their plants' growth and flowering habits. At this time he was ordering plants for his garden, but had not planted very much.

> I am trying to get together the material for a small practical book on Rhododendrons, with special reference to New Zealand, but also in order to give reasonably reliable information as to several most

APPENDIX EIGHT

important matters which cannot be found in any of the half dozen leading books and articles I have on the subject.

It is obviously of the first importance to have uniform colour descriptions which would convey correct impressions ... Of course it is a matter of the very first importance for anyone who is trying to make a beautiful and artistic garden to know what colours there are, and to have them on his palette. The best remarks on this subject are to be found in a recent book by an American – Mrs Francis King. She says: 'The past mistress of the charming art of colour combination in gardening is, without doubt, Miss Jekyll. Her book "Colour in the Flower Garden" is the last word in truly artistic planting.'

Truby's letter included a list to be filled in recording name, flowering duration and remarks for sixty rhododendrons, which presumably were commonly available in New Zealand. There is no record of the number of respondents, nor is there any evidence that King made any progress with his 'small practical book'. Was he proposing to do to rhododendrons what he had done with women and Plunket?

Truby King's hybrid rhododendrons ordered for Melrose

Adenoptorum	Dunedin nursery (? Bennett)	1932	5
Alarm	Bennett, Dunedin		1
Albessens	Taylor & Sangster, Victoria	1924	1
Album Elegans	Bennett, Dunedin		1
Album Triumpans	Taylor & Sangster, Victoria	1924	1
Alfreda	Bennett, Dunedin		1
Alice	Van Houtte, Netherlands	1924	6
Altaclarense	Wallace, Tunbridge Wells, UK	1924	1
Altaclarense	Wallace, Tunbridge Wells, UK	1926	1
Argenteum	Taylor & Sangster, Victoria	1924	1
Ascot Brilliant	Wallace, Tunbridge Wells, UK	1924	1
Ascot Brilliant	Wallace, Tunbridge Wells, UK	1926	1
Assorted	Dunedin nursery (? Bennett)	1922	15
Aucklandi	Seton, Fairfield, Otago	1924	1
Aucklandi	Wallace, Tunbridge Wells, UK	1924	1
Aundyomena	Taylor & Sangster, Victoria	1924	1
Azaeloides	Wallace, Tunbridge Wells, UK	1924	2
B. de Bruin	Wallace, Tunbridge Wells, UK	1924	1
Beauty of Tremough	Wallace, Tunbridge Wells, UK	1924	1

Betty Wormald	Koster & sons, Boskoop	1926	3
Blandyanum	Bennett, Dunedin		1
Blatteum	Bennett, Dunedin		1
Bodartianum	Wallace, Tunbridge Wells, UK	1924	1
Boule de Neige	Bennett, Dunedin		1
Boule de Neige	Dunedin nursery (? Bennett)	1932	2
Brayannum	Van Houtte, Netherlands	1924	1
Broughtonii	Seton, Fairfield, Otago	1924	1
Broughtonii Aureum	Taylor & Sangster, Victoria	1924	1
Broughtonii Aureum	Wallace, Tunbridge Wells, UK	1924	1
C B Van Nes	Van Nes & sons, Boskoop	1926	3
C S Sargent	Wallace, Tunbridge Wells, UK	1924	1
Chevalier Felix de Sauvage	Van Houtte, Netherlands	1924	6
Chionoides	Bennett, Dunedin		1
Christmas Cheer	Wallace, Tunbridge Wells, UK	1924	1
Christmas Cheer	Wallace, Tunbridge Wells, UK	1926	3
Christmas Cheer	Van Nes & sons, Boskoop	1926	4
Compte de Gomer	Van Houtte, Netherlands	1924	3
Cornubia	Wallace, Tunbridge Wells, UK	1924	1
Corona	Wallace, Tunbridge Wells, UK	1924	1
Countess of Haddington	Bennett, Dunedin		1
Countess of Sefton	Bennett, Dunedin		1
Cunningham's Dwarf White	Wallace, Tunbridge Wells, UK	1924	1
Cunningham's White	Van Nes & sons, Boskoop	1926	1
Cynthia	Taylor & Sangster, Victoria	1924	1
Daluense	Dunedin nursery (? Bennett)	1932	5
Defiance	Bennett, Dunedin		1
Dhuleepsingh	Bennett, Dunedin		1
Diphole pink	Wallace, Tunbridge Wells, UK	1926	1
Doncaster	Van Houtte, Netherlands	1924	15
Dr Rocks	Dunedin nursery (? Bennett)	1932	5
Dr Stocker	Wallace, Tunbridge Wells, UK	1924	1
Duchess of York	Wallace, Tunbridge Wells, UK	1924	1
Earl of Athlone	Van Nes & sons, Boskoop	1926	3
Essex Scarlet	Wallace, Tunbridge Wells, UK	1924	1
Essex Scarlet	Wallace, Tunbridge Wells, UK	1926	1
Essex Scarlet	Van Nes & sons, Boskoop	1926	1
Fragrans Rosia	Taylor & Sangster, Victoria	1924	1
Fragrantissima	Bennett, Dunedin		1
Fred Waterer	Taylor & Sangster, Victoria	1924	1
Fred Waterer	Bennett, Dunedin		1
G A Sims	Wallace, Tunbridge Wells, UK	1924	1
General Cavendish	Van Nes & sons, Boskoop	1926	3
George Hardy	Wallace, Tunbridge Wells, UK	1924	1
Ghent Azalea	Taylor & Sangster, Victoria	1924	1

APPENDIX EIGHT

Gloriosum	Taylor & Sangster, Victoria	1924	1
Gomer Waterer	Wallace, Tunbridge Wells, UK	1924	1
Helen Cook	Taylor & Sangster, Victoria	1924	1
Helen Schiffner	Wallace, Tunbridge Wells, UK	1924	1
Himalayica	Taylor & Sangster, Victoria	1924	1
Hugh Wormald	Koster & sons, Boskoop	1926	3
hybrids (unnamed)	Dicksons, Edinburgh	1924	44
Ivery's scarlet	Wallace, Tunbridge Wells, UK	1924	1
Ivery's scarlet	Van Nes & sons, Boskoop	1926	1
J B Poe	Wallace, Tunbridge Wells, UK	1924	1
J G Millais	Wallace, Tunbridge Wells, UK	1924	1
J H Agnew	Taylor & Sangster, Victoria	1924	1
J H Agnew	Wallace, Tunbridge Wells, UK	1924	1
Jacksoni	Wallace, Tunbridge Wells, UK	1924	1
Jacksoni	Van Nes & sons, Boskoop	1926	4
James Marshall Brooks	Van Houtte, Netherlands	1924	1
Joe Ganet	Bennett, Dunedin		1
John Waterer	Taylor & Sangster, Victoria	1924	1
John Waterer	Bennett, Dunedin		1
Kathleen Fielding	Koster & sons, Boskoop	1926	3
Kewense	Wallace, Tunbridge Wells, UK	1924	1
King George	Wallace, Tunbridge Wells, UK	1924	1
King George	Van Nes & sons, Boskoop	1926	3
King of Purples	Wallace, Tunbridge Wells, UK	1924	1
Lady Alice Fitzwilliam	Wallace, Tunbridge Wells, UK	1924	1
Lady Annette de Trafford	Van Houtte, Netherlands	1924	1
Lady Armstrong	Van Houtte, Netherlands	1924	3
Lady Armstrong	Bennett, Dunedin		1
Lady Cathcart	Bennett, Dunedin		1
Lady Claremont	Bennett, Dunedin		1
Lady Clementina Mitford	Wallace, Tunbridge Wells, UK	1924	1
Lady Grey Egerton	Wallace, Tunbridge Wells, UK	1924	1
Limbatum	Van Houtte, Netherlands	1924	1
Loderi	Wallace, Tunbridge Wells, UK	1924	1
Loderi white	Wallace, Tunbridge Wells, UK	1924	1
Luscombi splendens	Wallace, Tunbridge Wells, UK	1924	1
Madam Carvalhoe	Taylor & Sangster, Victoria	1924	1
Madame Masson	Van Houtte, Netherlands	1924	3
Maddeni	Taylor & Sangster, Victoria	1924	1
Marquis de Lothian	Bennett, Dunedin		
Marquis de Lothian	Dunedin nursery (? Bennett)	1932	1
Marquis of Lothian	Seton, Fairfield, Otago	1924	1
Meticar	Taylor & Sangster, Victoria	1924	1
Michael Waterer	Bennett, Dunedin		1
Minnie	Taylor & Sangster, Victoria	1924	1

IN A STRANGE GARDEN

Mme Cachet	Bennett, Dunedin		1
Mme Masson	Bennett, Dunedin		1
Mme Miolin Carvalho	Bennett, Dunedin		1
Mount Blanc	Taylor & Sangster, Victoria	1924	1
Moupiense	Wallace, Tunbridge Wells, UK	1924	1
Mrs E. C. Stirling	Wallace, Tunbridge Wells, UK	1924	2
Mrs G Paul	Wallace, Tunbridge Wells, UK	1924	1
Mrs Holford	Bennett, Dunedin		1
Mrs John Clutton	Taylor & Sangster, Victoria	1924	1
Mrs John Clutton	Van Houtte, Netherlands	1924	6
Mrs John Clutton	Wallace, Tunbridge Wells, UK	1924	2
Mrs John Kelk	Taylor & Sangster, Victoria	1924	1
Mrs John Millias	Wallace, Tunbridge Wells, UK	1924	1
Mrs John Waterer	Van Houtte, Netherlands	1924	1
Mrs Lindsay Smith	Koster & sons, Boskoop	1926	3
Mrs Robert Wallace	Koster & sons, Boskoop	1926	3
Mrs Thistleton Dyer	Wallace, Tunbridge Wells, UK	1924	1
Mrs Tom Agnew	Wallace, Tunbridge Wells, UK	1924	1
named	Dunedin nursery (? Bennett)	1926	66
Neige et Cerise	Bennett, Dunedin		1
Nero	Bennett, Dunedin		1
No. 1 altaclarence	Wallace, Tunbridge Wells, UK	1924	1
Nobleanum	Taylor & Sangster, Victoria	1924	1
Nobleanum	Wallace, Tunbridge Wells, UK	1924	1
Nobleanum	Van Nes & sons, Boskoop	1926	3
Old Port	Taylor & Sangster, Victoria	1924	1
Perfection	Taylor & Sangster, Victoria	1924	1
Perspicuum	Wallace, Tunbridge Wells, UK	1924	1
Pictum	Bennett, Dunedin		1
Pictum	Dunedin nursery (? Bennett)	1932	6
Pink Pearl	Van Houtte, Netherlands	1924	6
Pont d'Or	Dunedin nursery (? Bennett)	1924	20
Prince Camille de Rohan	Van Houtte, Netherlands	1924	1
Princess Alice	Taylor & Sangster, Victoria	1924	1
Princess Alice	Seton, Fairfield, Otago	1924	1
Princess Juliana	Wallace, Tunbridge Wells, UK	1924	2
Purity	Taylor & Sangster, Victoria	1924	1
Purpureum Grandiflora	Wallace, Tunbridge Wells, UK	1924	1
Queen Wilhemina	Van Nes & sons, Boskoop	1926	3
Rosa Mundi	Wallace, Tunbridge Wells, UK	1924	1
Rosamund Millais	Koster & sons, Boskoop	1926	3
roseum Amabile	Bennett, Dunedin		1
roseum Novum	Van Houtte, Netherlands	1924	1
Rosy bell	Wallace, Tunbridge Wells, UK	1924	1
Shilsoni	Wallace, Tunbridge Wells, UK	1924	1

APPENDIX EIGHT

Sinbad	Bennett, Dunedin		1
Sistereanym	Taylor & Sangster, Victoria	1924	1
Smithiiaureum	Wallace, Tunbridge Wells, UK	1924	2
Spencer	Taylor & Sangster, Victoria	1924	1
The Bride	Taylor & Sangster, Victoria	1924	1
The Maroon	Van Houtte, Netherlands	1924	1
The Queen	Taylor & Sangster, Victoria	1924	1
Unknown Warrior	Van Nes & sons, Boskoop	1926	3
Various	Silberrad, London	1923	
Vasayi	Wallace, Tunbridge Wells, UK	1924	1
Victorianum	Wallace, Tunbridge Wells, UK	1924	1
Virginalis	Bennett, Dunedin		1
Viscosum	Wallace, Tunbridge Wells, UK	1924	1
Wilsonianum	Wallace, Tunbridge Wells, UK	1924	1

Truby King's species rhododendrons ordered for Melrose

R. ambiguum	Wallace, Tunbridge Wells, UK	1924	1
R. ambiguum	Wallace, Tunbridge Wells, UK	1926	2
R. arboreum	Seton, Fairfield, Otago	1924	1
R. arboreum	Dunedin nursery (? Bennett)	1926	1
R. arboreum kermesianum	Wallace, Tunbridge Wells, UK	1924	1
R. augustini	Wallace, Tunbridge Wells, UK	1926	1
R. augustini	Wallace, Tunbridge Wells, UK	1924	1
R. aureum maculata	Taylor & Sangster, Victoria	1924	1
R. aureum marginatus	Bennett, Dunedin		1
R. auriculatum	Wallace, Tunbridge Wells, UK	1924	1
R. barbatum	Taylor & Sangster, Victoria	1924	1
R. barbatum	Wallace, Tunbridge Wells, UK	1924	1
R. boothii	Wallace, Tunbridge Wells, UK	1924	1
R. bullatum	Wallace, Tunbridge Wells, UK	1924	1
R. calophytum	Wallace, Tunbridge Wells, UK	1924	1
R. calophytum	Taylor & Sangster, Victoria	1924	1
R. campanulatum	Wallace, Tunbridge Wells, UK	1924	1
R. campylocarpum	Wallace, Tunbridge Wells, UK	1924	2
R. campylocarpum	Van Nes & sons, Boskoop	1926	1
R. campylocarpum	Wallace, Tunbridge Wells, UK	1926	2
R. catawbiense	Van Houtte, Netherlands	1924	2
R. catawbiense Album	Taylor & Sangster, Victoria	1924	1
R. caucasicum Sulphur	Wallace, Tunbridge Wells, UK	1924	2
R. chartophyllum	Dunedin nursery (? Bennett)	1932	5
R. chartophyllum praecox	Wallace, Tunbridge Wells UK	1926	1
R. coriaceum	Taylor & Sangster, Victoria	1924	1
R. davidsonianum	Dunedin nursery (? Bennett)	1932	5
R. decorum	Wallace, Tunbridge Wells, UK	1926	1
R. decorum	Dunedin nursery (? Bennett)	1932	5

R. discolor	Wallace, Tunbridge Wells, UK	1926	1
R. falconeri	Wallace, Tunbridge Wells, UK	1924	1
R. fargesi	Wallace, Tunbridge Wells, UK	1924	1
R. fastigiatum	Dunedin nursery (? Bennett)	1932	5
R. fastuosum	Taylor & Sangster, Victoria	1924	1
R. ferruginum	Wallace, Tunbridge Wells, UK	1924	1
R. fictolacteum	Dunedin nursery (? Bennett)	1932	5
R. flavum	Wallace, Tunbridge Wells, UK	1924	1
R. forsterianum	Taylor & Sangster, Victoria	1924	1
R. fortunei rose colour	Wallace, Tunbridge Wells, UK	1924	1
R. fulgens	Taylor & Sangster, Victoria	1924	1
R. heliolepis	Dunedin nursery (? Bennett)	1932	5
R. hippophaeoides	Dunedin nursery (? Bennett)	1932	5
R. hippophaeoides	Wallace, Tunbridge Wells, UK	1926	1
R. hirsutum	Taylor & Sangster, Victoria	1924	1
R. hirsutum white	Wallace, Tunbridge Wells, UK	1924	1
R. intricatum	Wallace, Tunbridge Wells, UK	1924	1
R. intricatum	Wallace, Tunbridge Wells, UK	1926	1
R. kaempferi	Wallace, Tunbridge Wells, UK	1926	1
R. ledifolium	Wallace, Tunbridge Wells, UK	1924	1
R. luteum	Wallace, Tunbridge Wells, UK	1926	3
R. moupinense	Wallace, Tunbridge Wells, UK	1926	1
R. neriiflorum	Wallace, Tunbridge Wells, UK	1924	1
R. nuttalli	Taylor & Sangster, Victoria	1924	1
R. oreotrephes	Dunedin nursery (? Bennett)	1932	5
R. ovatum	Wallace, Tunbridge Wells, UK	1924	1
R. racemosum	Wallace, Tunbridge Wells, UK	1924	1
R. racemosum	Dunedin nursery (? Bennett)	1932	10
R. rubiginosum	Dunedin nursery (? Bennett)	1932	5
R. smirnowii	Wallace, Tunbridge Wells, UK	1924	1
R. smirnowii	Dunedin nursery (? Bennett)	1932	5
R. sutchuense	Wallace, Tunbridge Wells, UK	1924	1
R. yunnanense	Dunedin nursery (? Bennett)	1932	5
R. yunnanense	Wallace, Tunbridge Wells, UK	1924	1

Total 527

Endnotes

Chapter One: A young man in the colonies

Note: Several biographers refer to Thomas King as having been a member of the British Parliament before emigrating to New Zealand. This is impossible as the minimum age for representation is twenty-one, and Thomas was twenty when he arrived in New Zealand. This was pointed out to me in correspondence with the House of Commons.

1. J. B. Priestley, *Victoria's Heyday* (London: Penguin, 1972).
2. Mary King, *Truby King – The Man* (London: George Allen & Unwin, 1948), p. 12.
3. Margot Fry, *Tom's Letters: The Private World of Thomas King, Victorian Gentleman* (Wellington: Victoria University Press, 2001), p. 52.
4. Ibid., p. 53.
5. Ibid., p. 196.
6. King, *Truby King – The Man*, p. 20.
7. Ibid., p. 22.
8. Ibid., p. 22.
9. Ibid., p. 23.
10. Obituary, *Taranaki Herald*, 29 April 1893.

Chapter Two: Little Truby

Note: Several biographers erroneously credit Truby King with the *Eccles* scholarship at Edinburgh University. It was the *Ettles* scholarship.

1. King, *Truby King – The Man*, p. 28.
2. Ibid., p. 29.
3. Ibid., p. 31.
4. Letter dated 21 June 1874, King Family Papers, ATL.
5. King, *Truby King – The Man*, p. 36.
6. Ibid., p. 50.
7. Ibid., p. 64.
8. Ibid., p. 68.
9. Ibid., p. 76.

Chapter Three: Who am I?

1. King, *Truby King – The Man*, p. 81.
2. The Crozier collection, Dr Paul Crozier, Kingseat Hospital.
3. D. M. Wilson, *A Hundred Years of Healing, Wellington Hospital 1847–1947* (Wellington: Reed, 1948).
4. Theodore Gray, *The Very Error of the Moon*, (Ilfracombe, 1959), p. 98.
5. Wilson, *A Hundred Years of Healing, Wellington Hospital 1847–1947*.

Chapter Four: An asylum by the sea

1. Dr Brunton, in 'The Scylla-Charybdis Syndrome', quoting the first keeper at Oakley Hospital, 1853, p. 3, the Crozier collection.
2. *Appendix to Journals of the House of Representatives* 1886, section H.
3. Brunton, 'The Scylla-Charybdis Syndrome', p. 11.
4. Cheryl Caldwell, *Truby King and the Seacliff Asylum 1884–1907*, University of Otago, BA Hons thesis, 1984, p. 48.
5. Gray, *The Very Error of the Moon*, p. 98.
6. Frank Tod, *Seacliff, A History of the District to 1970* (Dunedin), 1970, p. 29.
7. *AJHR* 1889, section H.
8. *AJHR* 1905, section H.
9. Caldwell, *Truby King and the Seacliff Asylum*, p. 4.
10. Tod, *Seacliff, A History of the District to 1970*, p. 29.
11. Barbara Brookes, 'Frederic Truby King and the Seacliff Asylum', New Perspectives on the History of Medicine, (Melbourne: University of Melbourne), 1990.
12. Ian Church, 'Truby King's initiatives, modernised fishing in Karitane', *Otago Daily Times*, 20 October 2001.
13. Kath Lonie, former resident of Seacliff village, personal communication, 2000.
14. Dr Brunton, 'The Scylla-Charybdis Syndrome', 1893, p. 11.
15. Letter to Mrs Cracroft Wilson, Christchurch, Plunket archives, Hocken Library.
16. Lionel Terry, 'God is Gold', quoted by Frank Tod, *Seacliff, A History of the District to 1970*, p. 78.
17. Dr Charles Moore, Medical Superintendent, Seacliff 1960–70, personal communication, 2000.
18. Lionel Terry, quoted by Frank Tod, *Seacliff, A History of the District to 1970*, p. 92.
19. Lionel Terry, quoted by Gordon Parry, *A Fence at the Top* (Dunedin: John McIndoe, 1982), p. 51.

20. Ibid., p. 51.
21. Eleanor McLagan, *Stethoscope and Saddlebags* (Collins, 1965).
22. Ibid.

Chapter Five: Colonising the Catlins
1. A. R. Tyrrell, *Catlins Pioneering* (Dunedin: Otago Heritage Books, 1989).
2. King, *Truby King – The Man*, p. 227.
3. Ibid., p. 229.
4. Mrs Stott, Lauriston farm resident, personal communication, 2000.
5. Ibid.
6. Letter to Andrew Sutherland, Plunket archives, Hocken Library.
7. King, *Truby King – The Man*, p, 231.
8. Memorandum of Association, Plunket archives, Hocken Library.
9. King, *Truby King – The Man*, p. 225.
10. The Argyle Gold Dredging Company, Plunket archives, Hocken Library.
11. Allister Evans, 'Waikaka Saga', Waikaka Historical Committee, Dunedin, 1962.

Chapter Six: A sound mind in a healthy body
1. *AJHR*, 1886, H-7.
2. Truby King, *Annual Report on the Lunatic Asylums of the Colony*, *AJHR*, 1902, H-7, p. 5.
3. Cheryl Caldwell, *Truby King and the Seacliff Asylum*, p. 29.
4. Frank Tod, *Seacliff, A History of the District*, p. 31.
5. King, *Truby King – The Man*, p. 151.
6. Truby King, *AJHR*, 1906, H-7, p. 19.
7. Caldwell, *Truby King and the Seacliff Asylum*, p. 63.

Chapter Seven: Some curious attitudes of his own
1. Sir Randall Elliot, son of Truby King's personal physician, personal communication, 2000.
2. Truby King, *The Feeding of Plants and Animals* (Dunedin: Whitcombe & Tombs, 1905).
3. Ibid.
4. Dr F. C. Batchelor, address to the Society for the Promotion of the Health of Women and Children, 19 May 1909, p. 7.
5. Truby King, address to the Society for the Promotion of the Health of Women and Children, 19 May 1909, p. 11.
6. Beryl Hughes, *The Book of New Zealand Women* (Wellington: Bridget Williams Books, 1992), p. 80.

7. Truby King, 'The Evils of Cram', *Dunedin Evening Star*, 1906.
8. Baroness von Marenhltz Bulow, 1848. www.geocities.com/froebelweb/webline.html
9. Gordon Parry, *A Fence at the Top* (Dunedin: John McIndoe, 1982), p. 49.
10. Kieran Egan, 'The Flaw in Progressivism', p. 9. www.educ.stu.ca/people/faculty/kegan/flawc1-part_2.html

Chapter Eight: Conservation at Karitane
1. King, *Truby King – The Man*, p. 108.
2. Truby King, lecture in *Tree Culture in New Zealand*, 1902.
3. McLagan. *Stethoscope and Saddlebags*.
4. Mary King White, oral history, ATL AB879, 1992.

Chapter Nine: The adoption of Mary
1. Hamish McDoull's great aunt, via Hamish, personal communication.
2. McLagan, *Stethoscope and Saddlebags*.
3. Eliza Gordon, *Dictionary of New Zealand Biography*, Auckland University Press, www.dnzb.govt.nz

Chapter Ten: A prototype for Plunket
1. Truby King, speech at the annual conference of the National Farmers Union, Wellington, 1904.
2. Pierre Budin, *The Nursling, the Feeding and Hygiene of Premature and Full Term Infants* (London, 1907), translated by Malone.
3. Ibid.
4. Ibid.
5. Lynne Milne, *The Plunket Society – an Experiment in Infant Welfare*, University of Otago, MA thesis, 1976, p. 34.
6. Ibid., p. 41.
7. Parry, *A Fence at the Top*, p. 18.
8. Milne, *The Plunket Society – an Experiment in Infant Welfare*, p. 41.
9. Ibid., p. 42.
10. Ibid., p. 44.
11. Ibid., p. 45.
12. Truby King, 'Karitane Products', p. 4.
13. Milne, *The Plunket Society – an Experiment in Infant Welfare*, p. 46.

Chapter Eleven: The Plunket movement
1. Milne, *The Plunket Society – an Experiment in Infant Welfare*, p. 48.
2. Ibid., p. 50.

3. Ibid., p. 54.
4. Ibid., p. 55.
5. Ibid., p. 55.
6. Ibid., p. 71.
7. Ibid., p. 77.
8. Plunket archives, Hocken Library.
9. Parry, *A Fence at the Top*, p. 45.
10. Ibid.
11. King, *Truby King – The Man*, p. 100.
12. Dianne Armstrong, personal communication, 2000.

Chapter Twelve: The elusive Bella

1. King, *Truby King – The Man*, p. 44.
2. Ibid., p. 48.
3. Ibid., p. 49.
4. Ibid., p. 48.
5. Mary King White, oral history, ATL AB879, 1992.
6. Obituary, *Otago Daily Times*, 17 January 1927.

Chapter Thirteen: Taking Plunket abroad

1. King, *Truby King – The Man*, p. 232.
2. Ibid., p. 233.
3. Ibid., p. 233.
4. Ibid., p. 234.
5. Ibid., p. 234.
6. Ibid., p. 243.
7. Ibid., p. 245.
8. Ibid., p. 255.
9. Ibid., p. 264.
10. Ibid., p. 277.
11. Ibid., p. 281.

Chapter Fourteen: The later years of Plunket

1. Truby King, Plunket archives, Hocken Library.
2. G. M. Smith, *More Notes from a Backblocks Hospital* (Caxton, 1941).
3. Helen Deem, Plunket records, Hocken Library.
4. Rachael Selby, *Reflections: Otaki Women Looking Back in 2000*, Otaki Women's Health Group, 2001, p. 1.
5. Lynne Giddings, *Women Together* (Wellington: Daphne Brassell, 1993), p. 259.

6. Plunket website, www.plunket.org.nz

Chapter Fifteen: A mausoleum in Melrose

1. Anene Cusins-Lewer, 'The Karitane Hospital in Wellington: Swaddled Babies and Muffled Walls', Victoria University of Wellington School of Architecture, p. 4.
2. Ibid., p. 4.
3. Chris Cochran, 'Truby King House', Conservation Report, Wellington, 1992, p. 8.
4. Ibid., p. 14.
5. Boffa Miskell, Truby King Park Conservation and Management Plan, Wellington, 1992, p. 8.
6. King, *Truby King – The Man*, p. 300.
7. Ibid., p. 310.
8. Cusins-Lewer, 'The Karitane Hospital in Wellington: Swaddled babies and Muffled Walls', p. 1.
9. King, *Truby King – The Man*, p. 306.

Chapter Sixteen: The manic gardener

1. Plunket archives, Hocken Library.
2. Margot Fry, Thomas King's biographer, personal communication, 2000.
3. Boffa Miskell, Truby King Park, Conservation and Management Plan, p. 32.
4. Plunket archives, Hocken Library.
5. Cusins-Lewer, 'The Karitane Hospital in Wellington Swaddled babies and Muffled Walls', p. 1.
6. Plunket archives, Hocken Library.
7. Ibid.
8. Truby King, excerpt from a letter in Scotland, quoting Kipling. Plunket archives, Hocken Library.
9. Ibid.
10. Plunket archives, Hocken Library.
11. Donal Duthie, Wellington garden historian, personal communication, 2000.
12. Truby King, letter to ? Bennett of Dunedin, August 1922, Plunket archives, Hocken Library.
13. A précis of the information tabulated in Appendix Eight.
14. Plunket archives, Hocken Library.
15. Dr James Ritchie, whose father worked with Truby King at Melrose, personal communication, 2000.

ENDNOTES

16. Plunket archives, Hocken Library.

Chapter Seventeen: The end

1. King, *Truby King – The Man*, p. 334.
2. E. N. Tibble, interviewed 22 December 1970, Crozier collection.
3. Ibid.
4. Dr Neil Begg, *The Intervening Years: a New Zealand account of the period between the 1910 visit of Halley's Comet and its reappearance in 1986*, (Dunedin: John McIndoe, 1992), p. 99.
5. Mrs James Begg, Plunket Society, *Otago Daily Times*, 11 February 1938.
6. The *Dominion* editorial, 11 February 1938.
7. Dr Watt, Director-General of Health, *Evening Post*, 11 February 1938.
8. Wellington Plunket Nurses, *Evening Post*, 14 February 1938.
9. Obituary, *New Zealand Medical Journal*, 1938.

Bibliography

Published documents

Begg, Neil, Dr, *The Intervening Years: a New Zealand account of the period between the 1910 visit of Halley's Comet and its reappearance in 1986*, Dunedin: John McIndoe, 1992.
Birchfield, Maureen, *She Dared to Speak*. University of Otago Press, 1998.
Boffa Miskell partners, 'Truby King Park Conservation and Management Plan'. Wellington City Council, 1993.
Brookes, Barbara, 'Frederic Truby King and the Seacliff Asylum'. New Perspectives on the History of Medicine, Melbourne: University of Melbourne, 1990.
Brookes, MacDonald, Tennant, *Women in History 2*. Wellington: Bridget Williams Books, 1992.
Budin, P. C. *The Nursling, the Feeding and Hygiene of Premature and Full Term Infants*. London, 1907.
Buelow, Bertha von Marenholtz, 'Reminiscences of Frederich Froebel'. www.geocities.com/froebelweb/webline.html
Daniell, Christine, *A Doctor at War – A Life in letters, 1914–43*. Masterton: Fraser Books, 2001.
Clouston, T. S., 'Female Education from a Medical Point of View'. Popular Science Monthly, 1883.
Cochran, Chris, Truby King House Conservation Report. Wellington City Council, 1992.
Crichton-Browne, Sir James, *Upon the Alleged Over-Pressure of Work in Public Elementary Schools*. London: HM Government, 1884.
Egan, Kieran, 'Getting it Wrong from the Beginning: the Mismatch Between Schools and Children's Minds'. www.educ.stu.ca/people/faculty/kegan/wrong-article.html
Egan, Kieran, 'The Flaw in Progressivism'. www.educ.stu.ca/people/faculty/kegan/flawc1-part_2.html
Else, Anne, *Women Together*. Daphne Brassell Associates Press, 1993.
Evans, Allister, Waikaka Saga. Waikaka Historical Committee, 1962.

Falkner, N. G., *Eliza Gordon 1877–1938*. Dictionary of New Zealand Biography.
Fry, Margot, *Tom's Letters: The Private World of Thomas King, Victorian Gentleman*. Wellington: Victoria University Press, 2001.
Fry, Ruth, *It's Different for Daughters*. 1985.
Gatley, Julia, 'And Save The Babies'. Historic Places Trust Magazine, March 1994.
Giddings, Lynne, *Women Together*. Daphne Brassell Associates, 1993.
Gray, Theodore; Stockwell, G. and Arthur, H., *The Very Error of the Moon*. Ilfracombe: 1959.
Hearn & Hargreaves, *The Speculator's Dream – Gold Dredging in Southern New Zealand*. Dunedin: Allied Press, 1985.
Hogan & Williamson, *New Zealand is Different: Chemical Milestones in NZ History*. Clerestory Press, 1999.
Ingram, I. M., 'Sir James Crichton-Browne: A Very Victorian Psychiatrist'. http://ourworld.compuserve.com/homepages/marcomm
King, Mary, *Truby King – The Man*, London: George Allen & Unwin, 1948
Kropotkin, Peter, *Ethics: Origin and Development*. 1924.
MacDonald, Penfold and Williams, *The Book of New Zealand Women*. Wellington: Bridget Williams Books, 1992
Maloney, William. J., 'The Nursling: Neonatology on the web'. www.neonatology.org/classics/nursling
McLagan, Eleanor, *Stethoscope and Saddlebags*. Collins, 1965.
Mein Smith, Phillipa, 'Truby King in Australia: A Revisionist View of Reduced Infant Mortality'. New Zealand Journal of History, Vol. 22, 1988.
Meller, Helen, *Medicine, Biology and Women's Bodies 1840–1940*.
Moore, C. W. S., 'Northern Approaches'. Otago Centennial Historical Publications, 1958.
Olssen, Erik, 'Truby King and the Plunket Society'. New Zealand Journal of History, Vol. 15, No. 1, 1981.
Parry, Gordon, *A Fence at the Top*. Dunedin: John McIndoe, 1982.
Preston, Frances I., *Lady Doctor: Vintage Model*. Wellington: A. H. & A. W. Reed, 1974.
Rowe, Alastair, 'Fifty Years of Rotary in Wellington'. Wellington, 1971.
Smith, G. M., *More Notes From a Backblocks Hospital*. Caxton, 1941.
Selby, Rachael, 'Reflections: Otaki Women Looking Back in 2000'. Otaki Women's Health Group, 2001.
Tod, Frank, *Seacliff, A History of the District to 1970*. Dunedin: 1970.
Tyrrell, A. R., *Catlins Pioneering*. Dunedin: Otago Heritage Books, 1989.
Tyrrell, A. R., *Catlins Rail*. Dunedin: Otago Heritage Books, 1996.

Verrier, Nancy, 'The Primal Wound: Legacy of the Adopted Child'. www.adoptiontriad.org/primal.htm

Wilson, D, MacDonald, *A Hundred Years of Healing, Wellington Hospital 1847–1947*. Wellington: Reed, 1948.

Young, W. Gray, 'Architectural Gardening'. Journal of the Proceedings of the NZIA. October 1916.

Young, W. Gray, 'Architectural Gardening'. Journal of Proceedings, NZ Institute of Architects, 1918.

Legal references

King, Thomas, Last Will and Testament. Archives NZ Ref ABAJ W4079.

AJHR, Appendices to the Journals of the House of Representatives of NZ, particularly Annual Reports of the Inspector-General of Mental Institutions.

Academic theses

Andrews, Christine Mary, 'Developing a Nursing Speciality. Plunket Nursing 1905–1920'. Victoria University of Wellington MA (Applied Nursing) thesis, 2001.

Caldwell, Cheryl, 'Truby King and the Seacliff Asylum 1884–1907'. University of Otago, BA Hons thesis, 1984.

Cusins-Lewer, Anene, 'The Karitane Hospital in Wellington: Swaddled babies and Muffled Walls'. Victoria University of Wellington School of Architecture.

Fleming, Philip J., 'Eugenics in New Zealand'. Massey University, MA thesis, 1981.

Milne, Lynne S., 'The Plunket Society – an Experiment in Infant Welfare'. University of Otago MA thesis, 1976.

Lectures

Brunton, Dr, 'The Scylla-Charybdis Syndrome'. Lecture to Clinical Psychology students, Sunnyside, 1971.

Mason, J. M., 'Sidelights on the Work of a Health Officer'. Australasian Medical Conference, Melbourne, 1908.

Oral histories

Mary White, Alexander Turnbull Library Oral History Archive, AB879 1992.

Dr Neill Begg, ATL AB863 314.05.

Sheilah Winn, ATL OHColl-0014/026.
Margaret Clayton, ATL OHColl-0014/026.
Olive Turner, ATL OHColl-0014/170+C19.

Archives
Plunket archives, Hocken Library.
King Family archives, Alexander Turnbull Library.

Truby King's published works
The Feeding of Plants and Animals. Whitcombe & Tombs, 1905.
The Evils of Cram. Evening Star, Dunedin, 1906.
The Feeding and Care of Baby. Initially printed in Dunedin in 1906, reprinted in London.
Baby's First Month. Department of Health, 1913.
The Story of Teeth. Whitcombe & Tombs, 1935.
From the Pen of F. Truby King. Whitcombe & Tombs, c. 1950.
Addresses delivered by Doctors F. C. Batchelor and Truby King, 19 May 1909. *Otago Daily Times*.

Unpublished works
Moss, M. S., 'Reminiscences of Sir Truby King' from a long-term clerical officer in mental hospitals, 1971.
Tibble, E. N., 'Reminiscences of Mental Hospitals', clerical officer, 1970–71.
Crozier collection. A collection of papers from Kingseat Hospital archives, made available by Dr Paul Crozier.

Websites
Plunket Society. www.plunket.org.nz

Newspapers
Otago Daily Times, Dunedin.
Evening Star, Dunedin.
Dominion, Wellington.
Evening Post, Wellington.

Index

Allen, Syd, Dr   70
Almond, Dr   94, 99
Archerfield School   114
Auckland   24–27, 34

Barbier   9, 10, 184, 187, 192
Barnett, Louis, Dr   128
Batchelor, Dr   85, 86, 202
Beardsworth   31
Begg, Neil, Dr   127, 168, 200, 273
Bennett, Agnes, Dr   85, 86
Beswick, Charlotte   **82**, 128, 132, 136, 146, 155, 220
Blair, Mr Justice   205, 228, 255
Bledisloe, Lord   197, 255
Boffa Miskell   185, 207, 271
Boffa, Frank   10
Budin, Pierre   119–123, 271

Catlins   58, 67–74, 174, 209
Charcot, Professor   35
Chilman, Mary (Mrs Thomas King)   23, 24, **25**, 29
Chilman, Richard   22, 23
Clouston, Thomas, Dr   40, 271
Cram, The Evils of   60, 86–101
Crichton-Browne, James, Sir   92, 93, 271
Crompton, Mr   32

Davies, Victor   190, 191
Deem, Helen, Dr (née Easterfield)   149, 166–8
Derrick, Dr T.,   228
Director of Child Welfare   165, 173, 203
Duncan & Davies   188

Dunedin   127, 134, 152

Edinburgh   36–43, 45, 36, 51, 83, 185, 195
Elliot, James, Sir   177
Eugenic movement   88, 115, 124

Falconer, Dr   120–125
Feeding of Plants and Animals, the   60, 81–86, 121, 211–216, 247
Ferguson, Lindo, Dr   87
Fraser, Peter   203, 205
Froebel, Friederich   88
Fry, Margot   185, 271

Giddings, Lynne   149, 170, 272
Glasgow   40
Gordon, Esther Loreena (Mary King)   116
Gordon, Leilah   116–118
Gordon, Ngarita   114, 116
Gordon, William   116
Gray, Theodore, Dr   48, 53, 200, 228, 272
Guyau, J. M.   95

Harris, Leslie, Mrs   132, 156, 160, 220
Hector, James   51
Hosking, Dr   35
Hughes, Lizzie   131–134
Hygeia   127, 145–149, 221–225, 249

Japan   59, 60, 113, 116

Karil, Karilac, Kariol   178, 229, 231, 233
Karitane   56, 57, 103–110, 130–141, 174
Karitane baby products   178, 179, 190, 199, 227–233
Karitane hospitals   169
King family, the
King, Bella (see also Millar, Isabella)   11, 45, **58**, 130, 138–148, **148**, 155, 159, 162, 179–182
King, Mary (Truby's adopted daughter)   11, 60, 73, 74, **82**, 111–117, 118–120, 130, 143–148, 155, 199, 229, 272
King, Thomas, snr   19–30, **25**, 34, 35, 78
King, Mary, snr (see Chilman, Mary)   23, 24, **25**, 29
King, Francis, brother   24, 29, 31, 58
King, Mary, sister   24, 27, 31, 58
King, Newton, brother   25, 29, 32, 35, 70, 74, 195
King, Sara, sister   24, 29
King, Herbert, brother   24, 58
King, Truby   **2**, **32**, **42**, **43**, **58**, **136**, **175**, **181**, **182**, **201**
   his parents   23–24
   schooling   31–35
   university   36–40
   in Scotland   36–41
   marriage   41
   Wellington Hospital   46–48
   Seacliff   49–66
   goldmining   73–75
   Plunket   127–150
   establishing Plunket in London   151–164
   knighthood   165
   Wellington   173–182
   the gardener   183–196
   death   200–209
Kingscliff   109, **110**
Kipling, Rudyard   189
knighthood   165

lactose   125, 126
Levinge, Dr   93
Lister Institute   169
Loretto School   94, 199

MacGregor, Duncan, Dr   51, 54, 58, 77, 115, 126
MacKinnon, Joanna   124–126, **136**, 128–141
Masterton   34, 35, 185
McKenzie, Mr   190, 191
McLagan, Eleanor, Dr   64–66, 114, 272
Millar, David   38
Millar, Isabella Cockburn (see King, Bella)
Millar, Mrs   38
Millar, Robert   38
Mitchell, Weir, Dr   202

Nanson, Richard   207
Nash, Walter   205
Nelson   26, 27, 155
New Plymouth   22–24

Parry, Gordon   231, 272
Pattrick, Miss   153, 156, 159, 228
Picture Shows, the Evils of   241–5, 248
Plunket
   early nutritional experiments   80, 84, 100
   the beginnings   119–126
   the Society's formation   129–130
   Lord and Lady Plunket   131–138, 154, 158–160
   first Karitane home   133
   spreading the word   138–142
   Plunket in London   151–159
   later years   165–172
   constitution   217
Pomare, Maui   169
'Primal Wound'   117

Richmond, Henry, Sir   20–23, 83

INDEX

Rollier, Institute   161, 162
Russell, Dan   181, 192

Savage, Michael Joseph   203, 204
Scot, Bill   233
Seacliff   11, 49–69, 72, 77–82, 84, 131, 138, 152, 162, 173, 174, 185
Seidberg, Emily, Dr   85, 220
Skae, Frederick   50
Smith, G. M., Dr   166, 272
Smith, Robert   35
Society for the Promotion of Health among Women and Children   129
Spencer, Herbert   88, 95, 96, 99
Stead, Edgar   197, 251, 255
Stout, Lady   135
Stout, Robert, Sir   121

Sutherland, Andrew   73
Taranaki   20–39, 195
Terry, Lionel   62–64
Theomin, Mrs D. E.   179, 220
Tod, Frank   53, 56, 272
Tolhurst, George   34, 35, 47
Tree Culture in New Zealand   104, 109, 247
Tweed, Dr   166, 205, 229

Watt, Dr   203, 205
Watt, Isaac Newton, Dr   26
Wellington   12, 22, 23, 47, 48, 62, 120, 131, 135, 173–182
White, Mary (see King, Mary)
Wilson, Alexander   91–100
Wrench, Winifrede Miss   152, 154

Young, W. Gray   175–180, 186, 273

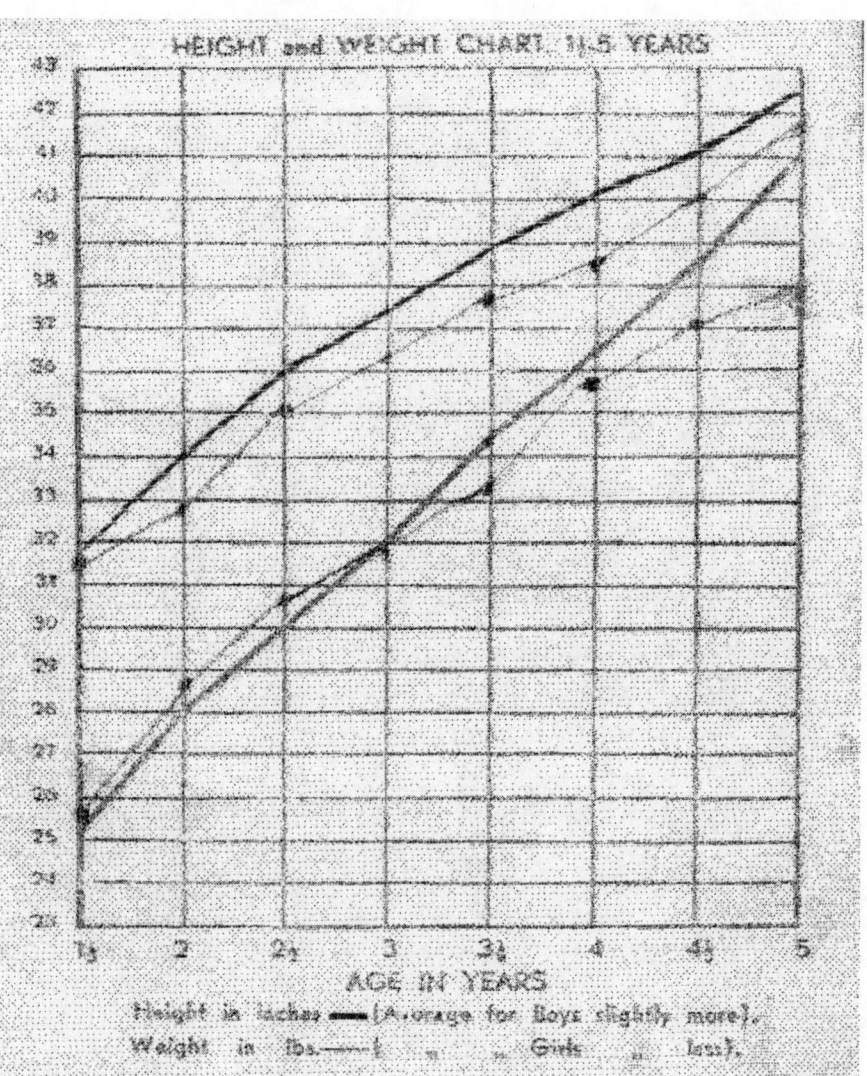

Your Baby Needs:

I.—AIR. Abundance of pure, cool, outside air, flowing fresh and free day and night.

II.—WATER. Must be boiled.

III.—FOOD. Suitable food, proper intervals. No food between the regular feedings. No night feeding.

Best Food—Mother's Milk.

Best substitute—Modified Cow's Milk, suitably graded.

N.B.—Bottle-fed babies MUST have some fresh fruit or vegetable juice daily. Orange, lemon, black currant and rose hip syrup are best; tomato and swede are good also. Your Plunket Nurse will advise the quantities required for age.
In sickness one may need to dilute, modify or change food or give only boiled water for a time.

IV.—CLOTHING. Must be non-irritating, non-constrictive, light but sufficiently warm.

V.—BATHING. Bath and dress very quickly in a cosy corner. No dawdling.

VI.—MUSCULAR EXERCISE AND SENSORY STIMULATION.—Not only must baby have plenty of vigorous exercise, in the way of kicking, working the arms and hands, moving the body, etc., but he must also have due stimulation of the skin and nervous system by plenty of outing in the open air and sunshine. The eyes must be protected from glaring light of any kind.

VII.—WARMTH. Warmed air and surroundings, as essential for pre-matures. Healthy babies, like adults, benefit enormously by being kept in pure, cool air, if properly clad.

VIII.—REGULARITY OF ALL HABITS. Regularity of feeding, with proper intervals and no food between meals. Regularity of exercise, sleep, etc. Regularity of action of the bowels. Secure at least one motion every day.

IX.—CLEANLINESS. Cleanliness in everything, especially with regard to food and feeding utensils.

X.—MOTHERING. Proper mothering and handling of a baby are essential for the best growth and development.

XI.—MANAGEMENT. Fond and foolish over-indulgence, mismanagement, and "spoiling" may be as harmful to an infant as callous neglect and intentional cruelty.

XII.—REST AND SLEEP. These depend mainly on the above. Remember to turn baby in his cot and remove wet napkins, cold bottles, etc.

N.B.—Baby must NEVER sleep in bed with his mother.

To Mothers

The most loving act a mother can do is to nurse her baby. Nothing can ever replace the milk and the heart of a mother.
Old French Proverb.

Name of Child *Ann Johnson*

Name of Parent *W. A.*

Address *36 Clifton St.*
Invercargill

N.B.—To prevent risk of mistakes by the mother, the Plunket Nurse will enter clearly in this book any recipe for food she may order.

Your Plunket Nurse is *Sr. L. Mulgrew*

Telephone No *1222*
1422 Private

Baby's Name: Ann Johnson
When first seen by Nurse: 4·12·46
Date of Birth: 16·11·46
Present Age: 2 4/7 week
Weight at Birth: 7-12
Present Weight: 7-11 Present Length: 19 5/8

PLEASE READ printed advice on inside cover of this book.

FEED baby regularly every four hours, five feeds a day, and no night feed.

GIVE baby one to two ounces of cool, boiled water some time during the day.

Head · 14½
Chest · 13
Abdomen · 12
front 2/6

It is most important that you keep your baby under regular supervision, therefore see your Plunket Nurse at regular intervals and follow her advice.

Always have this book ready when Nurse visits you in your home, and bring it with you when visiting the Plunket Rooms. To save Nurse's time enter the date of visit and baby's age in weeks.

FIRST ADVICE AND INSTRUCTIONS.

MOTHER to have plain, wholesome diet, including meat, fish, eggs, cheese, vegetables, including raw salads, fresh and dried fruits, wholemeal bread and better, wholemeal porridge, milk puddings. Use iodised salt in cooking and at table.

DRINK at least one pint of milk daily, and a glass of water each time you feed baby.

AVOID rich, fatty foods such as pork, pastry, rich cakes, too many sweets, too much cocoa or ovaltine.

REST for half to one hour daily with feet up.

RETIRE early at night.

SMOKING should be avoided.

SUGGESTED DAILY ROUTINE FOR BABY

6 a.m.: Change, feed, and put to bed to sleep.

9.30 a.m. Sun-bath when old enough; then bath, feed, hold out, and put to bed to sleep outside in sheltered spot if possible, or on a balcony or verandah.

2 p.m.: Change, feed, hold out, and put to bed, outside if possible. When older, put in playpen for exercise.

4 p.m.: Give fresh fruit juice.

5.30 p.m.: Wash face, hands, and buttocks; change into night clothes. Feed, hold out, and put to bed.

10 p.m.: Change, feed, hold out, and tuck down for night.

SIT baby up during and after feed to get up wind.

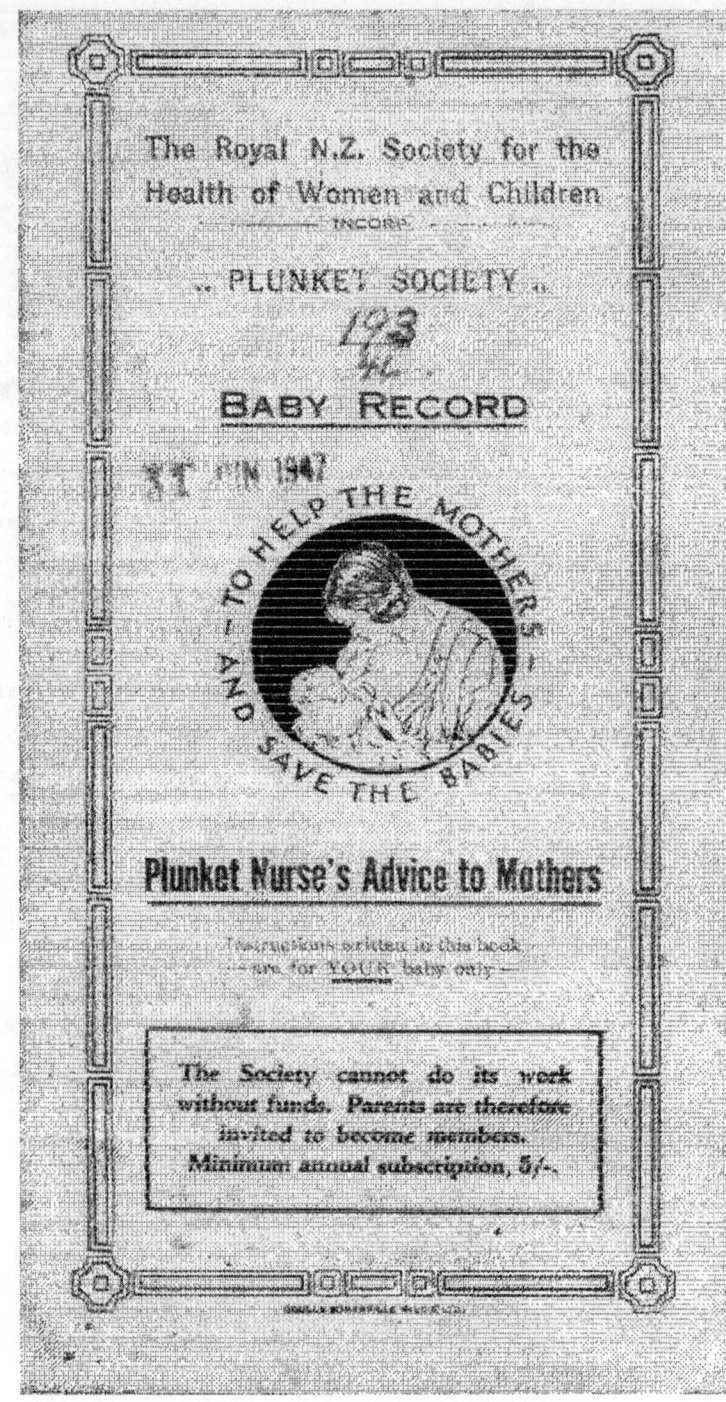

List of Illustrations

The author has made every effort to obtain permission from the owners of the images used. In cases where it has been impossible to ascertain ownership, full acknowledgement of the source has been given.

- p. 2   Truby King (ATL 18662)
- p. 25   Mrs Mary King, Truby's mother, c. 1850s. (ATL F11)
- p. 25   Thomas King, c. 1860s. (ATL F41318 1/2 S P Andrew collection)
- p. 28   Truby King's childhood home, New Plymouth. (*Truby King – The Man*, Mary King)
- p. 32   Frederic Truby King, aged eight years. (*Truby King – The Man*, Mary King)
- p. 41   SS *Selembria*. (*Truby King – The Man*, Mary King)
- p. 42   Three top Edinburgh medical graduates, 1886. Truby King is on the left. (ATL 4 3222 1/2)
- p. 43   Truby and Bella King, c. 1887. (*Truby King – The Man*, Mary King)
- p. 52   Seacliff, the grand baronial asylum. (ATL F4322)
- p. 58   Truby and Bella in the Seacliff garden, 1890s. (ATL 432)
- p. 68   Travel in the Catlins wasn't easy, c. 1912. (ATL F46155 1/2)
- p. 69   Truby King's timber mill at Tahakopa. (Stott family)
- p. 71   Even the swedes lined up for Truby King. (ATL C24179)
- p. 82   Mary King and Matron Charlotte Beswick in the Seacliff garden, c. 1910, dwarfed by giant Cardiocrinum, a rare member of the lily family from China. Photograph taken by Truby King. (White family)
- p. 110   Kingscliff, the house at Karitane. (ATL 60879)
- p. 117   Mary King in her early twenties. (Michael White)
- p. 136   Lady Plunket presents first Plunket medal to Miss MacKinnon. (*Great Days in New Zealand Nursing* ATL NZC610.73 Rat)
- p. 148   Bella King. (ATL 19919 1/2)
- p. 175   Byron Brown and Truby King at the Otaki Health Camp, c. 1926.
- p. 180   Melrose – The House of Windows, facing East. (ATL G48859 1/4)
- p. 181   King and Plunket acolytes on the Melrose verandah. (ATL 154985 1/2)

p. 182   Even doctors smoked in the 1920s. (ATL)
p. 186   The Melrose garden, c. 1934. (ATL F18464 1/1, Earle Andrew Collection)
p. 187   The Melrose garden at its best, c. 1943. (ATL F437 1/4, Pascoe Collection)
p. 201   Truby King in the 1930s, an old man. (ATL 1549861/2)
p. 204   Nurses keeping guard beside the coffin at St Paul's Cathedral. (*Evening Post* 14 Feb 1938)
p. 205   Funeral procession, Wellington. (ATL 48805 1/4)
p. 207   The unveiling of the Melrose commemorative plaque. (ATL C026305)
p. 208   The Karitane Hospital at Melrose. (Chris Chapman from Historic Places Trust, March 94 magazine)
p. 214   Potato diagram. (*Feeding of Plants and Animals*)
p. 230   The Karitane Products factory. (Chris Chapman from Historic Places Trust, March 94 magazine)
p. 236   The Melrose library, 1939. (ATL C15424, *Evening Post* collection)

Colour insert

1   The moon gate in the Melrose garden. (Lloyd Chapman)
2, 3 Curious brickwork adjacent to the Truby King house, Melrose. (Lloyd Chapman)
4   Ironwork surrounding the mausoleum at Melrose. (Lloyd Chapman)
5   Karitane isthmus, from a watercolour by Mrs Charles Moore, painted from Seacliff Hill. Kingscliff is among the trees on the isthmus. (White family)
6   Truby King's funeral cortège enters the Melrose garden. (ATL C11359)